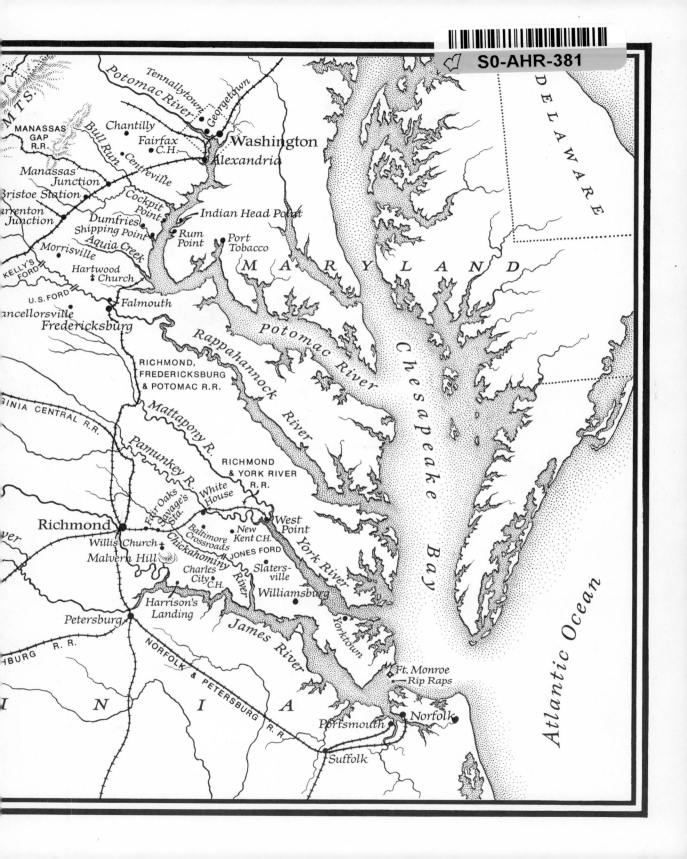

MTS.

MANASSAS
GAP
R.R.

Potomac River

Tennallytown

Chantilly

Georgetown

Washington

Fairfax
C.H.

Bull Run

Centreville

Alexandria

Manassas
Junction

Bristoe Station

Cockpit
Point

Indian Head Point

arrenton
Junction

Dumfries

Rum
Point

Port
Tobacco

Shipping Point

Aquia Creek

Morrisville

M A R Y L A N D

KELLY'S
FORD

Hartwood
Church

U.S. FORD

Falmouth

ancellorsville

Fredericksburg

Rappahannock River

Potomac River

RICHMOND,
FREDERICKSBURG
& POTOMAC R.R.

GINIA CENTRAL R.R.

Mattapony R.

Pamunkey R.

RICHMOND
& YORK RIVER
R.R.

White
House

Fair Oaks

Savage's
Sta.

Richmond

New
Kent C.H.

West
Point

Willis Church

Baltimore
Crossroads

Chickahominy River

JONES FORD

York River

Malvern Hill

Charles
City C.H.

Slaters-
ville

Petersburg

Harrison's
Landing

Williamsburg

Yorktown

James River

NORFOLK & PETERSBURG

I N A

HBURG R.R.

R. R.

Ft. Monroe
Rip Raps

Portsmouth

Norfolk

Suffolk

D E L A W A R E

Chesapeake Bay

Atlantic Ocean

GONE FOR A SOLDIER

David Herbert Donald has taught at Smith College, Columbia University, Princeton University, The Johns Hopkins University, and has served as Harmsworth Professor of American History at Oxford and as Commonwealth Lecturer in American History at University College, London. Now Charles Warren Professor of American History and Professor of American Civilization at Harvard, Dr. Donald is the author of *Lincoln's Herndon, Lincoln Reconsidered, Charles Sumner and the Coming of the Civil War,* for which he was awarded the Pulitzer Prize in 1961, and *Charles Sumner and the Rights of Man,* which was a National Book Award finalist in 1971.

Alec Thomas is a creator-producer of documentary films and multimedia productions. Among his works are the visual history book *Biography of a River: The People and Legends of the Hudson Valley* and the film *Freedom's Finest Hour,* which has been shown in schools and on television many times and which received the National Educational Association CINE Golden Eagle Award for excellence in 1965.

Alfred Bellard

From the
ALEC THOMAS ARCHIVES

GONE
FOR A
SOLDIER

THE CIVIL WAR MEMOIRS
OF
PRIVATE ALFRED BELLARD

Edited by
DAVID HERBERT DONALD

LITTLE, BROWN AND COMPANY · BOSTON · TORONTO
1975

FIRST EDITION
T 10/75

Portions of this book have appeared in *American History Illustrated* and *American Heritage*.

LIBRARY OF CONGRESS CATALOGING IN PUBLICATION DATA

Bellard, Alfred   d. 1891.
    Gone for a soldier.

    1. United States — History — Civil War, 1861–1865 — Per-
sonal narratives. 2. Bellard, Alfred, d. 1891.
3. United States — History — Civil War, 1861–1865 — Regimental histories — Army of the Potomac. 1. Title.
E601.B45 1975 973.7′81 75–19220
ISBN 0–316–08833–0

Designed by Susan Windheim

*Published simultaneously in Canada
by Little, Brown & Company (Canada) Limited*

PRINTED IN THE UNITED STATES OF AMERICA

To a delightful twosome, Julia and
Joseph August, whose finest endeavor produced ART.

With love,
Alec Thomas

Introduction by
David Herbert Donald

———◆———

I N THE VAST LITERATURE dealing with the American Civil War, *Gone for a Soldier* is a unique document. Through its combination of pictures and prose this memoir of Alfred Bellard, of the Fifth New Jersey Infantry, gives an unparalled firsthand account of what is was like to be a private soldier in the Union army. Bellard's recollections cover some of the most critical campaigns of the Civil War — General George B. McClellan's battles on the Peninsula, General John Pope's rout at Second Bull Run, General Ambrose E. Burnside's fiasco at Fredericksburg, General Joseph Hooker's bungled battle of Chancellorsville — but his memoir is not a story of generals or strategy. Instead, it is an account of the daily life of soldiers in the Army of the Potomac, showing what they wore, how they cooked, what they ate, how they behaved under fire, how they spent their leisure time, where they slept. *Gone for a Soldier* presents the Civil War as one private infantryman experienced it.

That private at the outbreak of the war was an eighteen-year-old carpenter's apprentice in Hudson City, New Jersey. Born in Hull, England, Alfred Bellard had come with his parents to the United States in the early

Bellard sent this patriotic ode to his father from the
lower Potomac

1850s. His father, James Bellard, was a skilled engraver and coppersmith who had his own shop in New York City. He was prosperous enough so that by 1860, when he was forty-three, he owned his house in Hudson City, on Beacon Avenue, which was valued at $3,000. Alfred naturally felt closer to his father than to his stepmother, Abby, who was only ten years his senior, but he was extremely fond of his half-brothers, Frank, who was born in 1857, and Walter, who was only two months old when the 1860 census was taken. To help manage her growing household, Abby Bellard had a fourteen-year-old live-in maid, who came from Holland, and she helped pay the family bills by renting one room to a young clerk.

Deeply attached to his family, Alfred Bellard, from the day he enlisted in August 1861, wanted to make sure that they knew where he was and what he was doing. He kept a brief diary, jotting in a pocket memorandum book the barest facts of his daily activities, and about once a week he elaborated upon these entries in long letters he sent to Hudson City, most of which he addressed to his father. Along with the letters he often enclosed what he called "sketches taken by myself on the spot," drawings that were sometimes hasty but were often so precise that they must have pleased his father's professional eye.

Bellard urged his parents to preserve his letters and sketches, and he was pleased when his father bought a sturdy notebook of some three hundred pages and began to have his letters copied into it. Alfred suggested pasting his sketches in the same book, and when there was an occasional gap in his own correspondence, he asked his father to include letters from his best friend in the army, Alfred H. Austin, because these would "look well in the letter book." It would also be a good idea, he thought, to have his pocket diaries, which he sent home as he completed each book, transcribed in the same notebook. All these records, he predicted, "will be interesting to me in after years to look at if I get safe out of this war."

At some point after Bellard returned to civilian life he reviewed these copies of his wartime diaries and letters and, adding information from his still vivid memory, drafted a more extended and coherent account of his part in the Civil War. Using an identical notebook, he filled 262 pages with his recollections, interspersing at appropriate points in the narrative his pencil sketches and wash drawings. For his memoir Bellard devised an elaborately decorated title page, but when it came to naming his book his imagination failed him and he called it simply: "Personal Recollections of the War. By a Private Soldier." We have used one of Bellard's own better phrases to retitle the memoir *Gone for a Soldier*.

It is reasonable to speculate that Bellard wrote his book about 1880, when some major changes began to occur in his life. After his discharge from the army in 1864 he gave up any idea of becoming a carpenter and took up his father's craft of engraving. Apparently he fared reasonably well for a time, for he was able to marry his childhood sweetheart, Annie E. Taylor, in 1866 and to occupy a house near that of his parents in Hudson City (which became part of Jersey City in 1869). But in 1878 the Bellards had their only child, Daisy, and the mother seems never to have recovered her health. Perhaps in order to be near his ailing wife and infant daughter, Bellard gave up his engraving business and opened a florist's shop in his house. Within two years his wife died and his business failed. During this trying time Bellard himself was not well, for the wound he had received at Chancellorsville began to trouble him, and in 1881 he filed his first application for a veteran's pension. Quite possibly the need to go back through his Civil War records for this purpose plus a desire to get his mind off his present troubles led him to write his memoir.

But if that was the case, no note of melancholy crept into *Gone for a Soldier*, which reads more like the work of a high-spirited recruit than of an ailing veteran. A major reason for the freshness of Bellard's recollections was, of course, the ready availability of his contemporary diaries and letters, so carefully preserved by his parents. Most of *Gone for a Soldier* is

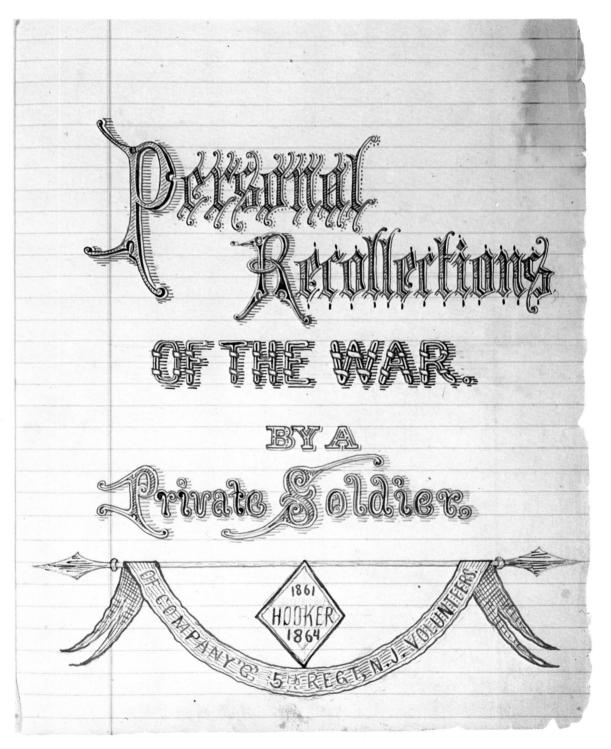

The title page from Private Bellard's original memoir

drawn directly from these sources, even to the extent of repeating such wartime clichés as "the sacred soil of Virginia" and "leaden pills," as Bellard insisted upon calling bullets.

Though *Gone for a Soldier* is based upon Bellard's diaries and letters, it differs from those documents in several significant ways. A glance at the parallel accounts of the fighting at Fredericksburg (see Appendix II), drawn from his diaries, his contemporary letters, and his memoir, shows how much he added in the way of vigorous, concrete detail. The expanded version contains not merely a number of additional important incidents, such as the firing of the New Jersey artillery upon the Confederate officers, and much more colorful detail, such as the card playing and singing during the informal truce with the Confederates; it gives a more complete general picture of the battle and describes more fully how the soldiers felt and behaved.

Other variations between the memoir and the letters show how Bellard's attitudes changed after he left the army. While a soldier, Bellard, like so many other members of the Army of the Potomac, venerated General McClellan and thought General Ulysses S. Grant overrated and incompetent. By the time he wrote his recollections, both his admiration for McClellan and his distrust of Grant had pretty well faded. Similarly, Bellard's letters were often critical of President Lincoln, but in his memoir all comment upon the martyred President was muted. As a final example, Bellard's letters repeatedly berated the Veteran Reserve Corps, to which he was assigned after having been wounded, as "a nuisance to the army," commanded by "a set of drunk officers," but in the memoir he recalled only the more favorable side of his service in the national capital.

Despite such changes, *Gone for a Soldier* substantially reflects most of the opinions and attitudes Bellard held while a private soldier. The memoir, like his letters, shows that on the whole he enjoyed army life. "About soldiering," he kept writing his parents, "I like it firstrate." He was thoroughly loyal to his regiment, which he boastfully called the "Bloody Fifth," and he felt completely at home in Company C, many of whose members came from Hudson City and nearby towns. The fact that Bellard had been born in England in no way made him distinctive; eleven others in his company were also English-born, and, indeed, sixty-two out of the original ninety-nine recruits in Company C came from abroad, chiefly from Ireland and Germany. It might seem that Bellard was much younger than his associates, since the average age of his company was nearly thirty; but that high average resulted from the fact that nineteen members of the company were over forty when they enlisted, and more than one-fourth of the men were, like Bellard, under twenty-one. Nor did Bellard feel uncomfortably over-shadowed by his comrades, though he was only five feet, four inches tall. The average height of the soldiers in Company C was only five feet, six inches, and only three men were six feet or more.

If Bellard found his company congenial, he also felt at home in the routine of army life. Of course he had occasional bouts of depression and he was more than once afraid, but on the whole he found his three-year tour of duty an exciting adventure. He enjoyed living out-of-doors, exposed to wind and sun. Though occasionally troubled by a foot injured during his childhood, he was rarely sick, and his friend Austin joked that Alfred's "health has been like his looks quite rugged." Bellard even liked army food — so much so that Austin predicted he would be drummed out of the regiment for "robbing the government by getting too fat."

"Soldiering agrees with me," Bellard admitted to his parents, "but I do not agree with soldiering. There is a little too much risk for me." One of the most charming things about *Gone for a Soldier* is the fact that Bellard never claimed to be a hero. Though he occasionally liked to boast that his company "fought like tigers," it is clear that he did not long to rush into positions of danger and was happy enough when his regiment formed part of the reserve brigade during a battle. Bellard did not try to become a leader among his fellow soldiers, and, despite a halfhearted and unsubstan-

Bellard's design of a battle flag for the 5th New Jersey Infantry

Bellard's private battle flag showing the engagements
at which he was present

tiated claim in the final paragraph of his recollections, he never served as a noncommissioned officer in his company. He was, in short, a good private soldier, with an excellent instinct for self-preservation.

Gone for a Soldier is also unlike many other Civil War memoirs in that Bellard never pretended that he hobnobbed with the great. He saw generals come and go, but he recounted no private conversations with them, no amusing anecdotes about them. President Lincoln repeatedly reviewed his regiment, but Bellard never claimed he heard any of Lincoln's celebrated stories or sage sayings.

Even more surprising, *Gone for a Soldier* made no attempt to second-guess the generals. Bellard's memoir contained no observations about strategy, virtually no judgments upon commanders. Even when Bellard reported his own experiences during a battle, he rarely attempted to give a general account of the strategy and tactics. Describing a major engagement, he confessed to his father, "is more than my brain can figure out on paper."

Finally, Bellard's memoir is exceptional in its avoidance of bombast. His friend Austin filled his letters with star-spangled rhetoric: "The cause of the Union is every where prospering and if we should fall it shall not be for those we leave behind to say otherwise than that *he like a soldier died.*" Fortunately Bellard had an aversion for such high-flown language, and his memoir, like his letters, soars close to the ground. Indeed, the peculiar fascination of *Gone for a Soldier* derives from the singular juxtaposition of Bellard's understated, unemotional prose and his exuberantly expressive, even gory, pictures.

So far as can be determined, Bellard wrote his memoir for his own satisfaction and made no attempt to publish it. After his death in a soldiers' home in 1891, the two notebooks containing his recollections and the copies of his letters and diaries dropped out of sight. Then in 1962 they turned up at a private sale of household effects in Mahopac, New York, where Mrs. Julia August, an antique dealer, purchased them for a small sum. During the next few years one or two local historians leafed through the books in her shop in Putnam Valley, New York, but nobody paid much attention to them until her son-in-law, Mr. Alec Thomas, who had just returned from the West Coast, discovered them. A producer of prize-winning documentary films, Mr. Thomas was instantly enchanted by Bellard's sketches, and upon reading the memoir decided that it ought to be published.

When Little, Brown and Company asked me to edit Bellard's manu-

CHANGE OF BASE

The morning of the 29th we fell back slowly, to our second line of Rifle pits at Savages Station. and taking our position we were in readiness for the Reb's but with the exception of a few straglers. none came in our front. although the right of our line on the rail road was engaged. when the right of our Army had fallen back. we commenced our retrograde movement. bringing up the rear with our Corps. A short distance to the rear we passed a large pile of Shot. Shell. and Powder. that was to be fired as soon as we were out of danger. in a few moments a terrific roar was heard caused by the explosion. and shells could be heard some time after exploding in different directions. where they had been thrown. A train was also loaded with Ammunition. and after setting fire to the Cars. started it down the track under a full head of Steam. At the Commissary depot. on the railroad. all the crackers and Junk that could not be carried away was burnt to the ground. and I do not think that in the History of the Rebellion there can be found any place. where so much Government Property was destroyed. or so many sick and Wounded left to the care of the enemy. And in the Battles that occured on the retreat all the wounded who could not walk

Destroying Provisions at Savages Station.

away themselves. were left behind. some of the poor fellows rather than be taken prisoners, attempted to walk. but were soon compelled to lay down, and the army passing them they were soon gobbled up by the advancing rebels. Our retreat lay through white Oak swamp. and having only one

A page from Bellard's original memoir

script for publication, my initial concern was to make sure that this intricately detailed, beautifully illustrated document was authentic. In months of intensive work on the memoir I have tested virtually every statement and fact in it against the published *Official Records of the Union and Confederate Armies*, against the large collection of manuscript records pertaining to the Fifth New Jersey Infantry in the National Archives at Washington, against the compiled service records of members of that regiment in the same repository, against the manuscript returns of the United States census, and against city directories of Hudson City, Jersey City, and New York City. In virtually every instance where Bellard's memoir can be checked, it has proved accurate. As an additional test of authenticity, Little, Brown and Company asked a leading handwriting and documentary expert to compare sample pages chosen at random from Bellard's memoir with his application for a pension, a document in the National Archives that is unquestionably in Bellard's own handwriting. The expert reported that beyond any doubt the memoir was written by Bellard himself.

Next to establishing the genuineness of Bellard's account, my concern was to present it to readers in a form that would be easily intelligible yet that would preserve some of the quirkiness of the original document. To attain this goal I have in editing not tampered with Bellard's prose, however idiosyncratic his spelling or ungrammatical his sentence structure. I have, however, silently corrected his wildly erratic spelling of place names, have standardized his capitalization, and have straightened out his confusion of "to" and "too," of "off" and "of," and of "quit," "quite," and "quiet." I am also responsible for dividing Bellard's non-stop chapters into what I hope are reasonably coherent paragraphs.

Instead of cluttering the pages with footnotes, I have supplied necessary background information in headnotes to Bellard's chapters and in other explanatory passages scattered through the book. The biographical index provides fuller identification of persons mentioned in the memoir.

Introduction

Working on this manuscript has been a joy, partly because Bellard wrote such a delightful memoir, partly because so many kind people helped me. My thanks go to Mr. Roger Donald, the editor-in-chief at Little, Brown and Company, who first interested me in Bellard's manuscript, to Mr. William D. Phillips, my able editor, upon whose time I have made too many demands, and to Mrs. Allison Selfridge, who skillfully copy-edited a manuscript that Bellard and I together had contrived to make virtually illegible. To Mr. Arthur J. Rosenthal, director of the Harvard University Press, and Mrs. Raya S. Dreben, of Palmer & Dodge in Boston, I am indebted for special assistance. Mr. Alec Thomas has been generous in his cooperation, and his aid has been invaluable in tracing the history of Bellard's manuscript. Without the assistance of the librarians at the National Archives, and particularly of Mr. Michael Musick of the Old Army Records, and without the help of Mr. Marcus McCorison, director of the American Antiquarian Society, I could never have identified the hundreds of persons and places Bellard mentioned. My wife, Dr. Aïda DiPace Donald, was of inestimable assistance in the difficult task of correcting proofs.

Contents

Contents

Gone for a Soldier

I

Enlistment

WHEN FORT SUMTER was fired into by the Rebels under Genl. Beauregard from Fort Moultrie in Charleston Harbor, my military spirit along with the rest of the people in the Northern States rose to boiling pitch, but being at the time bound down as an apprentice to learn the carpenter's trade, it was out of the question for me to enlist. The only way that I could show my military ardor being in helping to swell the crowds on the sidewalks, who had assembled to see the regiments off to the front. But soon after the battle of Bull Run, my boss, thinking perhaps that the war would be carried into our own State, left his shop and started for Canada. This left me free to go for a soldier, and accordingly on the 9th day of August 1861, myself and some eight Hudson City boys presented ourselves at a recruiting rendevous in Jersey City presided over by Lieutenant Russell for enlistment. After signing our names to the roll, we were ordered to report next day at the old church in Grand Street, Jersey City, for drill.

We were on hand early and found several already there, who having no homes in the city to go to, had slept there all night, mattrasses having been furnished for the purpose. After some prelimenaries had been gone through with, we formed in line for our first introduction to Uncle Sam's manual, Lieut. Hill being master of ceremonys, and for about an hour he put us through a course of sprouts in which we were initiated in the mistaries of keeping our heels on a line. Toes out at an angle of 45 degrees. Belly in. Chest out and such other positions as tend to make a full fledged veteran out of a raw recruit. After drill we were invited to partake of a lunch that had been prepared for us. Standing at the table we helped ourselves to a sumptious repast of ham, coffee and cakes, being our first meal in Brother Jonathan's service, our appetites being whetted by our unusual exercise in the setting up process. After the lunch had somewhat settled down, we had another short drill, after which we were dismissed and ordered to report ourselves on the 19th to proceed to Trenton.

Bidding goodbye to all my friends I found myself on the morning of the 19th at the rendevous in the old church. The company were already forming surrounded by their friends who had come to see them off for the seat of war. One of our men who seemed to be very anxious to be off for a soldier, had his ardor suddenly dampened by the appearance of his wife, who told the captain that her husband was nothing but a drunkard, did not support his family as he ought, and she wanted the captain to send him home, and in order to enforce the argument she pitched into him right and left to the great amusement of the boys, who soon saw that she was the better man of the two. As this Amazonian display was retarding the movements of the company, Captain Sewell ordered him out of the room, and Uncle Sam lost one would be recruit.

Marching to the Pennsylvania Railroad Depot, a special train was found in waiting. This was speedily taken possession of and surrounded with friends some of the women crying and wringing their hands, while the boys who were off for a soldier, were laughing and cracking jokes and doing their best to make everyone else feel as happy as themselves. At last the shriek of the locomotive whistle, announced that we were about to part, perhaps forever. The train moved out of the depot, amid the wild cheers of the men and the crying of the women and children. It was a sight never to be forgotten, for although only one company was leaving, the depot was crowded with friends and well wishers.

After a ride of about 3 hours we arrived safe at the Trenton depot and were marched to the headquarters of the mustering officer, Genl. Torbert. Here we went through rather an artificial examination to wit: The company was drawn up in line on one side of the room and when a man's name was called he would step up to the doctor, who put to him the following questions. Were you ever sick in your life, have you got the rhiumatism, have you got varicose veins, and other questions of like matters, instead of finding out for himself by actual examination w[h]ether you had or not. If the questions were answered in the affirmative and he had no reason to doubt it, he would give us a thump on the chest, and if we were not floored nor showed any other signs of inconvenience, we were pronounced in good condition and ordered to fall in on the other side of the room, where while waiting for the examination to end, we amused ourselves by grinning at each other.

When the doctor had pronounced us as fit for a soldier and in good condition, Genl. Torbert the mustering officer made his appearance and ordering us to hold up our right hands, read the oath to us swearing us in for 3 years or during the war, so help me "bob." As some of the boys held up their left hands, I supose it makes no material diference so long as the oath was mumbled out and the men stayed to hear it. At any rate we were now full fledged soldiers, in the pay of Uncle Sam, and only wanted our uniform and arms, to make us feel as if we were something more than the common run of mortals.

That part of the bussiness being settled we were marched out of the building and started for camp. We had only marched a few blocks when we were met by an old gentleman who wanted the boys to step into his place and have some refreshments. The invitation was gladly accepted as we were rather hollow at the time. We accordingly stepped into his place preceeded by the old gentleman himself. Upon entering his premises, we found ourselves in a large tent that he had fitted up for the purpose. Here we found a large table with an abundance of good things laid out presided over by 3 or 4 young ladies, who of course gave a better relish to the eatables, but being a bashful young gent myself it did not make any material difference so far as I was concerned, but judging from the looks at the time and the expressions afterwards, the supper must have been to some of the female fanciers an agreeable one. The old gentleman as I understood was too old to shoulder a musket and in order to show his appreciation of our services and to do something for his country had made up his mind to feed the boys who were on their way to camp, after a long or tiresome journey. After wishing us a safe return from our service, and the company giving him and the young ladies 3 hearty cheers in return, we again took up our line of march for camp.

By the time we arrived at the State Arsenal it was dark and in order to make our appearance in camp as martial as possible, drums were procured after some little delay, and about 9 o'clock we reached Camp Olden on the outskirts of Trenton and were at once assigned our camp ground. It had now commenced to rain and in order to make things as disagreeable as possible, we had to pitch our own tents as no quarters had been provided for us. Being new recruits at the bussiness, we did not make much headway, for while driving the pins down on one side of the tent, we would pull them out of the other caused by stretching the canvas too tight. At last with a great deal of swearing and the assistance of the officers, we managed to get them up and our baggage inside.

After digging a trench on the outside to keep the water from floating off our traps, we felt quite comfortable and were preparing to pass our first night in camp, when as ill luck would have it, your humble servant being unfortunate enough to have his name commence with the letter "B," was

My first guard duty

ordered out by the orderly sergeant for guard duty. Here was a pretty state of affairs. First night in camp, no uniform, no experience, and ordered out for guard. But as it was military rule (no compulsion but you must) there was no let up. Making the most of a bad job, I reported myself for duty. After being incased in harness, I was handed an old Harpers Ferry musket without a lock and placed on my post. As I was in citizens' dress and no overcoat, I can safely say that when I was relieved from duty, after standing two hours in a drenching rain, I was anything but a contented mortal.

Thinking after being relieved that I had done my share of duty, I was about to make myself comfortable for the night in my own tent, when I was given to understand that I would have to stay in the guard tent all night. I accordingly staid there, as orders were imperative.

The weather broke up fine in the morning and my last tour of duty was more of a pleasure than anything else. After being relieved in the morning, I was informed by the orderly that I was again detailed for guard, not having stood my 24 hours of duty, but thinking that 24 hours on post was a pretty long stretch I applied to my friend Austin who was also a sergeant, for information. He having served a 3 months term of service in the 12th N.Y. Millitia, soon gave the orderly to understand that 24 hours on duty did not mean to be on post for that length of time, but 2 hours on duty and 4 off. That settled the hash and I was soon relieved but ever afterwards he held a grudge against myself and Austin, which he was not slow to take advantage of whenever occasion offered.

The next day we were supplied with a blanket, tin-cup, plate, knife, fork and spoon, and having sometime to ourselves, put our tent in order, providing ourselves with a matrass each, procured from a neighboring farm house, at the expense of the state. There being plenty of farm houses round our camp, we never went short of fruit or corn, for soon after dark when the fog had fairly risen, we would sally out of camp in squads, visit the farms, and return to camp loaded with watermellons or corn, but some of the boys having a penchant for the ardent, instead of visiting the farmers' field, would sail for the city, and on returning would be sure to bring a brick with him [i.e., to be tipsy] carrying the same in his hat, and not being able to pilot himself through the cordon of guards usually found himself captured by them, and thrust into the guard house, where he would have ample time for reflection on the uncertainty of Jersey Lightning when taken in large doses.

A few days after we were supplied with Uncle Sam's suit of blue, and being a young soldier, I felt very anxious to show myself off in Hudson City, more especially as my father and some friends had visited the camp a day or two before. After several vain efforts to get a pass from the captain, being refused as often as I made application under the plea that we were expecting to go to Washington every day, I finally made up my mind that I would take french leave, and so picking out a foggy night, myself and two or three others donned our overcoats and on Sunday, August 25th we slipped out of camp one by one, by darting between the guards whenever their backs were turned towards us. In this way, all of us met outside of camp on the high road to the depot. While walking along the road and congratulating ourselves on our stragetic [strategic] movement in fooling the guards, who should we spy comming up the road, but my old friend the orderly. As we expected nothing less than detection and orders to return to camp, we determined to put a bold front on the matter and face the music, so pulling our cap peaks over our eyes and turning up our coat collars, we pushed on. Just as we got opposite the gent and were getting ready to run should he order us to halt, an unforseen obstacle that he did not observe met him halfway, and over he went (striking his toe against a rock that protruded from the path). This caused us to laugh louder than was necessary at his predicament, but other than a growl that he gave vent to on regaining his feet, we were not noticed and arrived safe at the depot without further trouble.

As the owl train came into the depot, our first idea was to get on top of the cars, and so steal a ride to Jersey City, but having some spare change myself to pay my fare with and seeing no guards on the train, I concluded to take an inside seat, and not run the risk of having my neck broken against some bridge before my time. On stating my intentions the rest of the boys came to the same conclusion, and in we got. The train started, and at 11 o'clock p.m. where [i.e., we were] fairly on our road home.

The conductor comming along for his fare, some of the runaways got under the seats to escape his eyes, but it was no go. The conductor simply said Tickets, and out they came. I soon found out to my sorrow that I was the only one of the party who had any money, and as the conductor was not a very strong Union man, I had to fork over the fare for all, or have them put off the train. As this was more pork for a shilling than I had bargained for, I then and there mentally vowed that when I traveled again I would look out and find what my traveling companions were made of, more especially as the amount has not as yet been refunded, although promised as soon as we got home.

We arrived in Jersey City [at] one o'clock in the morning and being rather early to wake folks out of their beds, we strolled around until 4 when we went home. The folks were very glad to see me and I spent a very pleasant time while there. My appearance on the street caused no little meriment on account of my uniform. In picking it out, I was in such a hurry to have it on my back, that I got an overcoat that was about two sizes too large for me, and the tails loosely flopped round my heels as I walked. I soon remedied that by cutting off about 4 inches of the tail.

After being home about two days, I heard from one of our company who had succeeded in getting a furlough that the Regiment would leave in a few days for Washington. So bidding good bye to my friends for the second time, I left for Trenton on the 28th being forwarded on with some recruits at the expense of the city, and arrived there that night. Upon reaching camp I found the boys bussy packing their knapsacks for a move. I went at once to the captain's tent and reported myself. After being interviewed, as to where I had been, and what I had been there for, I was provided with a knapsack and equipment, and ordered to pack up and be ready to move the next day.

II

Off to Washington

A s BELLARD'S MEMOIR SHOWS, *the stunning Union defeat in the first battle of Bull Run (July 21, 1861) did not dampen Northern enthusiasm for the war. Instead, it spurred recruiting. Within three months of that disaster, more than 100,000 fresh volunteers, including Bellard's regiment, began heading toward Washington.*

Bellard's experiences on his journey to the capital were fairly typical. The warmth of his regiment's reception in Philadelphia was equalled by the coolness of that in Baltimore, a hotbed of secession, where on April 19 a street mob had attacked a Massachusetts regiment on its way to defend Washington. Bellard's recollection of his trip south contains an error, due either to a faulty memory or an imperfect knowledge of geography, for his regiment passed through Havre de Grace before it reached Baltimore.

Once in Washington, Bellard's regiment came under the command of General George Brinton McClellan, to whom President Lincoln had entrusted the defenses of the capital after Bull Run. Fresh from victories in western Virginia, "Little Napoleon," as McClellan was admiringly called, was a superb organizer and disciplinarian. Promptly he put his raw recruits

*to work learning the manual of arms, the drill, and the routine of army life,
so that within a few weeks the motley assortment of troops around Washington began to take on the appearance of an army.*

———◆———

On the morning of the 29th our Regt. being full we received our
muskets and forty rounds of ammunition (buck[shot] and ball) and fell
into line. The Regt. being formed we marched to the depot and while waiting for the train, the commissioned officers were mustered into service. At
last a baggage train hove in sight into which we esconsed ourselves, and were
soon on our way to the seat of war. These cars had been fitted up for the
transportation of troops by having rough boards nailed across the car to
serve as seats, but these not being sufficient in number a great many of the
boys had to stand or squat on the floor. We amused ourselves by singing,
shouting, and making as much noise as possible, until we arrived at Camden,
N.J. about 5 p.m.

Marching on board the ferry boat we were landed in Philadelphia, Pa.
in a few minutes, the city of all others that took the lead in caring for the
soldier going to the front in health or returning home wounded or dying.
The Regt. was formed in line. Arms were stacked and 500 of the men were
marched into the Union Refreshment Saloon to refresh the inner and outer
man, 500 being accomodated at one time. First we were ushered into a wash
room where soap, towels and water were in abundance, and after a thoughro
[thorough] wash were introduced to the refreshment room. Two large tables
were loaded down with an abundance of good substantial eatables, at which
standing on both sides of the tables the men helped themselves to as much as
they could eat washing it down with plenty of good coffee. Young ladies
were in attendance at the tables and pressed you to take more than was
actually needed.

*Amid the crack of firearms and the cheers from
thousands of throats, the train slowly rolled out
of the city*

After the Regt. had been refreshed, we were again formed in line when
the order was given to load as a brush was expected while marching through
Baltimore. Being detained an hour or two we had an opportunity of witnessing the loyalty for which the people of Philadelphia are so famous. Men,
women and children turned out to bid us welcome and it made the men who
had just left their familys, forget their sorrow at parting for a time. Cigars,
tobacco, handkerchiefs and boquets were given away by the young ladies
(ad libatum). One young lady presented the writer with a bunch of cigars
that she passed up through the car window with the wish we might meet
again. At last the shriek of the locomotive gave warning to the mass of
humanity that the best of friends must part, and amid the crack of firearms
and the cheers from thousands of throats, the train slowly rolled out of the
city, much to our chagrin as we should have liked to have stopped there for
a day. During the firing one of our men received a pistol ball in the arm, and
was discharged in consequence.

At midnight we reached Baltimore and marched through the city in column of company to be ready in case of an attack. No demonstration was made however and we reached the Washington Depot in safety. Taking the train once more we arrived at Havre de Grace about daylight. The cars were run onto a ferry boat six at a time, on a double track laid on the boat and without any perceptable motion were landed on the opposite side of the river. Being now in a rebel climate, the boys amused themselves now and then by slinging leaden pills at the cows and sheep who were quietly gazing at the passing train. Their owner who was generally in the field with them would show his contempt for us by shaking his fist and other demonstrations. The country through which we passed seemed to be pretty much under cultivation in tobacco and corn, that being I believe their chief product.

About 4 p.m. on the 30th the train entered the Washington Depot, and the Regt. marched into the soldiers' rest, but instead of rest as the name implies, we got plenty of standing room. In this establishment we received our first sample of Uncle Sam's rations, and I can assure you it did not give us a very exalted opinion of it. On several large tables that ran the entire length of the building were tin plates upon which lay a large slice of very fat pork, and a 1/4 of a loaf of bread, while to wash it down, it had for a companion a pint cup of greasy black coffee. Not being very hungry myself, I forbore the pleasure of eating until a more favorable time. On one of the waiters making his appearance, he was asked if he considered that mess fit to eat. Upon answering in the affirmative he was immediately dumfounded by receiving about a pound of greasy fat pork over his mouth, when he made a bold dive for the door. This was the signal for a general fusilade, and bread and fat pork were flying in all directions. The man who got out of there without making the acquaintance of fat pork or having coffee spilt over his clothes was lucky. In after days we would have been glad to get that same fare and would have paid a good price for the privilidge.

The order to march was hailed with joy and after passing the capitol building we marched to Capitol Hill and went into camp. Our camp was situated on the hill near the Potomac branch and the Congressional Cemetary was near us on the river bank. We were now farely settled down to a soldier's life having our regular rations of 5 hours drill. The first drill was right after breakfast without arms. The officer in command would march us to the river, where instead of drilling in the facing [i.e., in uniform] etc, we would spend an hour in the water very pleasantly.

Close to our camp was the Washington Penitentiary and Lunatic Assylum in which the principle victoms seemed to be the Negroes. As the supply of water came from this place for the use of the camp, we had a good chance to see the workings of the institution. The grounds surrounding the buildings were used for growing corn, melons and tobacco. Every morning the prisoners marched out in charge of a white man, the overseer armed with a whip or stick to work the plantation. Some of the worst cases were chained together, and others were ornamented with a ball and chain. And any of them who became ugly or would not work received a cut from the whip as a reminder of his or her situation. In an old tobacco crib, that stood on one side of the entrance was an old crazy negro woman who made night hidious by her yels and screems. Any of our men who happened to be posted at this place generally supplied himself with plenty of tobacco, melons or green corn, it being the rule when relieved in the morning for the sentry to bring in some provisions under his coat tail.

Spirrits being plenty, in the shape of whiskey, one of our men who had imbibed rather too freely, was taken with the Jim Jams (Dilirum Tremens) and seizing a knife was soon running amuck through the camp looking for his enemy. He was finally captured and placed in the Lunatic Assylumn, from which he was discharged. Another of our men gave us considerable trouble by getting the night mare rather too often. In one of his spells he must have immagined that he was attacked by a party of Rebs, for he

15

Negro Prisoners,

*Others were ornamented
with a ball and chain*

jumped up and before any of us could divine his intentions he had secured a
large Bowie knife that lay under his head and went tumbling over the
sleepers flourishing it in his hand. He was immediately tumbled out of the
tent, and a dose of cold water dashed into his face, which had the effect of
bringing him to his senses, and he wanted to know very badly who it was
that had thrown sand in his eyes. The gent never found out what became of
the Bowie, and a single barrell pistol that he carried with him, the boys

having taken charge of the weapons, not wishing to wake up some night and perhaps find him at work on our scalps, dreaming that we were Indians.

Another genius in our camp, who was known to fame as Mickey Free, made himself very conspicuous by one or two of his exploits. On one side of our camp the remains of an old Negro burrying ground that had not been used or repaired for some time and in consequence some of the graves had been washed open by the heavy rains, exposing to view the coffins that had been deposited therein. Mickey being cook at the time and not having the necessary wood on hand to cook our breakfast with made a raid on the grave yard one morning and turning out one of the relicks, brought it into camp, when breakfast was soon under way. As he was also somewhat of a walkist, he nearly rubbed himself out at this camp by performing his favorite game. He made a bet one day that he could pick up 100 stones placed at a certain distance apart one at a time and deposit the same in a basket at one end of the line before he went for another in a stated time. He won the bet but came near pegging out, as he was seized with cramp immediately after. The doctor refused to prescribe for him saying that there was nothing the matter with him but rum, and if he did peg out, it would be a good riddance.

Various amusements were going on after parade to suit the tastes of the diferent companys. One of them held a camp meeting every eve, the chaplain presiding and quite a revival was in progress when we were ordered to move. Others got up impromtu variety theatricles (or free and easys) and I have no hesitation in saying that the last named agreed best with the majority of the boys. In this way we enjoyed ourselves splendidly until the 21st of September when we were ordered to pack up and be ready to move at a moment's notice to Alexandria, Va.

III

❖

Alexandria

FEARING THAT *the Confederates, flushed with success at Bull Run, might be planning an attack upon Washington, General McClellan during the summer of 1861 ringed the capital with a chain of forts. In the fortifications south of the Potomac he stationed his best and most reliable troops — including Bellard's Fifth New Jersey regiment. A vital link in the chain of defenses was Alexandria.*

By the time Bellard's regiment was posted in that sleepy little Virginia city, it had been in Union hands for nearly four months. In May, when Union troops occupied it, Colonel Elmer E. Ellsworth led the advance with his Zouave regiment, flashily uniformed in their baggy scarlet trousers, their short blue coats, and their red kepis. Intensely patriotic, Ellsworth was outraged to discover a Confederate flag flying from the three-story Marshall House, and he dashed up to the roof of the hotel to cut it down. As Ellsworth was descending with his trophy in his arms, a civilian Confederate sympathizer shot him in the chest, and he died almost immediately. The whole North mourned the loss of a gallant, handsome young soldier, who had been a personal friend of President Lincoln, and Union soldiers in Alexandria took revenge for his death by vandalizing the Marshall House.

———◆———

Striking tents on the morning of the 22nd we marched to the Potomac river and embarked on the Steamer Star that was moored at the Arsenal. As soon as the Regt. was on board the hawsers were cast loose, and we sailed down the river, arriving at the foot of King St., Alex[andria], in a drenching rain. Disembarking, we marched up King St. and halted at the Marshall House where Col. Ellsworth was shot. Part of our Regt. made this their head quarters for the night, and a more miserable and filthy place for quarters I never saw. The troops who had occupied it at various times before had used the corners of the rooms and hall way instead of sinks, and the stench that arose from it was enough to knock a person down. Curiosity seekers had also made sad work with the appearance of the building. The stairs on which Ellsworth was shot had been taken away by piecemeal. Walls broken. Carpets carried off bit by bit, and the flag staf on top of the house from which the Stars and Bars had floated when the Zouaves took possession had been demolished. Being one of the curiosity seekers myself I secured a piece of the carpet [and] flag staf and safe[ly] droping the same into my pocket so that in after years I would have a vivid reminder of the night passed in the Marshall House. At this time it was occupied by an old Negro woman, the former occupants having gone further south to a more healthy climate.

In the morning in company with one of the boys I took a strol over to the 1st New Jersey Brigade, who were encamped at the Fairfax Seminary near Fort Ellsworth. Arriving at their camp we had the pleasure of meeting some old faces from Jersey City, Hoboken and Hudson City, and upon invitation took breakfast with them. After refreshing the inner man and chating a short time with the boys, we returned to the city, only to find that the Regt. had moved in our absence and gone into camp. After some considerable scouting, we found them outside the city in a large field. Tents were pitched and dinner ready, so we got rid of that job.

After being in camp about three days, the 17th N.Y. Volls. who had been doing military police in the city for some time were relieved on account of their love for whiskey and the 5th N.J. detailed in their stead. Breaking camp the Regt. was scattered in diferent parts of the city. Two companys being sent to Fort Ellsworth a short distance out, while Co. "C" found quarters at the river front in a two story frame house. The first floor was the head quarters and the second floor accomidated the men. A shed that was attached to the rear of the building being used as a kitchen, the fire place being well supplied with hooks upon which the kettles were hung when cooking. Our dutys were to preserve order, arrest all soldiers without passes and see that no one, either citizen or soldier, was on the streets after 10 o'clock at night without the countersign. The tour of duty being 4 hours on post and 8 off. Upon being posted on our beats in the morning, at the corner of the street, our orders were to load with ball cartridge so that the people could see in passing that we were fully prepared to shoot should the occasion require it.

When we first took charge of the city lively scenes sometimes occured at night, but after we had thrown an ounce or two of lead at one or two of them who were too abusive, discretion got the better of their hot blood and we were respected all the more. One specimen of the southron chivalry who had more blood thirsty notions in his head than usual, met one of our company, who was on guard at the hospital, and began to abuse him in very round terms, giving the guard to understand that he was a secessionist. He said that the government had no right to take private houses for hospitals and that the hospital aught to be burnt down with all the yankees in it, and further, that he was afraid of no Northern soldier and would shoot the first man who said he would shoot him. He was promptly collared and presented to the provost marshall, who placed him under $1000 bail to learn him to keep his mouth shut, and to appear before the court marshal when wanted. What became of him I cannot say as we left the city shortly after.

The secesh women, in order to show their contempt for the yankee mud sills, had a fashion of pasting minature rebel flags, made of paper, on the hydrants at night and looking through the blinds at the aggravation of the soldiers on discovering them in the morning. One of them however came to grief. She had made a small rebel flag of silk, and while she was engaged in waving it in front of the nose of one of the boys, he very quietly relieved her of the obnoxious article, and no more flags were seen in that locality.

While doing guard duty in this city I found myself in rather a bad fix. Having got used to waking up at the least noise, the guards sometimes took a nap, in order to pass the time quickly. It so happened that myself, Buck and Peale [Peel] settled ourselves on a stoop for a quiet nap, relying on our ability to wake up and be on our posts at the proper time. About one o'clock in the morning we heard the patrol comming and being off our posts made haste to reach them before we were discovered. But vain effort, we were stuck fast and could not budge. Not knowing w[h]ether we were tied down or not and the patrol getting too close for our comfort, we unbuttoned our coats and crawled out, finding on regaining our feet that we had laid down on a pitch-pine stoop. The heat of our bodies had drawn out the pitch and of course fastened our coat to the wood. We just had time to drag off our coats and get onto our posts as the patrol came along, but thank fortune they had no suspicion of our doings.

After getting fairly acquainted, we rather liked the duty than not. On my post was the government bakery, and every night the bakers would give me a lot of rolls. Peale's post was supplied with a cigar store, the proprietor of which always gave us some cigars to smoke while Buck's had something for the stomach's sake. Being pretty well supplied with gass he had wormed himself into the friendship of a lawyer and every night when the signal was given three blocks of Alexandria was unguarded, while the guards themselves were round the corner, drinking the health of our friend the lawyer, up two flights of stairs.

We were furnished with the regulation frock coat for street duty with the brass scales for the shoulders. (The abomination of a soldier as it kept us continually digging away with our vinegar bottle and whiting to keep the tarnish off.) I had my likeness taken in this uniform and a fine looking burlesque it made. During our stay I made several trips to the camp of the first brigade meeting several old acquaintances in the persons of Conkling in the infantry and Bly, Eaton, Reinhardt and Sense [i.e., Senz] in the artilery. When off duty we had plenty of amusements in the way of swimming or fishing, there being plenty of either in the canal or river.

We were furnished with the regulation frock coat for street duty

Dame rumor was very bussy here as elswhere. At one time we were to proceed to Washington, drill, receive new rifles and uniforms, and after being brigaded, were to take position at the Chain Bridge. Madam

[Rumor] came again and said we were ordered to Missouri. This gained the most credence.

As we were getting ready for duty one morning one of our men having imbibed too much corn juice was taken with an affliction of the brain, that might have been a very serious affair for him. While my squad was forming on the street, previous to marching to our posts, this mad man made a rush and jumping from the window landed in the middle of us. Had not some of them seen him as he made the jump and got out of the way, he would have been impaled on our bayonettes. For this little escapade he was ordered to the slave pen, but he escaped from the guard before reaching there.

The appearance of the city was anything but prepossing [prepossessing] nearly all of the larger houses were empty and fast going to the dogs. The streets were paved with very uneven cobble stones, making the roads about as smooth as a corduroy. Sidewalks were nearly all brick. The principle part of the mechanics were negroes, showing that they were more inteligent than their masters gave them credit for. The government blacksmith shops and wheelrights were worked altogether by negroes. On the 12th of October, the 5th Regt. Pen. Volls. [Pennsylvania Volunteers] arrived in the city during a drenching rainstorm, and went into camp outside of the city. Although they were without arms, I suppose they came to relieve our Regt. as we left on the 18th although the citizens got up a petition to have us stay.

IV

◆

Washington

EVERYTHING BEING PACKED UP, we started about 3 o'clock on the afternoon of the 18th and leaving the city behind us started for the Long
Bridge. After marching about two miles, I had to fall out of the ranks as I
had rubbed all of the skin from one of my heels by wearing tight shoes. While
sitting on the road side resting Curtis of my company who was with the waggon train made room for me in one of the waggons and put my knapsack in
another, so I got along quite comfortable. At the entrance of the long bridge
we passed Fort Runyon, built by the Jersey Brigade in July. Crossing the
bridge, the Regt. marched up 14th Street and halted at Meridian Hill, where
they went into camp. This being our first night under canvass for some time,
the boys dedicated the occasion by music and singing, two violins and a flute
furnishing the music.

The next day we were brigaded with the 6th, 7th and 8th N.J. under
Genl. Casey and had our first brigade drill and review under command of
our provisional brigadier and staf, and also received our state colors. On the
21st we had a review of 8 Regts. before Prest. Lincoln and while returning
to camp, Genl. Casey rode up to Col. Starr and said concerning our Regt.

24

that he had better take his men home and drill them. The old gent little thought at the time, that the same Regt. would be called upon to force their way through the straglers of Casey's Division with the bayonette as they did in Apl. 62 at Fair Oaks, Va.

Genl. Geo. B. McClellan having taken command of the army, a grand

carrying the Log

Carrying the log

review was ordered and it took place in the rear of Washington. And a splendid sight it was. But as the general was riding the lines and while in the position of present arms, I was taken sudenly sick with a fainting feeling and fell down in my tracks, having to be escorted to the rear by two of my comrades, so as not to be in the way of the march past. Comming to before the review was over, I fell into line again, but soon had to leave and it took me about two hours to get to camp, when I should have done it in one.

It being supposed that the Rebels would cross the river to interfere with the elections that were about being held in Maryland, the Brigade left camp on Nov. 4th, for Port Tobacco on the Potomac river. The company I belonged to was left in camp to guard the property of the Regt. On the afternoon of the 10th, the Regt. came back looking as if they had seen some hard times, being mud from head to foot. As they were very hungry our provisions were placed at their disposal, and the way the crackers, pork and coffee disapeared was a caution. After the inner man had been satisfied I learned that they had marched 22 miles the first day, 25 the second and 16 the last making 63 miles in all to reach their destination. On the way back they took it more leisurely. Knapsacks were thrown in the waggons to lighten their loads. Mud, water and stumps were met on every hand and in some places the Brigade had to march in single file. This gave the last man a chance to try his wind and muscle in order to catch up with his command. No causelties [casualties] happened with the rebels but one of the 7th Regt. was killed, by being run over with a baggage waggon.

"The tenth Legion" 56th N.Y. Volls. went into camp near us, consisting of one Regt. of infantry, 2 companys of cavalry and 2 batteries of artilery, 1500 men in all. The infantry were splendidly armed with rifles and sword bayonettes.

At our first inspection by the Col. the old man gave us to understand what sort of stuf he was made of. One of the companys not being very particular about polishing their shoes were placed on double duty to refresh their memorys at the next inspection, while our company was excused from guard duty for 2 weeks for cleanliness. One or two unlucky ones however were given 2 weeks extra guard and to carry a log for one day. Corpl. Gill being one of the unfortunates formed his squad of about 10 men in line and

A piece of wood is run through his legs, and placing his arms under the stick on each side of his knees, his hands are then tied in front

marching them down to the guard tent, each of them were provided with a cord stick of wood instead of a gun, and had to parade in front of the guard tent for the rest of the day. While the corporal and his squad were serving out their punishment, a new Regt. marched past on their way to camp, and the corporal forming his squad in line, presented logs to them instead of arms.

Military punishments were various according to the offence committed or the whim of the officers. The buck and gag being the favorite. When a man was very drunk and abusive, a bayonette or piece of wood was placed in his mouth and a string tied behind his ears kept it in position, seating him on the ground with his knees drawn up to his body. A piece of wood is run through his legs, and placing his arms under the stick on each side of his knees, his hands are then tied in front, and he is as secure as a traped rat. For light offences, the culprits are made to stand all day on the head of a pork barrell or on the edge of it with the head knocked out, while sometimes an extra barrel is furnished with a hole cut out of the top for his head, and one on each side for the hands. After putting on this coat, he is mounted on the head of another and there he has to stand. For sentences of courtmartial a 24 pound ball is attached to his leg by a chain and this ornament he has to carry with him on all duty.

As orders were very strict in regards to going out of camp, various modes were made use of to get in a supply of the ardent [i.e., whiskey]. While on guard over the waggons one dark night, I heard some one comming through the woods very cautiously, as if they were afraid of being seen. As soon as they got near enough I sung out, Halt, who goes there. The answer was as usual, Friends. Ordering one to advance and give the countersign, I brought my piece to a charge, and afterwards to the port, to receive the

Punishment, Pork Barrells

Some fellow would find himself
flat on his back from the recoil
of his gun

word, but instead of the countersign, a suspicious looking bottle was placed in my hands, and taking a refreshing pul at the contents, I reported the countersign correct, and they passed on.

Upon being relieved from guard in the morning, the squad was marched to the rear of the camp, to what had been at one time a mansion, but at that time nothing remained but the bare walls, upon which we practiced target shooting. After every discharge some fellow would find himself flat on his back from the recoil of his gun, our muskets having the advantage of doing execution at both ends. On the 23rd we received each a pair of dark blue full dress pants that were about as rotten as they could be and hang together, also an extra blanket, pair of socks and gloves, the latter articles having been sent to our company by the ladies of Jersey City.

On the 24th I attended my first military funeral. A soldier having died in the Columbia College Hospital, a detail of 8 men and a corporal were taken from our company to pay the last tribute of respect to his remains. An ambulance was brought into requisition to answer for a hearse. Forming our squad on both sides of the ambulance, we marched about 2 miles to the soldiers' home, at reverse arms, and drums muffled. The body being laid in its narrow bed, a salute of 3 rounds was fired over the grave and we returned to camp to the tune of Yankee Doodle.

As the weather had turned very cold, stables were built out of brush to shelter the horses, and the officers had their tents floored. This looked as if the many rumors that were flying round camp of our staying there all winter was about to be verified, but alas for human expectation, for about the first of December, we had our baggage packed and were off once more.

V

Potomac Blockade

FOR ALL *General McClellan's recognized talents as an administrator, he had an incurable reluctance to use the army in a fight. As Lincoln was later to say, McClellan had a bad case of "the slows." Despite overwhelming Union superiority in numbers and equipment, McClellan permitted the Confederates in August 1861 to establish advanced posts on hills on the Virginia side of the Potomac, in full view of the Capitol. Later he did nothing when the Southerners began erecting batteries at Cockpit Point and other strategic locations commanding the Potomac some thirty miles down the river from Washington, and he seemed indifferent to the fact that the Confederates now could cut off river access to the Union capital.*

Under mounting pressure from the President and the Congress to re-open the Potomac, McClellan reluctantly dispatched troops, including Bellard's regiment, to the Maryland shore opposite the Confederate batteries, but the Northern soldiers could only watch impotently as the Southern guns continued to command the river. During the winter of 1861–1862 that Bellard and his fellow soldiers passed in relative idleness, the Confederacy seemed constantly to gain strength. On February 22, 1862, Jefferson Davis was formally inaugurated President of the Confederacy (he had hitherto served as provisional president), and he pledged never to yield in the struggle for Southern independence.

The Union government seemed to lack an equal determination. In December McClellan fell ill with typhoid fever and for several weeks was unable to give orders. Ineffectually Lincoln tried to take over the command of the Union armies himself. When McClellan recovered, he startled the President, who had hitherto trusted him, by announcing that he did not intend to push directly south against the Confederate forces confronting Washington but that, instead, he planned to move his army by way of Annapolis and the Chesapeake Bay in order to launch an attack upon Richmond from the east. Fearful that such a move would leave the capital unprotected, Lincoln took the extraordinary step of issuing his own war order, on March 8, 1862, directing the army to make no change of base until Washington was "entirely secure" and ordering McClellan not to move more than 50,000 soldiers away from the capital "until the navigation of the Potomac, from Washington to the Chesapeake bay, shall be freed from the enemies batteries and other obstructions."

Whether the President's order would have forced McClellan to attack the Confederate batteries at Cockpot Point cannot be known. As it happened, within twenty-four hours after Lincoln issued his order, the Confederate authorities decided to pull their army back toward Richmond, and they hastily evacuated their Potomac batteries. On March 10 — not on March 2, as Bellard erroneously reports — unopposed Union troops crossed the Potomac and occupied the deserted Southern positions.

———◆———

At about 11 a.m. the Regt. left camp and marched to the gas house dock, where they had to wait some 4 hours before they could get on board.

The weather being very cold, a number of the men procured canteens of whiskey and while waiting to go on board got gloriously drunk. As I was on camp guard at the time we left camp I had to march with the waggons and prisoners, and did not arrive at the dock until after the Regt. had embarked. By the time we arrived the whiskey had begun to operate and a fight had commenced between two officers who were jealous of each other. Swords were drawn and sheathed again without any whiskey being spilt. This started the ball rolling between two companys and a regular old fasioned free fight was the consequence for about half an hour, during which bloody noses and black eyes were freely given and received. The guards and prisoners arriving just as the fight between the men commenced, the guards were called upon to quell the riot. Both guards and prisoners mingled in and were soon lost sight of in the crowd. That was the last of the prisoners, as we could not find them after the row was over.

Thinking that I would take a little sleep, I mounted the huricane deck and lay down, but had no sooner picked out a soft spot on the deck, when some one tumbled over me. After several vain attempts to rest myself, I gave it up as a bad job and mingled with the crowd. While walking along on the lower deck, I was sudenly challenged by a member of Co. "B," as to what company I belonged to. Giving the desired information, I was refered to someone else. As he vouched for me I was passed on as all right company "C." Having a curiosity to know what this company had taken posession of the gangway for, I waited a while to see who the next unlucky chap would be, when up comes a soldier from one of the country companys. He was challenged in the usual manner and giving his answer as belonging to the Pie Eaters (as the country men were called) he was immediately knocked down by one of the impromtu guards, and another free fight took place. It wall [was] the result of whiskey caused by a dislike between the city boys and the country ones.

During the night some of them getting rather hot blooded, made a rush for the Colonel's quarters, calling upon him to come out so that they could chuck him overboard. The old chap did come out but with a drawn sword in his hand. Coming out as far as the door in his shirt tail, he made a cut with the sword and catching one of them over the head, split it. This had the effect of cooling them off and they had more respect for the old man ever afterwards. One or two of the men in roaming round the boat looking for more whiskey got too near the edge and losing their equilibrium, they fell with a splash into the freezing water, one of them breaking his thumb in the tumble. This sobered them up with a jump and the poor fools had to stand by the gas house fire all night to get dried off.

About daylight we steamed down the river passing Alexandria which was white with snow. Sailing about 30 miles, we disembarked at a place called Indian Head, Md. The Regt. having to march 10 miles lower down to Rum Point Landing. I was again called into requisition as guard, and after getting as many prisoners together as possible we started after the Regt. with the waggons. And such a march, over an old country road, over stumps, ditches, and often times in mud over our boot tops. We finally reached the Regt. Several times on the road we had to pry the waggons out of the mud, that the mules with all the beating and swearing were unable to do. On the road we passed what the natives call a village. One [building was] a house occupied by a white family and the other one tenanted by negroes. At the time our Regt. arrived, some of the regts. that had been there for some time previous were engaged in building a corduroy road, as the roads were almost impassable in rainy weather. As we had no tents put up and being too tired to build a shelter, besides being out of rations, I went over to the 6th Regt. that lay alongside of us, and being acquainted with several of the boys, I succeeded in getting my bread basket filled, and a good night's rest under canvas.

The next day the 4th, the tents had not been unpacked, so we set to work and built ourselves a substantial brush shanty to keep off the wind and rain, and with a large fire in the center, made a very respectable shelter that was both warm and cozy. Rations were then given out by the quarter master, but one of the companys by some hook or crook had got the best of us to the tune of 4 boxes of hard tack. As there was no use growling about it, the boys sailed in and not only got our own back, but some two or three sides of bacon as interest. At night, the scene at this camp or bivouc presented a very picturesque sight. Barrels, boxes, tents and stacks of muskets were strewn around in beautiful confusion, enumerable camp fires showing them off to the best advantage. On the afternoon of the 5th we were again on the move, and marching about 4 miles we entered a beautiful pine grove interspersed with holly, hemlock and cedar trees, which was to be our future home for the winter. After stacking arms, the tents were brought out and pitched and we were at home once more. The rebels were on the other side of the river at Cockpit Point where they had a battery for the purpose of blockading the Potomac River but the day that we arrived, some 40 shells had been thrown at an oyster boat without doing any further damage than sprinkling them with water.

The next morning the regular details for picket were made, this being our first duty of that description. One full company took charge of Rum Point Landing, about 4 miles from camp, to protect the government stores and other property that were landed at that place, previous to being transported to camp. This was a lively spot for our troops on account of the sutlers and contrabands who made this their head quarters. There was also a detail of 108 men taken from the brigade for picket duty along the shore, 3 men being placed on one post for 24 hours relieving each other as they saw fit. Occasionally the pickets would take a boat out for a sail on the river, but this was sure to draw the rebels' fire from their batterys, and was at last abandoned. It was rather risky bussines to sail on the river, as the Johny's had 3 batterys on the oppisite side of the river, manned with heavy guns. One at Cockpit directly oppisite our camp with 5 guns, one at

Winter quarters, Lower Potomac

Shipping Point, lower down the river with 3 guns, and still another, and the most formidable at Aquia Creek.

As the weather was getting rather cold the tents were raised up about two feet by driving split pine tree saplings into the ground and fastening the tent on top. Bunks were put up, and a large fire place was built on the rear of each tent, made of logs and mud. These lasted a long time when well plastered with mud, and with a roaring fire in them made our quarters quite warm and comfortable.

On Christmas day, Co. H of our Regt. were well supplied with good things as their friends had sent them out about 18 boxes containing plenty of poultry and various other good things, making the mouths of the less fortunate companys water. As I received a box myself about this time it did not affect me quite so bad as some of the rest. In order to make it look as much like Christmas as possible, a small tree was stuck up in front of our tent, decked off with hard tack and pork, in lieu of cakes, oranges, etc. Our band of 15 pieces arrived about the time and the boys were highly elated at the prospect of plenty of music. And it was noticed that when the Regt. marched out to parade with our band at the head of the line, the boys had more rubber in their heels than formerly.

On the 31st we were inspected and mustered by Lieut. Col. Mott, who in order to show his authority and enforce military disipline, placed the writer on fatigue duty from inspection until sundown or retreat. (That is to carry a log of wood on his shoulder). All this for having a little dust on the nipple of his gun.

The rebels had a little target practice today in firing at 5 schooners that were running the blockade. Although they were fired at repeatedly, no damage was done. The steamer Pensacola also passed the batterys, having a barge of hay on the rebel side of her to keep the shells from doing any damage when the steamer came down. It was a very dark night, nothing was heard but the cry of the screech owl, when all of a sudden, boom, boom, bang was heard as if heaven and earth had come together. The camp was alive in a moment. Men were running here, there, and all over, shirt tails flying, and all trying to find out what the row was about, not knowing but what we had been attacked, but up in the heavens could be seen like shooting stars the fiery fuse of the shells as they were hurled at the passing steamer. What with the flash of the guns and the explosion of the shells, it was a grand sight, and one never to be forgotten by any who were there to see. I have heard a more terific bombardment since, but none that made such a lasting impression.

In January 1862, our old muskets were turned over to the quarter master and the Austrian rifle issued in there stead. They were a very handy piece to carry being short, light and very easily cleaned, being finished in the rough (that I suppose was owing to there not having the time to finish them). The bayonettes were longer than the U.S. pattern, 4 bladed, and as sharp on the point as a needle. A wound made with one of them would be bad to heal, as the would [wound] would close when the bayonette was withdrawn.

Feb. 1st the cooks were routed out at 11 p.m. to cook rations for the Regt. and were at it all night. About 1 a.m. it commenced to rain and snow and turning into a steady rain the Regt. was not ordered out, as the roads were too muddy for either marching or working.

Whenever the weather permitted, our men were bussy in building a bakery and guardhouse. They were built of logs plastered with mud, and thatched with long river grass that grew plentiful on the river bank. The oven was built entirely of mud and turned out bread enough to supply the Regt. every day with one loaf for each man. This was quite a treat, as we had nothing but hard tack since leaving Wash.

Our first death took place in this camp in the person of private Bell, who died of consumption and was buried with military honors. A subscription was raised in the company to send his body home, but on informing his wife of our intentions we received a letter in reply, that she would rather have the cash than the body. So poor Bell was left alone in his glory on the Maryland shore, and the men pocketed their greenbacks themselves.

In anticipation of a forward movement, general orders were read out on dress parade, that the 3rd brigade, N.J. Vols. were to hold themselves in readines for active service, and that all enlisted men, who had pistols were to give them up, and place reliance only on the musket. Very good advice, but a gun is not quite so handy for foraging as a pistol, so instead of complying with the order, I handed mine to the captain's cook, who took care of it for me until we got on the move.

Although the whipping post had been abolished for soldiers, it would seem that for citizens it was a matter of taste. The orders at this time were that no liquor should be sold to soldiers, and anyone caught selling it would be severely dealt with. Two men from Washington however, not having the dread of punishment before their eyes, took it into their heads that they would make a few surplus stamps for themselves by ignoring the order, and accordingly provided themselves with a good stock of the raytion witch [which] they proceeded to dispose of to the soldiers at a fabulous price. Col. Starr having got wind of the little arrangement had them arrested and placed in our guard house for safe keeping. The Regt's. court martial was convened and the prisoners tried. They were each found guilty and sentenced to receive 20 lashes on their bare back and to be set adrift in the Potomac in an open boat without oars. The sentence was confirmed by the authorities at Washington and on the 13th was executed.

Two young pine saplings were selected close to our guard house. The shirts of the prisoners having been taken off, they were tied fast to the trees and the flogging commenced, two of the guards being detailed for the job, one of whom had a coach whip and the other a long waggon whip. Lieut. _____ a coward and poltroon, being officer of the guard, acted as the great "I am." This officer afraid of being shot had bought a steel plated vest to ward of the bullets but on trying it one day in the wood, to see how it would stand lead, a rifle ball went clean through it and the brave lieutenant resigned. At the first cut the ridges were raised and the men writhed in their bonds, but on the lieutenant's ordering the guards to lay it on harder (under the penalty of receiving a dose themselves) they fairly howled. The blood was now running down their backs freely. When they had received the 20 lashes their backs looked like raw beef. When the sentence was executed they were cut loose, and after putting on their shirts they were escorted to the guardhouse muttering threats of vengeance on the military authorities. Whether the setting adrift part of the sentence was carried out, I never learnt as the men were taken from camp under guard, and were seen no more.

*Although the whipping post had been abolished for soldiers,
it would seem that for citizens it was a matter of taste*

One of the houses at this point was used by the darkeys or
"contrabands" for sleeping apartments for the women

Feb. 22nd weather very changeable being about one fine day to 3 of rain or snow. On this day it was raining pretty lively, but the air resounded with the booming of cannon in honor of the birthday of him whose name will never die (Washington) whose example it is that within a few days has caused the Union Troops to gain victories, that will make the Traitor Jeff.

41

[Davis] quake in his boots, while he takes his seat in Richmond as the bogas President of a deluded and misguided people.

But to return, our company being detailed for picket at Rum Point Landing, we had, taking it altogether, a very good time. The mud was very bad being up to our ancles, and tramp, tramp, through this was not very pleasant. But all that was forgotten when the sutler's stores arrived. The boys offered their services to load his waggon which was accepted, and boxes of pies and barrells of cake were taken from the boat and placed in his waggon. There not being room for all of it the rest were placed under the dock (in a safe place as the sutler thought), as a sentinel was pacing his beat close by. The sutler being ready to return to camp, the boys thought it was high time that he forked over, but being offered the large ammount of one pie for about a dozen men, they got rather cranky and made a rush for the waggon intending to upset his apple cart, but his horse was whipped up and his goods saved. The sutler being gone, our attention was taken up with the cakes under the dock, and the way those cakes disapeared was a caution. When the sutler came back and found that his cakes had dis-apeared, a look of blank astonishment settled on his face, and making his way to the captain's quarters stated his grievances to him. The only satis-faction he got was, that government troops were not there to guard sutlers' stores, but the government's, and if he did not want his things stolen, he must guard them himself.

One of the houses at this point was used by the darkeys or "contra-bands" for sleeping apartments for the women. And it was a sight to look through the cracks in the boards on some warm night, if his nasal organ was not too sensative, to see the manner in which they were bundled together, black legs, arms and woolly heads sticking out in all directions.

The shanty used by the reserve picket for sleeping purposes or to keep out the cold wet weather, was built entirely of corn stalks, fastened over a

*Two ships' howitzers
having been attached
to the 2nd company*

wooden frame. It was very warm and would have been very comfortable, had it not been for the large amount of fleas and other varmint that infested it, and made the boys pass the hours in scratch, scratch, scratch.

Two ships' howitzers having been attached to the 2nd company of our Regt. big things were expected from the Bloody Fifth (as we were styled by the other Regts) when we got into action. At some distance from our camp, an earthwork had been thrown up having for an armament two whitworth guns, and wishing to test their range, Genl. Hooker and staff had the gunners fire at the Rebels at Cockpit batterys oppisite comming very near cutting down the flag staff, from which the rebel flag floated in the breeze. The fire was returned but did not come anywhere near, but that was not always the case for on one occasion as the 7th N.J. were forming for dress parade, a shell came screching across the river and dropped close to the band, who were playing at the time. That tune was cut shorter than usual, and coat-tails was about all that could be seen as they disapeared behind the tents.

On Sunday March 1st the Rebs were quieter than usual, and although their flag was flying, no men could be seen. In the afternoon the gunboat Annacosta [Anacostia] came stealing down the river, firing a few shots occasionally at the battery, but instead of being returned, everything was quiet and not a soul could be seen on their works. The boys hearing the firing had assembled on the hill and were expecting to see a little fun. The gun boat went closer, and closer to the works but not a shot was fired. At last a boat was manned and pulled for shore. On the Jolly Tars gaining a foothold on shore at the foot of the works, which was in plain view from our position, we were sure that the rebels had skedaddled, but when the rebel flag was hauled down and our own glorious banner was unfurled to the breeze, three rousing cheers were given by the boys in blue, who were now on the hills by thousands, which was returned by the blue jackets on the forts.

While this was going on at Cockpit the rebels were firing Shipping Point lower down. The steamer Page that had been laying still all winter was burnt along with two schooners. Magazines were blown up and several mills and store houses destroyed making a total wreck of the entire concern, being determined that the yankee mud sills should not reap the benefit, if they could not.

At 12 that night we were ordered out and told to be in readiness to march at 4 a.m. It is needless to say that there was no sleep that night in anticipation of such an event. The long roll had been beaten on several nights at 12 o'clock to test the men and see how prompt they would be in case we were called upon to march or repel an attack. The consequence was, that when the drummer beat the roll, we were in line of battle in 15 minutes, with arms in our hands ready for action. At 4 o'clock we were in line and after loading with ball, but placing no caps on the nipple, we wheeled into column of platoons and were off for Dixie in earnest.

At the landing we found one of the White Hall ferry boats, having a gun mounted fore and aft, having in tow a canal boat, in which we were to make our debut on the sacred soil of Virginia. After we had stowed ourselves away

44

as best we could in the hold, owing to the limited accomidations, it commenced to rain, and kept it up until noon. The Regt. being all on board, we were towed over expecting every minute that we would be upset as the river was very rough and the bottom of the boat flat. At last by good luck we got over and after waiting about an hour for the gun boats to get into position to cover our landing we disembarked.

Upon striking terra firma we found ourselves on a narrow neck of land, running some distance out into the river, that had been at one time a fishing station, the ground being covered with old nets that were fast going to decay for want of use. The point had been covered with trees, but [they] were cut down by the rebels to prevent our getting artilery over it, in case we made an attack on their works. In less time than it takes to write it, we were in the formidable Cockpit Battery, but instead of finding no guns as we

DESTROYING COCKPIT POINT. BATTERY.

At the landing we found one of the White Hall ferry boats,
having a gun mounted fore and aft

45

supposed, there were 5 of them. One of them a very large one, having this inscription engraved upon it, "Captured from the Yankees at Bull Run." This gun had burst while they were firing at our ships killing two men and wounding two more. The rest were the ordinary size gun and were in good condition but spiked.

Stacking our arms we began to look around us. The rebs here as they have done several times since, prepared a trap for us in order to thin us out, should we be too inquisitive. Some of the boys were on the point of looking in the magizine when one of the naval officers who seemed to think that something was wrong told the boys to keep back until he took a survey of the door. After looking at it for a short time he discovered a string fastened to the door. This he cut, and on going in, a fine trap was discovered. On the floor of the powder magazine were 4 or 5 capped shells, while on a board over them was placed a solid shot, attached to the door by the string. It was expected by the rebs. that not thinking of anything of the kind, we would open the door in our eagerness when the string being tight, would roll the ball off the board and falling on the capped shells on the floor, would have blown everything up, sky high, and thinned out the 5th Regt. but thanks to providence it was discovered in time. One moment of delay on the part of the officer and the writer would have been numbered with the things that were.

After satisfying our curiosity in the magizine, we set to work dismantling the works. The cannon were dismounted and by the aid of the steamer were rolled over the bank, going down with a crash through the brush wood into the river, from which they were afterwards taken out and forwarded to Washington. About 800 shot and shell, a large lot of picks, shovels, spades, axes, camp kettles, trunks and other articles were found and placed on board. The rifle pits were leveled and the gun carriages and barracks burnt. The battery was built on a perpendickular bluff. The only way to reach it from the river, being by a series of steps cut in the earth of which one man could climb at a time. The guns were placed so far back from the edge that they could not be depressed sufficiently to do any damage to vessels sailing near their side of the river, in fact the nearer a vessel got to the battery the safer it was.

The camp had every appearance of being deserted in a hurry. In strolling around after the guns had been sent into the river I found in some shantys bread in the ovens half baked, in others dough in the pans all ready to bake. Tin cups half full of soup. Tin plates. Knives. Forks. Spoons etc. The bread was very heavy and looked as if they had been trying to make short cake and had no success. Quarters of beef were hanging on trees and in fact everything had an air of skedadling. Cartridges by the tub full. For coffee burnt rice seemed to be the staple, some of which we found ready ground in a coffee mill. Shoes seemed to be plenty, as they were strewn all round. Clothing was also plenty but did not look very military. Grey coats, caps and pants, some black striped and in fact all kinds that are used by farmers. The houses were built very comfortable, bunks put up and well filled with straw, but as for regularity there was none. The quarters seemed to be built in any place that the occupants fancied. About a mile back, a scouting party detailed from the Regt. to look out for the enemy found a steel gun stuck fast in the mud. Taking it altogether it was a pretty well fortified place and would have stopped the river effectively had they staid, but movements elsewhere hastened their departure.

In the afternoon the Regt. embarked for home and reached there about dark, presenting a very grotesque appearance as they were on the march on account of the variety of plunder that they carried home with them. Our tent boys carried off an iron tea kettle, 2 axes and 2 spades, while others were saddled with bunches of tin ware on their backs. Picks. shovels, trunks and frying pans were suspended from guns, while some were puffing and blowing under the weight of shells and solid shot, that they were carrying off as mementoes of our first attack upon a rebel battery. Upon reaching camp, the Col. addressed the Regt. stating that he was well pleased with the soldierly bearing of the men, and hoped that in our next expedition we would lose no more men than in this one.

While our Regt. was at Cockpit the 1st Mass. Vols. of our division took possession of the battery at Shipping Point making quite a haul. The rebel sutler left in such a hurry that he left all of his goods behind, and the Mass. boys had the satisfaction of taking back some 40,000 cigars besides other truck too numerous to mention. Large knives made out of old files that the rebels wore to kill the Yankees with, [which] were left behind being too clumsy to carry and fell into our hands as curiosities. Two men were nabbed by the Mass. boys. One of them came back to get some tobacco, not knowing that we had possession and of course got in limbo. Two companys of the 6th N.J. were sent over afterwards to look up the rebels but found nothing but a Texas cap, made of red cloth with a single star in the centre. The river was now open for the first time since we arrived, and steamers were plying up and down all day, making things quite lively and looking more like civilization.

As we had no excitement after the rebels had left but drill, the boys commenced ball playing as a little recreation from the routine of camp life. Matches were got up between different companys and regts. and once between two brigades when the Jersey Blues came out ahead. Shooting was also indulged in, the sportsman bringing home possum, rabbits and other game. Turkey buzzards, eagles, crows, wild geese and ducks, etc. were seen flying round very often. Fishing was also very good, there being plenty of yellow perch, cat fish, roach and eels and other small fish, and many a dinner of fish was set down to with a gusto that was not seen with the army grub. Small game was roasted without cleaning. After getting a bed of hot coals, the possum or rabbit was rolled in mud until it was about an inch thick and well plastered on. It was then put in the coals and covered up. When done, the crust of mud was cracked open, which took all the hair with it and left the skin clean. Cutting it open the insides were taken out whole and your game was ready for the table.

VI

Yorktown

With the potomac *again under Union control, General McClellan was free to start his long projected campaign to take Richmond from the east, by moving up the Peninsula between the James and York Rivers. In the middle of March 1862 he began sending troops down the Potomac to Fort Monroe, a powerful bastion at the extreme eastern tip of the Peninsula that remained in Union hands. By May 1 he had an army of 112,000 men, including Bellard's regiment, on the Peninsula.*

By that time, however, McClellan's plan for a quick strike at Richmond had gone awry. He had expected powerful Union flotillas, with complete mastery of the James and York Rivers, to bring up supplies as his army advanced. But in early March the Confederates demonstrated how fragile was Union naval superiority. Seizing the powerful steam frigate, the Merrimack, which had been sunk and abandoned when the Federals fled from Norfolk in 1861, the Confederates equipped the vessel with iron plate and a cast-iron ram and rechristened it the C. S. S. Virginia. On March 8 it made its debut in Hampton Roads by attacking the wooden vessels of the Union blockading squadron. Within hours it sank the Cumberland *and ran aground the* Congress *(which Bellard mistakenly called the* Flushing*). Re-*

turning to the attack the next day, the Virginia *encountered the newly arrived Union ironclad, the* Monitor, *a strange-looking vessel that reminded Bellard of a cheese box on a raft but that was as powerful as her Confederate rival. After an inconclusive duel, in which both ironclads suffered damage, the commanders broke off the engagement, and the* Virginia *steamed back to her harbor at Norfolk. So long as the* Virginia *remained afloat, McClellan could not use the James River as his line of supply, since the Confederate ironclad might at any point cut it off.*

Nor was Union control of the York River more certain. The Confederates had erected formidable batteries at Yorktown, on the south bank of that river, and also at Gloucester, on the opposite shore.

McClellan was left, then, with no option but to drive directly up the Peninsula, bringing his supplies by land. On April 4 his first two columns pushed out toward Richmond. But they and the troops that followed them, including Bellard's company, encountered two obstacles. The very next day the spring rains began, and the good roads McClellan needed to transport his artillery and heavy equipment turned into muddy ruts. Second, they discovered that the Confederates had constructed a line of defensive fortifications across the Peninsula, running from Yorktown south along the Warwick River. When McClellan began his campaign this line was manned by a handful of Confederate troops, but their commander, General J. ("Prince John") Bankhead Magruder, who was fond of amateur theatricals, had his thin regiments march "through a clearing, in sight of the Federal advance guard, double-quicked them around a little forest out of sight, and then marched them through the clearing again — over and over, like a stage manager using a dozen adenoidal spear carriers to represent Caesar's legions." Convinced that the enemy was "in strong force and very strong position," McClellan settled down to nearly a month's siege of Yorktown, which, of course, lost any advantage that surprise might have given his expedition. By early May the Confederates succeeded in reassembling their main army, under General Joseph E. Johnston, to the east of Rich-

mond. Quietly Magruder withdrew his tiny force from the Yorktown defenses just one day before McClellan was ready to begin bombarding it.

———◆———

On the 5th of April, tents were struck, knapsacks packed, and everything got ready for a move, and the next day we left our camp and marched to the landing. There we found the Wm. Kent, a north river steamer used by the government as a transport. We marched on board and lay in the stream until one o'clock the morning of the 8th, when we started and had pleasant sail down the river to within about 25 miles from Fortress Monroe, when we anchored for the night near the Maryland shore, the captain being afraid to go on. The wind having raised, it caused such a commotion in the water that the boat was rolling and tossing all night, having such an effect on the boys that half of them did not know whether they were standing on their heads or heels. We were packed like herrings in a box, and where we dropped we had to stay, as if we attempted to take a walk, we would loose our foot of plank, if indeed you were not thrown down by the rough sea.

At about 8 o'clock the morning of the 9th we again started southward with a very rough sea and raining, having done so since the 5th. The water as we sailed down the Chesapeake Bay was fairly alive with wild geese and ducks, making the bay black with them, but as we were not on a duck shooting expedition they were left to themselves. At about noon we arrived safe at Fortress Monroe, when a sight met our eye, that put us in mind of New York. Ships were here in swarms. Gun boats, tug boats, sloops, ships, ocean and river steamers, steam frigates and last but not least the Monitor. The cheese box that had a few days before sent the Rebel Ram Merimac howling home. The Merimac could be seen indistinctly in the distance afraid to come out. Several vessels had been sunk, and one, the Flushing had her bow just out of the water.

At this point, we had a good view of the Rip Raps, w[h]ere the unlucky soldier, condemned to hard labor is made to carry stones from one pile to another, and then carry them back again, and so on all day. A very pleasant occupation for some but excuse me. As we were short of provisions, a detail was made, and sent in a boat to the fort to bring us some rations, but while there imbibed too freely in the ardent and were brought back in a very loose condition. We got our grub however, other soldiers from the fort bringing it out to us.

We lay there until the 12th when we started for Ship Point, finding the rest of our division already there, awaiting their turn to land from the transports. This was the rebels' first stronghold outside of the Fortress. A large breastwork was built around the point, with embrasures for cannon. Inside the works their quarters had been built, consisting of log houses, shingled. Everything seemed to have been built for a permanent garrison.

Here we disembarked, and marching a mile went into camp, using the shelter tents for the first time. This tent is a great institution, as no matter where the soldier goes, he is always sure of shelter from the storms and dews, as every man carries a half tent on his back when on the march. It is put up in a few minutes and does away with having to build a brush shelter while waiting two or three days for the waggons to bring up your tents.

Stopping at this camp until we had got the trees pretty well cleared

And last but not least, the Monitor

off, we sailed across Cheeseman's Creek in pontoons and camped on the other side in regular military order, having a company street in front of each row of tents. Oysters were plentiful in the creek and soldiers could be seen in all directions taking these delicious bivalves for camp consumption. The weather being very warm the grass was quite green and peach, pear and cherry trees were in full bloom. The firing from the direction of Yorktown could be heard quite plain, and to make it look something like wartime, Co. "B" of our Regt. was sent on a scouting expedition loaded with ten days' rations.

One of our men had an experience that must have shook his nerves somewhat. After every court martial it was usual to read off on dress parade the findings and sentences of the court. One eve. on parade when the adjutant was about to read the orders, the prisoners who had been tried by the court were marched to the front and centre of the Regt. under guard. Among the number was a man who had fallen asleep on his post (the penalty of which was death). The adjutant read off the charges and specifications preferred against him, and the pleadings of the prisoners, when he came to the findings and sentences of the court, which was, that after mature deliberation, the court finds the prisoners of the charge, Guilty, of the specifications, Guilty, and the sentence of the court was that he be shot to death by musketry, at such time and place, as the commanding genl. should direct. I can't say how he looked when this verdict was rendered against him, as his back was towards us, but the next order would have a tendency to brighten him up, which was that the execution of the sentence be revoked, and the prisoner be returned to duty.

On the 21st we had orders to move, and as it had been raining all day the roads were simply horrible. Before leaving camp, some of the boys had made an effigy of Jeff Davis, by getting together some old clothes, an[d] stuffing them with straw. This after being duly labelled was hung on the limb of a tree and left behind. After dinner we took up our line of march, made slow and tedious, by the condition of the roads.

On the way we passed 3 earthworks that had been built close to the road under cover of the woods. They could not be seen until we were close up to them. Had they been mounted and manned, they would have been ugly customers to pass, but the rebels had fallen back so quick to Yorktown that they had no time given them. The trees on our line of march gave unmistakable signs of shot and shell, some cut in two, others half way and some had their branches hanging over the road.

We encamped that night in a peach orchard about 1-1/2 miles from Yorktown. While hunting in the dark for sticks to pitch our tents, it commenced to rain, and in half an hour the ground was flooded. Not having had time to trench, and being in low ground, my knapsack was soon floating in 3 inches of water, and blankets and everything else was soaked. There was no chance to lay down, so we sat on our knapsack and listened to the rain as it rattled down on our tents. We had not fairly settled ourselves for the night, when myself and others of the first letters of the alphabet were detailed for entrenchment duty.

Arming ourselves with picks and spades, we started off in the mud, rain and darkness to find the trenches. After proceeding a short distance we lost sight of the first party under command of a captain, and had to grope our way blindly. After we had floundered through the mud for about a mile and a half, we came to a halt for consultation, as we did not know where to go. Nor did we wish to make the acquaintance of any stray rebel who might take a notion to gobble us up. Seeing a light ahead of us, we were debating w[h]ether to advance or not, when a cavalry vidette came looming up in the darkness. We thought that we were gone in sure this time, but when he got close to us, we saw that it was one of our own cavalry. He wanted to know what we were doing there, and being informed that we had come from camp to work on the trenches but had lost our way, he told us to go back to camp, giving us the cheering news that if we had gone for that light, we would have been gobbled up to a certainty, as it was one of the fortifications in the rebel lines. Of course we were glad of the chance to get back to camp, and put for it the best we could. After considerable hunting round in the mud, we found our water lots and put up for the night. The next day it cleared up fine and we put our tents up properly, got our wet goods dry, and were ready for anything.

Upon getting fairly to bussiness, details were sent out every morning and night for duty on the works digging trenches and forts. While one party dug, another would stand guard so as not to be taken by surprise. Fortifications were built very fast, and by the 25th of April, our brigade had one fort finished and mounted, while others were under way. Between all the forts was a long line of zigzag rifle pits that connected each fort, and extended the entire length of our line of works, while a short distance in the rear was cut a military road, that would enable our troops to march from one point to another without being seen, both infantry, cavalry or artilery.

We sometimes experienced lively times while on picket, or digging trenches. While some of our men were at work on one of the earthworks, one of them more venturesome than the rest, mounted the magizine of the fort in plain sight of the rebels. In a moment the shells were flying around lively. Some of them fell in the fort, but did no damage beyond throwing more dirt around than was needed.

At 2 o'clock in the morning the brigade would be ordered out as reserve in case the pickets were driven in, and stood in line until all danger of a night attack was past, when we were dismissed in time to put our tents and traps in order, when we would be ready for breakfast. (This reserve bussiness we had about every 3rd day.) After breakfast, a detail was sent out to build roads (and sometimes the whole company) about a mile from camp. While on this duty, and in the woods cutting down trees, I was very much annoyed by an insect that they call down south, a wood tick. They make their way under the skin, and if not pulled out at once, leave a nasty sore, causing a great deal of scratching, being worse in fact than a bed bug, but something of the same breed.

On the 26th, our Regt. was detailed for picket in the trenches. Starting

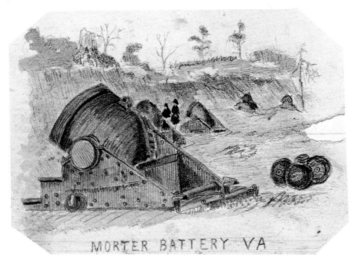

Morter Battery, Va.

early in the morning we passed the forts and were soon at the front. One wing of the Regt. was posted in a ravine out of the way of any stray shots, to act as reserve, while the rest of the companys were stationed at diferent places along the line, one half of whom did the picketing, while the others took post in the rear as a reserve for the company. Our company was stationed in one of the military roads that had just been cut, the ground being completely filled with diferent kinds of shells, showing that it had been under water at some ancient date.

On each of our posts was stationed one of Berdan's sharp shooters, who were always on the look out for game, and woe to the rebel who put himself in their way. One of them who was armed with a telescope rifle had placed a negro picket "Hors de Combat" the day before. In front of our line stood a large hollow tree, having loop holes cut into it so that a rifle could be run through and discharged at our men without danger to the negro who fired it. On this occasion our sharp shooter had fired twice at the black without hitting him, but in the afternoon he left the tree and was taking a walk for the benefit of his legs, when he was suddenly flopped on his face before he had taken six steps. Two white men who with him tried to haul him back, but a few doses of leaden pills being thrown that way, he was left alone until darkness gave them a chance to take him away.

On our left was an apple orchard and the rebel pickets and artilery were posted in it. The post that I occupied was on a bluff with a few bushes in front that kept us from being seen but was no protection against bullets that soon made our acquantance in earnest. Shells crashed through the

In front of our line stood a large hollow tree, having loop holes cut into it so that a rifle could be run through and discharged at our men

Sharp shooters Tree at Yorktown

woods, and bullets whistled all round us, but no one was hurt, except one of the Mass. men who was digging in the trenches.

Towards night our pickets were advanced and posted on the earthworks that had been thrown up during the day, and what with the rain that had drizeled all day, and the cold, we put in a sorry night, and a muddy one, being compelled to lay on our bellys on the muddy banks. It might have been worse, but before going on post we were supplied with a ration of whiskey that the Lieut. had drawn for us, and that helped to keep out the cold. Another ration had been left with the reserve for use in the morning but during the night one of our sergeants who was a temperance man (so called) had slept too near the kettle containing the beverage and was found by the Lieut. in the morning in a very loose state, while the whiskey had evaporated.

Firing was kept up at intervals all night, but towards morning a volley was fired at something that was seen in the field in front. That had the effect of bringing the reserve to their feet. As no enemy appeared it died out in a short time. As soon as it was daylight the shells and bullets began to fly around pretty lively, and for a short time whistled over our heads very uncomfortably. But with the exception of one man of Company I who had a gash cut in his leg no one was hit. We captured one prisoner who informed us that he had been under fire all day both from our men and his own. The rebels he said had 2000 men on picket, and that a great many more would desert but were afraid of getting shot by our sharp shooters in comming over. He was a native of Jersey City and was known to several of the Regt. As he had been pressed into the service he was very glad to get out of it so easy.

The 6th N.J. relieved us before noon when we returned to camp. When they returned from picket they brought in two of their men who had been wounded by shells. Heavy seige guns are passing our camp every day, some of them so large that it takes 16 horses to pull them over the roads. On the 29th one of our batterys opened on the rebels to try their range, and a great racket was kicked up for about half an hour. The gun boats on the river sent in a shell now and then and every time they struck the rebels would set to and yell with gusto.

The morning of May 4th our Regt. was turned out to do duty in the digging brigade. Arming ourselves with picks, shovels and axes, we started to the right for the purpose of throwing up earthworks near the river. While resting ourselves in a peach orchard, it was discovered that the works of the enemy had been abandoned for the glorious stars and stripes were seen flying from their works, where the day before the stars and bars floated defiently in our face. As there was no more use for the shovel brigade in that quarter we about faced and returned to camp, when we dropped the pick and shovel, and took up the rifle and knapsack. Tents were struck, rations issued out, canteens filled, and after receiving 100 rounds of ammunition [we] were ready for the fray. The only time that I was on the shovel brigade was the night we arrived and the day we left, so that I did not do much of the digging, being excused from that kind of duty by the Lieut.

Sharpshooter firing at the gunners

Arming ourselves with picks, shovels and axes

VII

On to Richmond

WHEN THE CONFEDERATES *evacuated Yorktown, they fell back to a secondary line of defense, about halfway up the Peninsula. Their withdrawal left the south bank of the James exposed, and recognizing that it was only a matter of time before Federal troops would occupy Norfolk and the navy yard, they destroyed the Virginia in order to keep the iron clad from falling into enemy hands. The Union fleet was now free to push up the James River in support of McClellan's advance. At the same time the capture of Yorktown opened up the York River, and McClellan shipped four divisions up that river in the expectation that they would land far behind the Confederate lines.*

Meanwhile the body of McClellan's army marched up the Peninsula, with General Joseph Hooker's division, to which Bellard's regiment belonged, in the lead. About two miles east of Williamsburg, the ancient capital of Virginia, Union soldiers ran into the new Confederate defenses. Astride the road from Yorktown the Southerners had erected the formidable Fort Magruder, which General Hooker described as having a "crest measuring nearly half a mile, with substantial parapets, ditches, magazines, &c."

Protecting the approaches to the fort was an abatis of felled trees, with dangerously sharpened branches pointed toward the advancing Union soldiers. Since McClellan was still in Yorktown, Generals Hooker and Philip Kearny commanded the Federal assault upon the fort.

Bellard's account of this brief but hotly fought battle of Williamsburg (May 5, 1862) is necessarily secondhand, since he was not able to keep up with his company. It is nevertheless generally accurate, though his tale of Roberdeau Wheat's "Louisiana Tigers" advancing under a Union flag is dubious. More reliable is Bellard's description of the "repeating gun" — a kind of ancestor of the Gatling gun — used by the Excelsior Brigade, which consisted of New York regiments recruited by the swashbuckling General Daniel Sickles. These guns in theory could fire a hundred shots a minute, but in practice they proved too cumbersome and inaccurate to be of much value. Bellard's enumeration of the heavy casualties sustained by his regiment is accurate.

Though Colonel Samuel H. Starr's official report of the battle mentioned cowards and shirkers in the Fifth New Jersey Infantry, he probably did not have Bellard in mind. During the engagement at Williamsburg many of the inexperienced Union soldiers like Bellard became separated from their units. But, remarked Colonel Gilman Marston of the Second New Hampshire Infantry, which Bellard so informally joined, "every man that had a musket to fire went into the fight with whatever regiment or company he happened to fall in with, and so continued until night put an end to the contest."

———◆———

The assembly soon called the men to arms, and by 12 o'clock noon we were on the move, the cavalry being in the advance with our division. After a short march across a level plain we reached the famous fortifications of

Yorktown, and formidable they were. Three lines of zig zag earthworks encircled the little village of Yorktown and extended from the York to the James River. There seemed to be no lack of guns, as they could be seen as far as the eye could reach, all in good order but spiked. Ammunition was also found in abundance.

The rebels had again planted some of their infernal machines, through

Torpedos were planted in any place that was likely to be visited by our men

which some 3 or 4 men lost their lives. Torpedos were planted in any place that was likely to be visited by our men, on the walks by the forts and between the graves where rebel soldiers had been buried. Wherever a torpedo had been buried, a short stick or branch was standing up, and woe be to the man or animal who tread on it or kicked it. On the main road to Williamsburg they were planted in the middle of the road, and when the infantry marched past, were marked by pieces of rags tied to a stick as a warning that we were treading on dangerous ground. In case two or three were together as sometimes happened, a soldier was stationed to warn men off.

We had no chance to examine the works as we marched through without halting. Blankets, clothing, knapsacks, and in fact everything pertaining to the make up of a soldier was strewn around in beautiful confusion.

Mickey Free being somewhat of a walkist determined to show the boys what he could do in the way of a load, and begun to pick up every blanket that he could see until he had enough for a horse. As the weather was rather warm he soon got tired of his bargain and threw them off one by one until he was as clear as the rest. While passing through a deserted camp of the rebels I picked up a dragoon helmet but as it was too heavy to carry, had to leave it behind. We could have got plenty of war trophies had we the means of sending them home. At about 11 o'clock we bivouacked in the woods, near a

By morning we were drenched
through completely

brick church for the night. It commenced to rain during the night and by morning we were drenched through completely.

Before daylight we were off again and splashed through mud and rain for Williamsburg, passing on the road some two or three earthworks from which the rear guard had harrassed our cavalry but were driven out. At about 7 or 8 o'clock our advance guard came up to the rebels, who were found in their entrenchments about a mile from the city. Directly in front of us standing in a large open field was Fort Magruder, their principle work while severall others were on either side of it. Between us and the fort was several rifle pits, occupied by sharp shooters, and in order to make themselves more secure, and at the same time hold us in check, the woods for about a hundred yards on each side of the road had been cut down, forming an effectual abatis, being in some places 8 or 10 feet high.

After making their way through this mass of felled timber the 5th N.J. was posted on the right of the road to support a battery, while the 6th, 7th and 8th N.J. were on the left in the rear of the ravine. Fighting soon became general, and the wounded were sent to the rear, while the dead lay where they fell. The first man I saw carried off was an artileryman who had one leg taken completely off at the knee, and was being carried to the rear by two of his comrades. Shot, shell and bullets were now flying round lively, and it was about as dangerous to be in the woods on account of the falling trees and limbs that were cut off by the shells, as it was in the front.

As the rearguard of the rebels was not strong enough to keep us back reinforcements soon came pouring in from the retreating army, and a charge was made on our line. Giving one of their blood curdling yells the rebels came on. The celebrated Louisiana Tigers carrying the stars and stripes to prevent our firing upon them. The ruse however did not succeed and buck and ball was poured into them so thick from the 6th, 7th and 8th who were immediately in their front, that they were well satisfied to get back as quick as their legs could carry them. That being a failure, a charge was made on the 5th but their far reaching Austrian rifles soon sickened them, and they fell back to their entrenchments. In the afternoon the battle had become furious and the rebels making their third and last charge, captured a battery of the regulars' (the gunners having run away from their pieces) and immediately turned the guns on our Regt. Vollunteers had been called for by Genl. Hooker to man the battery, which was readily responded to. But it was too late, as it was already in the rebels' hands and firing into our men, who fell back under a galling fire.

As the fight was going against us and the men being about used up, the regimental bands were ordered to consolidate and play. On wanting to know what they should play, he answered, Toot, Toot, Toot something, and Toot they did. And as soon as the bands struck up, three cheers for the red, white and blue, two guns were run out on the road. A shower of grape and cannister was sent into the advancing rebels who were seen comming down the road. And as cheer upon cheer rent the air, the infantry, who had a few moments before been on the skedadle, now rushed in with renewed vigor, as did also the stragglers who had previously been got together as a sort of forlorn hope.

The Johnys were checked. And as Kearny's Division came on the field, having marched past the entire army to come to our relief. As they were comparitively fresh the Johnys were soon on the run, and darkness coming on the fight was over. Throwing ourselves down in the woods on the wet ground, we were soon in the arms of morpheus, and slept soundly till morning, when we discovered that the enemy had fled during the night.

As there was no more fighting to be done, we went over the battle field to bring in Privates Donaldson and Franz [Frantz], who had been badly wounded. Franz was wounded in the groin by a musket ball that had first passed through his cap pouch and then entered his body. In carrying him from the field one of the men who was carrying the stretcher droped his corner, and poor Franz fell to the ground, putting him in dreadful agony.

He was at last got into an ambulance and taken to the field hospital, where he died next day. Private Donaldson was shot in the body, and died at Fortress Monroe a few days after the battle. Lieut. Hill was wounded and sent home. Three of our Regt. who had started to find their way through the fallen timber to reach the Regt. found the rebels instead and were taken prisoners, but as the rebs had no time to take them along they were parolled on the field.

An artileryman who had one leg taken completely off at the knee

Dead men were laying in all directions. In walking over the field, some would be seen with their legs or arms shot off, others with the top or side of the head cut off as with a knife (which in this case was a piece of shell), while one man of our Regt. had his entire chest smashed in as flat as a board. In the fallen timber a reb was found who had one hand in the pockets of a Union soldier and had been shot while leaning over a log and rifling the pockets of his enemy. In a ravine that was so ably defended by the rest of our brigade, the dead rebels were piled one on the other. They were buried where they fell by throwing the dirt from the hill on top of them and so covering them up.

Our division went into camp on the field, and the sad task of burying the dead commenced, the 8th N.J. having lost the most. A large trench about 100 feet long and about 8 feet in width and 18 inches [deep] was dug, and into this wholesale grave about 80 men were placed side by side, with their uniforms on and the earth being covered over them. Mounds were raised over each body, after which a piece of cracker box with the name, co. and regt. of the dead man was placed at the head of his grave.

On the march from Yorktown, I had on a pair of tight boots, and by the time we encamped they had become so tight from being wet, that I could not pull them off, and as sand had got into them in some way, I was hardly able to walk. As there was no way of pulling them off, some of the men cut them off with knives, and when they did come off at last, some of the skin went with them. There being no clothing with the army, I had to get a pair of dead men's shoes from the battle field, and at last succeeded in getting a pair of 12, which I wore until we got close to Richmond, causing considerable amusements and remarks, by the slip slop manner in which I had to march.

At this battle, the Excelsior Brigade had a pattent gun that was calculated to annihilate an entire regt. at once. By the manner in which it worked, it was nicknamed the coffee mill. It consisted of a single barrell, mounted on a swivle, with some arrangement in the breech filled with bullets. When the crank was turned the barrell swung from side to side, throwing the balls about 100 yards apart. It did not answer however and was condemned. While the men were using it, the rebs came on them so suddenly that it could not be dragged away, and in order that the rebels should not use it against us, the barrell was taken out and so rendered useless. It was recaptured later in the day and sent to Washington.

While carrying water for the wounded, the day after the battle, some fellow took a fancy to my knapsack and when I returned it was gone. I did not care so much for the knapsack, blanket or dress coat, for they could be picked up all over, but I was rather mad to loose my revolver, papers, etc, as it was presented to me by my Father, while on a visit to our camp at Trenton.

During our stay at this camp, I visited Fort Magruder, the most formidable one at the battle, and the one in front of our Regt. It had been manned by field pieces and rifle men during the fight but was now deserted with the exception of the wounded rebels, who were quartered there. It was well built, having a deep ditch or moat running all round it filled with water. The Rebs as reported threw some of their dead [in it], thus saving the trouble of burrying them and keeping their exact loss from being known. As the fort was built close to the turnpike, one of our mule drivers got too close to it, and his waggon and mules went over board, loosing one of the mules by the experiment.

Our Regt. lost in the Battle of Williamsburg about 103 in killed, wounded and missing. While we lay still, Genl. McClellan paid a visit to Genl. Hancock's Brigade that lay close to us, and gave them great praise for what they had done at the battle, although they were on the extreme right and had to fight but a short time, while Hooker's Division who had been at it from 8 a.m. to 5. p.m. were never mentioned.

Although present at this battle and under fire, I was not with my Regt. My left foot that was lamed when a boy gave out with the continual marching through mud and the tight boots, so that I could not keep up. When I got to the front with some two or three others, we found the chaplains of the regts. there, who refused to let us go in, as it was not know[n] at what place our Regt. had gone to. So we staid there until we should see some of our officers. The shells were flying all round us and the trees and limbs falling, so that it was about as dangerous in the rear, as in the front. Happening to look up at a shell that had burst I saw a piece comming towards us, and I got out of the way just as it imbedded itself in the mud where I had been standing. Had I stood there a minute longer, I would have been finished. The other two of my company getting tired of waiting, said they were going through the fallen timber to find the Regt. They went, and found the rebs instead being taken prisoners. I formed in with the 2nd New Hampshire that lay in the road and staid with them until all straglers were ordered to fall in and from across the road to support the two guns that had been brought into service. Just as our army was falling back, and the rebs advancing, Kearny's men comming in at that time, we were ordered back.

———————◆———————

After breaking through the Confederate defenses at Williamsburg, the Army of the Potomac continued slowly to push up the Peninsula. It seemed to privates like Bellard that they spent the rest of May making a series of short and apparently pointless marches. In fact, General McClellan was moving his headquarters from Fort Monroe to White House, a landing on the Pamunkey River, which is a tributary of the York. He chose this spot because it was the head of navigation, so that he could continue to supply his army by water. White House was, moreover, on the Richmond & York Railroad that led directly to the Confederate capital. Finally, it was a position from which McClellan could extend the right wing of his army northward to meet the reinforcements he hoped President Lincoln was sending overland to him. Carefully the general deployed most of his troops in an arc just north of the Chickahominy River.

But in order to protect his left flank, McClellan sent Erasmus D. Keyes's corps across the Chickahominy to the Fair Oaks Station on the Richmond & York Railroad, and Samuel P. Heintzelman's III Corps, to which Bellard's regiment belonged, crossed over too. An army divided by a river is always an attractive target, and Confederate General Johnston saw an opportunity to crush the Union divisions south of the Chickahominy before McClellan could reenforce them. Nature came to the aid of the Con-

*We passed one of their guns that had
become disabled and left behind*

federates on May 30 with the tremendous rainstorm Bellard describes. The
usually sluggish Chickahominy became an unfordable torrent, and the
bridges that McClellan had painstakingly constructed across it were unsafe
for the passage of troops and artillery. Seizing the chance, Johnston on
May 31 struck at Keyes's corps in what became known as the battle of Fair
Oaks (or Seven Pines).

As the dazed Union soldiers of Silas Casey and Darius Couch fell back,
Hooker's division, including Bellard's regiment, raced forward to help them,
as did General Edwin V. Sumner's II Corps from north of the river. The
rescuers found the roads from the front clogged with deserters, among
whom Bellard derisively noted the "ZouZous" or "Red Leggs," those same
haughty Zouaves who had scorned more ordinary infantrymen.

Bellard's account of his regiment's role in the battle of Fair Oaks is in
precise accord with the official reports of that engagement. General Heintzelman wrote that in order to get to the front the Fifth New Jersey Infan-

72

try had to force its way through the fugitives with bayonets. Heintzelman also recorded that on the next day (June 1, 1862), Hooker himself led the Fifth and Sixth New Jersey regiments in a gallant charge that helped end the Confederate advance. From a Confederate victory the battle of Fair Oaks was turned into a draw.

Bellard's almost too graphic account of the dead and wounded after the battle was not the result of some morbid obsession. Colonel Starr, reporting four days after the fighting, declared that the greatest of the many sufferings to which his men were subjected was "the incurable stench to which they have been and are exposed, arising from the unburied dead bodies of men and horses . . . thickly scattered over the ground for hundreds of acres around." Bellard's own regiment had sixty men killed or wounded at Fair Oaks.

———◆———

On the 10th of May we commenced the series of short marches for which the Army of the Potomac was so famous. Leaving camp in the morn-

THE MARCH R FROM WILLIAMSBURGH VA
May 1862

The march from Williamsburgh, Va., May 1862

ing we marched up the Williamsburg road and were soon at the entrance of the city, meeting Lieut. Hill of our company in an ambulance on his way to Yorktown. After shaking each of us by the hand, he burst into tears, as the Regt. marched past him. We marched through the city, with bands playing and colors flying much to the disgust of the secesh women, one of whom said that she wished we would never get back. A great many wounded rebs were found in the city, and some of our men who had been parolled. About two miles from the city we passed one of their guns that had become disabled and left behind, and in various places on their line of retreat could be seen baggage waggons, guns, blankets and in fact everything that could retard their progress. Marching about 14 miles we bivouaced for the night.

On the 11th we moved camp to Slatersville and encamped there until the 14th when we took a trip of two miles, the weather being fine but plenty of mud. The 15th we tramped 7 miles through mud, slush and a heavy rain storm, and went into camp near West Point where we heard a rumor, that Magruder had asked for 3 days to consider terms of surrender. But that was all camp rumor and amounted to nothing. Officers were now supplied with the new regulation hat, and various remarks were passed on their appearance not very complimentary to the wearer. On the 18th we took another small march, this time to within two miles of New Kent court house. The 19th we went through it, and found that it consisted of a court house, jail, hotel and the inevatable blacksmith shop. It was deserted at the time, not a soul being seen. Marching a short distance, we bivouaced near Cumberland Landing on the Pamunkey River.

The 20th [we] moved to Baltimore Cross roads and lay there to rest and draw clothing of which we stood much in need, especially myself with my number 12 shoe. Our first regular ration of whiskey an[d] quinine was issued at this camp, as we were getting into the swampy country. On our march we passed an earthwork that had been thrown up across the road to retard our progress, that was made to cover two guns. It had evidently not been used. The rebs had also set fire to the woods on their retreat, and on one day's march we [went] along the road with a smouldering fire on each side of us. Heavy trees had also been felled across the roads, but our pioneers had cleared the way before we got there. We had an old fashioned thunder storm on the 22nd in which rain and hail vied with each other in trying to make us miserable. As we were well used to it by this time, we did not mind it much. We took another tramp on the 22nd of five miles through the gluey mud of Virginia, and on the 25th we moved to Poplar Hill, 14 miles from the city of Richmond.

Tents were pitched and we were not long in making ourselves as comfortable as possible. The fields and woods were perfectly covered with fruit bearing trees and shrubs of diferent kinds, such as peach, apple and pears, while the blueberry, blackberry and wortleberry bushes were perfectly loaded down with fruit. We also found plenty of reptiles such as snakes, newts, sand lizards, and frogs, but were not much bothered with them, except one man, who was bitten by a snake one night, and his leg swelled up to an enormous size but was not painful.

While on the march we passed two rebel officers who had come into our lines with a flag of truce and when we saw them were in charge of a guard and blindfolded. This gave us an impression that we were near the enemy and we expected soon to see some fun.

As our division artilery had been considerably cut up in the last fight, details were made out of the infantry to fill up the ranks, and a detail from our Regt. swelled the ranks of Bramhall's battery from Rahway, N.J. The rest of our brigade received the new Springfield rifle, and we were now one of the best armed brigades in the service.

On the 29th heavy cannonading was heard in the direction of Richmond 14 miles away. The 30th I was detailed on picket, and I shall never forget that night so long as I live. It had been raining more or less all day, but at night it seemed to concentrate all its fury. I was posted in a clump of

Two rebel officers who had come into our lines with a flag of truce

bushes alone, but so long as that storm lasted there was no fear of anyone being found asleep on his post. From dark until daylight the thunder crashed as if heaven and earth had come together, and by the flash of the lightning that came about every second the country could be seen for miles around. The lightning was simply terrible, the forks seeming to lick up the ground in all directions. When the flash was gone everything was dark as pitch and you could not see your hand before your face. The rain poured down continually, so that my position was anything but pleasent. About midnight, I heard someone calling for my post, but not knowing what was wanted or who it was, I did not answer for some time. At last I recognized the voice of the officer in charge of the picket. When I answered, finally by the aid of the lightning he found his way through the mud to my post. After indulging himself in a good swear at having to come out in such a night to relieve pickets he advanced the post further out in the field, where I found no shelter whatever and could be seen to advantage by any prowler who might be around. Leaving two men with me to help keep watch, he left for his quarters.

Thinking that I had done my share of picket duty for one day, having been on from about 9 a.m. to midnight, I looked around for something to keep me out of the wet, and finally found two three cornered rails. These I laid down on the ground and wrapping myself up in my blanket, laid down to get a little sleep and rest if possible. But I got neither. The rain pouring down soon had my blanket as wet as a dish rag, and the crashing of the thunder every few minutes would wake me from any doze, that I may have indulged in, while the edges of the rails found their way into my bones, precluding any possibility of rest, by keeping me on the twist every little while. Towards morning the rain ceased. The sun came out, the water in my clothes fairly steamed, and by nine o'clock when I was relieved, my uniform was as dry as a bone.

At about noon of the 31st, heavy cannonading was heard in the direction of Richmond, and about 3 o'clock we were ordered out in light marching order. Tents and blankets to be left behind. Nothing to be carried but ammunition, grub in the haversack, water in the canteen, and our blankets rolled and slung over the shoulder. After receiving a double ration of whiskey we were on the road to Richmond on the double quick, it being rumored that our army was whiped and falling back. Quick time had to be made in order to save the day.

Picket May 30th Poplar Hill.

*The rain poured down continually, so that my
position was anything but pleasent*

When we had arrived within a mile of the fight, we met a stream of stragglers and wounded men, all making their way to the rear, as fast as shank's mare could carry them. They were so thick in one place on the road that our Regt. being the advance, had to force their way with the bayonette. The reports from the front that we got from these men was not very encouraging. One of them, an officer of the Red Legged ZouZou's, gave us the pleasing information that he was the only one left out of the Regt. while another of the same Regt. said that he was col., capt., cook and all hands. But this was rather stre[t]ching matters, when close behind him came a large squad of Red Leggs, and the Blue, Red Leggs being in the majority. Any soldier who was wounded in that fight did not lack for help to get out, as everyone seemed ready to give them a lift in order to get as far away from danger as possible themselves. Asking some of them how the fight was going on, we were told that we had better turn back as the army was cut to pieces, and the rebs had driven us back a mile. One of them said that the Rebs wanted to know "Where's your Hooker's Division now." Col. Starr told them at last that he would sabre the first man who said anything to us about being licked. That put an end to it.

When we arrived at the front, it was dark and the firing had ceased, so we bivouaced in the woods for the night close by the road. Stacking arms in line of battle, the first thing in order was water, but we met with poor success, as none was found except what lay in the gullys in the road over which we had just marched. And when we took a drink of it, the sand could be felt and almost heard as it rattled down your throat. In the morning a large pond of good clear water was seen close to us, laying along side of it all night, but [we] could not see it on account of the darkness. After refreshing ourselves with hard tack and salt junk and washing it down with the above kind of water, we rolled ourselves in our blankets and forgot our troubles in sleep.

About 8 o'clock in the morning of June 1st, a rattling volley of musketry was fired in our front, showing that there was some rebels there yet.

Close behind him came a large squad of Red Leggs, and
the Blue, Red Leggs being in the majority

The long roll was beaten by the drummers, and in less than 15 minutes we were in line of battle, stocks broken and ready to march. Forming in column of division (that is two companys front) we advanced over a wheat field to the music of the rebel bullets that had begun to fly pretty sharp. In marching over this field I experienced for the first time a sensation of fear. I got so sick at the stomach that I thought I should have to fall out of the ranks to relieve myself, but we had no sooner got under fire, than it all vanished, and I was myself again.

On the edge of the wheat field was a thick pine wood, in which our skirmishers and the rebs were pegging away at each other. Marching through this we came to a waggon road that had been cut through for the use of the farmers, and just wide enough for one waggon. Turning up this road we marched in column of fours into the woods, but had only gone a short distance when we were saluted with a volley of balls that knocked over twenty-one men of Co. A. who were just forming the skirmish line in front of the Regt. and wounded a few of the other companys. Line of battle was formed at once to meet them, but not a reb could be seen. Suddenly a volley was fired directly in our rear which caused a little confusion, but the rear rank was about faced, and after firing from our two lines a short time and not being able to see our enemy, the order was given to fall back.

As we neared the field, General Hooker, who was standing there and thinking perhaps that we were on a skedadle, said for God's sake boys, don't fall back. That was not our mottoe, for when our Col. came out of the woods, the 5th and 6th N.J. were formed on the edge of the woods in the shape of a letter V. with the point towards the enemy. Advancing in this way we soon came up to the Johnys, when we received another dose of cold lead from both sides of our V. This seemed to be our luck for the day, and to make matters worse, we could not see a solitary reb. I supose they were laying down and the color of their uniforms helped to hide them as well, being something the same color as the ground, while we wore the blue and marching were in plain view.

A halt was ordered and firing became general. Being unable to see them as yet on account of the brush, we were ordered to lay down and during the fight as I was laying on my belly, a bullet came skipping along in front of my face, plunging in the ground about 4 inches from my nose. It flung the dirt over my face in fine style, and came out again near my foot, striking my toe as it went whistling on its way to the rear. That I thought was rather too close for comfort.

Our Col's. horse, an Indian pony, captured from the Indians during his frontier life with the 2nd U.S. Draggoons, showed his dislike for the bullets by turning his tail to the enemy whenever the firing was rather lively, putting the Col. to some trouble, as he had to turn half round in the saddle to see what was going on, as he was in command of the brigade, Genl. Patterson having been taken sick that morning with the diarrhea.

As we advanced into the woods, orders were given at last to fix bayonettes and a charge was made by our two Regts. and two more on our right. Charging with a yell, we drove them through the woods, and into the open field beyond, where they were met by the Excelsior Brigade of our Division (Sickles) who also had orders to charge, and were driven from the fields. So complete was the rout that the rebel army was panic stricken, and Richmond could have been taken at that time, had our army been pushed forward with one or two fresh divisions as reserve. This ended the fight.

The ground over which we advanced was covered with dead and wounded rebels. One of them I remember distinctly, as he lay in front of the left company, into which I had been detailed to fill their ranks. [He] was so horribly mutilated that a blanket was thrown over his head to hide the sight.

Our brigade being relieved by the Excelsior, we were ordered to the rear to draw rations and ammunition, while myself and some five others were detailed to pick up the wounded and carry them to the hospital. In the woods we found one of the 6th who was badly wounded in the groin by a musket ball. Placing him in a blanket we carried him to the field hospital. The surgeon on looking at him, said it was no use doing anything for him, as he could not live, and told him, that if he had anything to send home, to give it to the chaplain, whom he sent. About 3 weeks after the same man went home to recruit up. After considerable trouble we found our Regt. and received a day's ration of tack with 20 rounds of leaden pills thrown in.

In the afternoon, Genl. McClellan rode by our Regt. and was loudly cheered by the boys. Taking off his cap he said, Boys, we've licked them, right, left, and centre, and we're going into Richmond. This sounded well and put the boys in good humor. At the head of our Regt. he dismounted and had a long chat with our Col. who was a West Pointer, having been 25 years in the regular service.

On the morning of the second we were sent off on a reconnoitering expedition to find what had become of the enemy. Marching up the Williamsburg and Richmond Turnpike, past the camps of Casey and Couch's divisions, and over the dead rebels who were still lying where they fell, we came across their pickets at the same line they had held previous to the battle. Having ascertained the information that we were sent out for, Genl. McClellan ordered us back, and we bivouaced on the ground lately held by Genl. Peck's brigade in the rear of Seven Pines Tavern. As our tents were still at Poplar Hill 14 miles to the rear, we slept on the ground with the sky for a quilt, and slept soundly till morning.

The 8th Alabama Regt. that had been opposed to us in the fight was pretty badly cut up, losing nearly all of their men as well as the Col. The latter's horse was captured by some of our men and turned over to Col. Starr. He had been shot in the nose. The only exhibition of brutal passion that came under my notice was at this fight. One of the wounded rebs who was lying in the woods got rather too independent for a man in his position, and he riled one of our men so much that he raised his musket for the purpose of dashing out his brains, when he was stopped by one of our officers, who happened to see it in the nick of time.

While the battle was going on, the Columbian Hotel stage from Richmond was driven on the field to take off the wounded rebels, the driver being under the impression that we were whipped and skedadling to Yorktown. It was soon captured and filled with our men (not wounded) who rode along the line showing off their prize.

The firing must have been pretty lively, for in some places the pine trees about 4 inches thick had been cut in two by bullets while others were filled with bullet holes. And it was a wonder to me that any of us got out of it safe. To show how some of their regts. were peppered, I will take a grave made by themselves during the night they held the ground. Close to one of our forts were nine graves filled with men who had belonged to one of the North Carolina Regts. At the head of each grave was placed a piece of board, upon each of which appeared the names of from 10 to 12 soldiers who had been killed. The dead rebs were still laying where they fell on the second

The dead rebs were still laying where they
fell on the second day after the battle, and
presented a horrible sight

day after the battle, and presented a horrible sight. They had swelled to double their natural size, and as a consequence their clothing had burst,

Dead Reb in a Cracker box

thus exposing their bodies to the sun, and turning them as black as ink, caused it was said by drinking gun powder and whiskey.

By this time our details were ready to bury them having attended to our own dead first. They were now so far decomposed and made such a horrible stench, that it was as much as we could do to get them under cover. The way we managed it was this. Upon finding a body, a hole was dug about 18 inches deep close to him, two or three pieces of wood or fence rails were placed under the body, and at the word Roll rolled in, the men taking to their heels the instand it went over the edge, for in nearly all cases it burst, upon striking bottom. Another one would be served in the same way, some distance off, by which time the stench from the preceeding one had cleared off a little, when it was covered up. All of the horses killed at this battle, and there was quite a number of them, some batteries having lost them all, were covered over with brush and fence rails and burnt. Our stomachs being so strong by this time that we cooked our coffee over their ribs.

A short distance from our camp was the remains of what had been at one time Casey's quarter master's stores. They had been pretty well ransacked by the rebels however, while they held the ground. Hard tack and salt horse were strewn all over, dead rebels being sandwiched in between. One of them who must have been helping himself to some tack, was shot dead while in the act, as he lay with half of his body in the box and the other out.

At a house close to our camp, we found two dead men. One of them lay on his back on the floor having been shot in the side which exposed his entrals, and they lay strewn around him. The other one sat on the door step, inclining forward as if he was asleep. One of our men thinking that he was so, called to him, but receiving no answer, he shook him by the shoulder, when the body fell over dead as a door nail.

Others that lay around in plenty, had legs and arms shot off, while I saw one or two with the top of their heads cut off clean as a whistle. All of the bodies had been rifled of buttons and other knicnacs, every one of them having their pockets turned inside out. When I went over the field to find some mementoes of the place, I could not find as much as a button.

There was so many dead burried round our camp, that it was our morning's work to clean the ground of worms, that had been washed from the graves during the night by the rains. Our well, that was merely a barrell sunk in the ground had to undergo a general skimming before we could get water for coffee. The rain also washed the dirt from the shallow graves, and every morning a detail was sent out to cover up arms, legs and heads that had protruded from the ground during the night.

The Col. having had our tents and baggage brought to us, we made ourselves quite comfortable and got out of the wet. As we were close to the enemy, orders were issued to wear our equipment at all times, but so far as I was concerned, [I] slept with them off, as it was far more easier and comfortable. The wounded were being sent to the White House by train everyday, being carried to the cars by stretchers, ambulances and mules, the latter having a seat or sling on each side of him in which the wounded were placed.

———◆———

The Union and Confederate armies spent the three weeks after the battle of Fair Oaks regrouping and recovering, and only desultory skirmishing occurred during this time. Slowly McClellan brought the larger part of his army south of the Chickahominy River, in a move that put him closer to Richmond but that left the V Corps, under General Fitz John Porter, dangerously isolated north of the river. On the Confederate side, after Johnston was wounded at Fair Oaks, General Robert E. Lee took command of the Army of Northern Virginia. Building entrenchments around Richmond so that a skeleton force could hold the capital, Lee called back General Thomas J. ("Stonewall") Jackson from his daring campaign in the Shenandoah Valley and prepared to fall upon Porter's exposed force with overwhelming strength.

For a time on June 25 it seemed that McClellan might upset these careful Confederate plans by taking the offensive south of the Chickahominy. He ordered the III Corps under Heintzelman to advance. In the ensuing battle of Oak Grove, Hooker's division, which still occupied the battleground of Fair Oaks, bore the brunt of the fighting. Hooker sent Sickles's brigade forward along the Williamsburg road and ordered General Cuvier Grover's brigade to support Sickles on the left; Hooker's third brigade, to which Bellard's regiment belonged, was held in reserve, possibly because, as Colonel Starr reported, the men of the Fifth New Jersey Infan-

*The other one sat on the door step inclining
forward as if he was asleep*

try were "sickened, weakened, and exhausted." When superior Confederate
forces stopped Hooker's men, General Kearny's division came to their assistance. As the fighting died down at nightfall it became clear that McClellan
had not initiated a new offensive; he only wanted Heintzelman, as he said, "to
drive the enemy's pickets from the woods in his front, in order to give us
command of the cleared fields still farther in advance." The day's exercise
cost Bellard's regiment five casualties.

More significant, the little battle at Oak Grove confirmed Lee's sense
that he could safely reduce his forces in front of Richmond in order to

attack the Union army on the right flank, north of the Chickahominy. Bellard's regiment was not aware that on June 26 Lee struck Porter's corps at Mechanicsville and that on the next two days he continued his attack at Gaines's Mill. It came as a surprise, then, to learn that McClellan decided these battles made his base at White House untenable. As the general moved his headquarters and supplies by ship down the Pamunkey and York and up the James to Harrison's Landing, the Army of the Potomac began its slow and painful retreat southward across the Peninsula.

◆

Our picket duty now began in earnest with entrenchment duty between, each brigade going on duty every third day. Picket skirmishing seemed to be indulged in more for amusement than anything else, for whenever the Excelsior Brigade went out it was the signal for a skirmish and they would have it hot and heavy until the Jersey Brigade went out and relieved them, when we would have the pleasure of driving the rebels back to their own

Ambulances and mules, the latter having a seat or sling on each side of him in which the wounded were placed

By this time we had our works in good condition and were ready for an attack at any time

lines, when the firing would gradually cease, and with the exception of an occasional shot, would remain quiet until Excelsior went on again, when the same routine would be gone through with.

On the 16th, two rebel regts. came charging out of the woods to capture a new redoubt that we had just built, but were driven back with a few charges of grape and canister. The night of the 17th the rebs made a grand rush on Sickles's brigade driving them back and capturing some 40 of their men. Our brigade going on the next day, we slowly pressed them back and occupied the old line. In this affair the rebels used explosive bullets, one of them exploding over our heads as we lay in reserve at the lookout tree.

By this time we had our works in good condition and were ready for an attack at any time. A continuous line of zig-zag rifle pits formed a cover for our infantry, while we had two redoubts built for guns besides two guns planted on the Williamsburg road and one in the opening of our works on the left. Abatis had been formed in our front, by cutting down about 150 feet of pine timber. In front of our fort we had made a chevaux de Friese by sharpening the branches of trees and pinning them down with the points towards the enemy. In the rear of the works were two large rifle pits to be used as a cover for the reserve.

On the 18th the 16th Mass. who had been sent from Fortress Monroe to reinforce our division were put to their mettle by sending them on a little reconoisance. Deploying out as skirmishers, they advanced over the open field, being supported by the 2nd New Hampshire Regt. and two pieces of artilery. Upon entering the woods, the pickets opened fire and the regt. disapeared. They had not gone far before the rebel pickets were driven in and a rebel regt. confronted them. The fight now commenced. The two guns firing over our men's heads drove the rebels back, when the 16th went in and drove them over their rifle pits and into their lines placing quite a number Hors de Combat. After a short fight in which they showed that they meant business, the regt. retired behind our works with a loss of about 50 men.

On the 21st the pickets were attacked, and again on the 23rd considerable lead was thrown, with but few casualties, owing to the barricades that
our men had erected to protect them from the enemy's fire. On the 24th a
heavy rain storm prevailed in the morning, and that afternoon we struck
tents and marched to the rear about a mile. Here we were ordered to pitch
tents. We proceeded to do so, and had got the officers' tent in position, when
the order was countermanded, down they came again and were packed once
more. We marched to the right about 3 miles and occupied the camp of the
Irish Brigade who had gone still further to the right to support the first

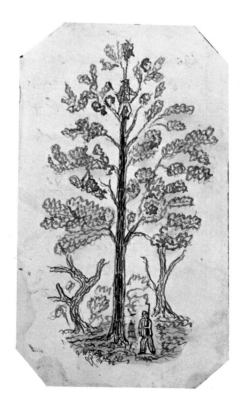

*The lookout on our tree
reporting rebel regts*

We made our way through the woods and across swamps

Jersey Brigade, which had been badly cut up, the fourth Regt. of N.J. being nearly all taken prisoners, besides losing their colors.

Remaining in this camp all night, we returned to our own camp in the morning and were sent out on picket, the 5th being on the outposts. In marching along the edge of the woods to take our posts, we were told by the pickets on duty to keep low as the sharpshooters seemed to be more lively than usual that morning having shot one or two men already. The bullets now began to whistle round our ears, the rebs having caught a glimpse of us while we stood talking to the pickets. With stooping down low we managed to reach our posts in safety. The sharpshooters had got so troublesome by this time that our whole division was ordered out in anticipation of an attack. The lookout on our tree reporting rebel regts. on the march, one of the Mass. regts. was now sent forward as skirmishers, and in a few minutes were firing away at the pickets and sharpshooters, the latter being hid among the branches of trees. One of them having been shot through the head, hung by his heels from a branch and was taken down and brought into our lines. He seemed to be of a diferent type from the rest as he was a fine looking man and well uniformed. He had on a fine pair of boots, but they did not stay there long, as one of our men thinking that he had no further use for them helped himself.

Grover's and Sickles's brigades having been sent into the woods to support the skirmishers, the fighting became general. As volley after volley was fired into them, it had the effect of driving the rebels back. They were reinforced however and came charging on our men yelling like a lot of Indians. It was no use as our line held firm. When the fight had been going on for sometime, Genl. Kearny came riding through the woods at the head of his division. He ordered our pickets to fall back on the reserve, stating that he would take care of the rebels, and we had hardly got into line, when we heard Kearny's men hard at work on the left. The two divisions now drove the rebels from the picket line, through the woods, and over an open field. The Johnys going over it on a run holding their colors down so as not to be seen by our men.

When the firing had ceased we were ordered to take our old position, but had not been their long before we were ordered to advance. We made our way through the woods and across swamps, sometimes over our boot tops in water. The fighting had been done over this swamp, but not a sign of a dead or wounded man could be seen. Rebel coats and blankets, rolled up, were laying round in plenty, but no men. Pools of blood here and there told where some poor fellow had met his fate and that was all.

Upon reaching the advanced line of battle we found our men posted behind a brush fence with an open field in front, on the other side of which was the enemy. We were now ordered to take position on the left, to connect with Kearny's division, but not knowing the road, were soon marching straight for the rebel lines, and would in all probability have been captured in a few minutes, had not some of Kearny's men who were in sight told us of our mistake. We hastily countermarched, and formed line on Kearny's right.

While resting ourselves, we could hear the rebs marching through the woods, the orders of their officers being plainly heard. Their forts were also practicing on two pieces of artilery that our men had run out on the Williamsburg road, and the crashing of the shels as they went through the trees over our heads, was more musical than pleasant, being as we were between two fires.

About 7 p.m. the rebs made an attack on our left, and we were ordered to their support on the double quick. On reaching there we formed line on their right with an open road in front of us, and although the regt. on our left was hotly engaged, not a shot was fired by us, nor was there a sign of a reb. The firing on our left was a perfect roar that soon put the rebs on the back track. When all was quiet, pickets were posted. And as we had been up all the night before the rest of the Regt. who were not on duty, we lay down and soon fell asleep.

All went well until about midnight when we were suddenly awakened by a crash of musketry from our right and centre, that brought us up standing. Quickly grabbing our rifles, we fell back a pace or two to see what was the matter, for we were fairly stunned at the moment. In jumping up I struck my head against the roots of a tree that had been uprooted, nearly knocking me down again, and sent my cap spinning. As it was dark it took me some time to find it. In our front was a perfect stream of fire, through which our pickets could be seen making tracks for the Regt. It was a splendid sight when out of range, but just then, with the bullets whistling and singing past our ears, it was anything else. Our rifles were quickly brought to the shoulder, a flash followed, and with that dose of blue pills, the game left. We heard no more of them that night except the orders of their officers, and the beating of their drums. Our causalties were only a few men wounded owing to our laying down when the first volley was fired.

We were shortly afterward relieved by a regt. from Couch's Division, who brought picks and shovels with them to throw up entrenchments so that we could hold the ground that we had won. Returning to camp we turned in for rest and sleep. In the morning we were marching out again to act as reserve but there being no need of us we returned to camp. With the exception of one or two volleys and the occasional picket firing everything was quiet until the 27th when the rebels made a charge upon Couch's Division, who had relieved us on the advanced line. After a few rounds had been exchanged the line broke and fell back to our former position, thus losing all that had been gained. The 55th N.Y. being very conspicuous in their red pants made a very gallant retreat past our camp, going for the rear as fast as their legs could navigate.

A few nights before this a grand racket was created by one of our pickets firing at what he supposed was a rebel cavalry charge, but it turned out to have been a horse belonging to the rebs who had broken loose, and being shot at by our men, he started on a full gallop, thus making a great noise as he dashed through the woods in the dead of night. As he went tearing along, he drew the fire from one end of the line to the other. The whistling of the balls gave the rebs the impression that they were the object of attack, and they joined in the row too.

While our men were at work cutting down the trees for abatis, the body of a rebel was found laying at the root of one of them. The flesh had been entirely eaten away by the worms, leaving nothing but his skeleton encased in his uniform and blanket, the latter being kept continually on the move by the mass of worms under it. Some thoughtless man had taken the skull from the body and stuck it on the stump of a pine sapling that was directly in the rear of our picket line. My attention was called to it one day while on picket by the sun shining on the polished bone. Taking it for a large ball I went over to it, when I saw what it was. There was nothing on it but a small tuft of hair like a scalp lock.

On the 28th while on picket we had our first intimation of a retreat. During the day a large seige gun was brought from the right and placed in position in our fort with ammunition placed in readiness, but towards night the gunners received orders to move and they struck for the rear. In a short

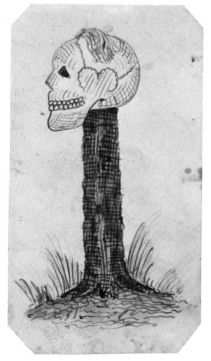

Some thoughtless man had taken the skull from the body and stuck it on the stump

time orders were given us to return to camp and pack up our tents and blankets. Everything that could not be carried off was to be burnt or destroyed. Knapsacks and tents were slashed and cut to pieces with swords and bayonettes, crackers and provisions of all kinds were thrown down all the wells we could find, filling them up to the brim, making a general destruction of everything. The last to disapear was the brigade sutler's tent. As he did not have waggons enough to carry off his produce, he had to stand by and see the boys help themselves to cans of butter, milk, cheese and in fact every thing he had on hand, after which the tent was ribboned. On the completion of our job we returned to the front with our haversacks well filled with grub and awaited our turn to take the back track.

VIII

Change of Base

As McClellan's army retreated *across the flooded and almost impassable White Oak swamp, the Confederates pursued closely. Bellard's regiment, which helped cover the Union withdrawal, was under fire every day, but it took no major part in the battle of Savage's Station (June 29, 1862) and saw only limited action at Glendale the next day. By July 1 the Army of the Potomac had reached Malvern Hill, a virtually impregnable position. Flushed with victory, Lee tried an assault. McClellan's artillery, supported by fire from the Union gunboats on the James, mowed down the advancing Confederates, so that there was little fighting for infantrymen like Bellard to do.*

Though Malvern Hill was clearly a Union victory, McClellan withdrew his army the next day to Harrison's Landing, in the shelter of the Union navy. There the Army of the Potomac remained until mid-August. The Fifth New Jersey Infantry desperately needed the respite. The regiment had begun the Peninsula campaign with about eight hundred men, but by July death and sickness had left only 441.

Now a veteran, Bellard could write knowingly about entrenchments, abatis, and chevaux-de-frise (obstacles composed of spikes attached to a wooden frame, used to check the advance of enemy cavalry). As a seasoned infantryman, he had nothing but scorn for the cavalry. With surprise he reported the rare cavalry charge made by Colonel Richard H. Rush's Lancers (Sixth Pennsylvania Cavalry), and he noted as a curiosity the first dead cavalryman he saw during the entire Peninsular campaign. Bellard and his fellows also observed with growing cynicism the conduct of General Francis E. Patterson, commander of the Third Brigade in Heintzelman's Corps, to which the Fifth New Jersey Infantry belonged, for that officer, after making boastful pronouncements, always seemed to fall ill when the firing started.

———◆———

The morning of the 29th we fell back slowly to our second line of rifle pits at Savage's Station, and taking our position we were in readiness for the rebs but with the exception of a few straglers, none came in our front, although the right of our line on the rail road was engaged.

When the right of our army had fallen back, we commenced our retrogade movement bringing up the rear with our Corps. A short distance to the rear we passed a large pile of shot, shell and powder that was to be fired as soon as we were out of danger. In a few moments a terific roar was heard caused by the explosion, and shell could be heard some time after exploding in diferent directions where they had been thrown. A train was also loaded with ammunition and after setting fire to the cars started down the track under a full head of steam. At the commissary depot on the railroad all the crackers and junk that could not be carried away was burnt to the ground, and I do not think that in the history of the rebellion there can be found any place where so much government property was destroyed, or so many sick and wounded left to the care of the enemy. And in the battles that occured in the retreat all the wounded who could not walk away themselves were left behind. Some of the poor fellows rather than be taken prisoners attempted to walk but were soon compelled to lay down, and the army passing them they were soon gobbled up by the advancing rebels.

Our retreat lay through White Oak Swamp, and having only one road to march on with safety it was a slow job. Upon nearing Willis Church (or Glendale) we came to a halt in a large wheat field and bivouaced for the night, everything being quiet except a few shots that were fired by the regulars who were on picket at some prowling bushwhackers. Getting up next morning I felt rather thirsty and seeing a house a short distance from our Regt. I took a strol for the purpose of getting some milk, but when I got to the place, I found that the regulars had been there before and had taken everything that was worth taking and more too. The spring house where the southerners keep their milk, cheese, hams, etc. was completely gutted, and even the woman's clothes, with the exception of what she had on her back, had been made into gun rags and appropriated by the troops, her trunks

Dragging a large size howitzer across the road
by hand

and wardrobe having been turned inside out to furnish them. When the matter came to the ears of the Genl. a guard was placed on the house and the straglers driven out. It was generally reported that her husband was a guirella and had fired at our pickets the night before, hence the destruction.

About 10 o'clock the rebs commenced shelling our waggon train, and our brigade was ordered out to drive them back. By a flank movement we succeeded and the train was safe. The teamsters had already commenced to cut the traces of the horses, ready to save themselves on horseback at the expense of the ammunition. Our Col. was equal to the emergency however, for seeing their intentions he threatened to put an end to their lives if they did not keep with their waggons. A company of heavy artilery having no horses were dragging a large size howitzer across the road by hand when our brigade came up on a double quick to get to our position. They were ordered by our Col. to halt until we had passed, and they indulged in some tall swearing at having to wait, but to no purpose as we had to reach our position in a hurry.

As there was only one road the infantry marched through the wheat fields, which was now about ripe, making roads through it as clean as if it had been cut with a scythe. It was a disastrous march for the farmers but it had to be done to save our army. After marching through woods and fields for about 2 miles we took up our position at the edge of a wood, with an open field in front, with a rail fence for protection. The position was well chosen having a cross fire on the enemy from no matter what quarter they came from. The fighting soon commenced and was kept up until dark. A charge was made on our line during the day, but they met with such a storm of shells and bullets that they fell back to the shelter of the woods and staid there. Although the balls flew thick around us part of the time, only one man was wounded and that by a shell.

At dark the Battle of Willis Church or Glendale as it is sometimes called ceased. The cries of the wounded as they cried for water or help could be heard all night long. Every little while a lantern would flash through the trees, as the hospital men were flitting through the woods picking up the wounded, and burying the dead. In the field in our front and in the line of fire of both armys stood a house with the family living in it. As it was in danger of being hit and the inmates killed, some of the officers told the people to seek some place of safety, but as the[y] would not do it of their own sweet will, they [were] compelled to vacate.

At daylight July 1st we were off again on the way for Malvern Hill, our destination, passing on the road several lines of battle that were drawn up to cover our retreat, with artilery planted in their front and cavalry and infantry as skirmishers in front of the artilery. On reaching one of the hills we halted to rest and the sight that met our eyes was magnificent. From our position we had a good view of the grand Army of the Potomac or at least what was left of it. Waggons and artilery were parked. The cavalry were encamped, while the infantry were drawn up in long lines of battle, one behind the other, waiting for the enemy. The sun flashing on the bayonettes and brass guns presented a beautiful sight but was soon destined to pass in oblivion.

The rebel artilery opening fire about 10 a.m. we were ordered to our position supporting a battery. On the march we passed a grove of wild plum trees to which we helped ourselves. As they were still green, they were rather sour, but helped to refresh us. When we had reached our position line of battle was formed in front of a battery of field pieces posted on the brow of a hill. Our line was about the centre of the slope behind a ravine filled with small scrubs and vines. Directly in front of us lay the 2nd N.Y. of our brigade who were posted behind a fence, and the ground rising in front of them, they could not be seen by the rebs. In front of us was a large open field over which the rebels would have to come to take our artilery while above us on the brow of the hills were a line of field batterys extending nearly the entire length of our army, with a few siege guns placed in the most promi-

Passing on the road several lines of battle, that were drawn up to cover our retreat,
with artilery planted in their front

nent positions. On the river to our left five gun boats were in position, and
did good service with their large shells, preventing the rebels from getting
around our left wing. For a defensive position it was all that could be
desired and could not have been better if made for the purpose.

At 10 a.m. the rebs opened on us from a piece of woods in which they
had a battery. In a few minutes the firing became general from both sides,
and a more terific roar of artilery I never heard. It was deafening. There

being about 300 cannon going off on both sides, and as ev[er]y gun made two explosions (that is one for the gun and one for the shell when it burst) there was a lively racket. The battery that we were supporting fired off the six guns at once and I believe that was the case with all of them. The gunners got so warmed up to their work that they took off their jackets and worked in their shirt sleeves.

In the afternoon the rebs made some furious charges to capture our batterys. Brigade after brigade would charge from the woods into the open fields, only to be driven back with great slaughter being beaten in detail. A

Above us on the brow of the hills were a line of field batterys extending nearly the entire length of our army

brigade of our men were marched into the open field in front of us to form a new line of battle. They were greeted with such a storm of shot and shell that they were glad to get back. The shells flew so thick around them from the rebel batterys in the wood that no regt. could stand it, and they fell back, the men running back in a doubled up position to escape as much as possible the flying missiles that threw up the dirt all around them.

Our situation at this time was anything but pleasant, for the shot and shell that were intended for the advance brigade came bounding over the field and fell into our lines, one of them killing two men and wounding the third. The shell went through the breast of one man, cut the lower part of the body off another and took the hand off from the third after which it ploughed its way in the ground without bursting, thus saving more of us. Part of our line being hard pressed in the afternoon Sickles's Brigade of our division were sent to their support and went over the field on the double quick.

Rush's Lancers made a charge during the day and I believe the only one they ever did make. From our position we had a good view of the field over which they passed and it was a sight worth seeing as they came into view from behind a clump of woods in line of battle, the lance set for the charge with the red pennons floating in the breeze. The enemy fled when they saw this formidable array comming, before they got within striking distance, preferring the shelter of the woods to being impaled on the head of a spear.

While the fighting was going on some stray pigs became frightened and ran between our lines. A hunt commenced for fresh meat and whenever one of the boys would get near porky, a bayonette was thrust at him generally sticking piggy enough to make him squel but not bringing him to the ground. As this was torture to the pig, the Col. stoped it telling the boys he did not mind how many they killed but he did not want to see them butchered. They were accordingly shot and soon helped to fill up the inner man of those who were lucky enough to get a piece.

Towards dark our batterys opened on the rebels with renewed vigor and until 9 p.m. the bombardment was terific awful to hear, but still worse to be under as the rebs found to their cost. Their loss in that fight was awful and put a check to their advance as an army.

Before daylight on the morning of the second, we left our position and took the road at the foot of the hill for Harrison's Landing. As it had commenced to rain, the roads were in a horible condition. Marching was almost an impossibility. At the foot of the hill, at Malvern Hill Tavern, the artilery, baggage waggons and infantry were in a disorganized mass, all jumbled together without regularity or purpose and everyone for himself. The artilery was driven along the road as fast as the horses could pull it, and the infantry had to keep their eyes open, and get out of the way to avoid being run over or crushed to death between two guns. The mud in some places was over our boots making marching no light matter.

After a great deal of sweating (and perhaps some swearing) we reached a wheat field a short distance from the landing and went into camp. The rain was now comming down beautifully and such a thing as keeping dry was out of the question. So in order to make ourselves as comfortable as possible, we set to work pulling wheat, getting together quite a stock. It was spread on the ground making a very respectable footing and bed, and over all we pitched our tents and were happy enough, with one little exception. We had nothing to eat. There being no rations to be got, we pulled a lot of wheat and boiling it we made a very decent meal. When the inner man had been attended to, we turned in and went to sleep to the music of the rain pattering on our tents. The next morning we were up bright and early and found that it was raining still, but as our rations came up we were once more in clover.

Towards noon we were surprised by a shell flying into camp, followed by several more from somewhere in our rear. We of course expected that the rebs were trying to drive us into the river and we were in for another fight, but it turned out that the rebs had pushed forward a battery of artilery supported by a regt. of infantry and were trying to give us a little surprise. But instead of that the surprise was on the other side, for our men got into their rear and captured battery, infantry, reserves and all. After that coup de etat all was quiet in the Army of the Potomac.

On the anniversary of the National Independence we moved camp about a mile nearer Richmond and put in the day picking blackberries that were in abundance. These were eaten in the shape of a company pudding. The gun boat Marritanza observed the day by capturing the rebel gun boat Teaser on the James River. Amongst the spoils was a balloon made of silk

Rush's Lancers made a charge during the day

dresses provided by secesh women. Salutes were fired by the gun boats, artilery and infantry. On the 5th we moved into the woods and encamped in the rear of some old rifle pits that had been thrown up by some former troops.

On the 7th we commenced building our advanced line of works that we were to occupy during our stay. Trees were cut down and placed in position for the inside of the works, being securely pinned together to hold them in place. When the logs had been put in position and securely fastened, a ditch was dug on the outside, the earth being banked against the logs, making a very substantial and strong work, about six or eight feet thick at the base and four on top. The brush wood was cleared away from our front and the trees were cut down for about 200 yards making a very effectual abatis. In front of our brigade we built a battery or redoubt to hold seven guns, and on the left of our position we had three twenty and three thirty pound parrots [Parrott] guns. By the 8th we had our works finished and were ready for Johny at any time he took a notion to advance.

On the 9th while clearing the ground for our camp, the fallen timber in our front by some means got on fire, and the wind blowing towards us soon brought it over the breastworks and into the brush that covered our intended camp ground. In a few minutes brush and grass was on fire, and leg bail was taken for security, losing haversacks, blankets, and other articles that had been forgotten in our haste. Returning armed with brush we succeeded in subduing the flames, but not until it had burnt all the brush and in some places the logs of the breastworks.

Tents were pitched on the 10th and we began our regular routine of drill and guard. Wells were made outside of the works by digging a hole and sinking a barrell, from which we procured our supply of water. It was very unhealthy however as it was nothing but surface water that came out of the woods and swamps that surrounded our camp on all sides.

Whenever we were off duty we amused ourselves by sporting in the

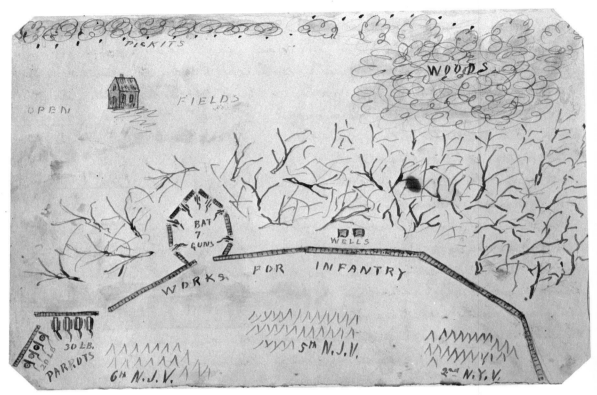

By the 8th we had our works finished and were ready for Johny at any time he took a notion to advance

water or fishing. Some would enjoy the swiming, while others would prefer the shower bath and falling water, others washing their clothes in the brook below the dam, while quite a few would ply the hook and line for fish. Our watering place was a large pond of running water that had been dammed off for running mills. As the dam was about 15 feet high the boys would stand under and the water dashing over them made a very effectual shower bath. Below the dam clothes were washed in the running brook, having clean water all the time, and the surrounding trees and bushes furnished the cloths line upon which they were hung to dry. In order to have a good diving place we built a stone pier on one side of the pond, over which we fastened a plank, having it extend some distance over the water. As it was an excellent spring board we had a good jumping off place, and on any fine day the boys could be seen running along the plank and plunging into the water, like so many frogs. Our Regt. being on the advance picket on the 21st two of us took a strol through the woods, going some distance away. We found the bushes packed with berries. Blackberries were found all over and some of them that grew in the shade, were as large as good sized plums. Blueberries and huckleberries were so thick that the bushes hung down under the weight of fruit. Having a tooth for such things we went out about a mile and after eating as many as we could manage we returned to our posts with our haversacks crammed for the rest of the boys.

Augt. 2nd our Division was ordered out in light marching order but returned to camp in about 3 hours, having taken the wrong road, through the incompetancy of the guide. On the 3rd we were again on picket, but had no opportunity of picking berries this time, as our company was stationed on what they were pleased to term the telegraph picket, that is, a line of posts consisting of three men each extending from the pickets in the woods to our camp. The idea was, to give an alarm in the shortest possible time of any attack on the outposts in front.

None was made however until dark, when an army of Virginia mosquitoes made a general attack on our post, that was on the edge of the wood. We were completely surrounded and had to keep our arms continually in motion trying to brush them off. Not being able to stand it any longer we built a wood fire, making plenty of smoke in the hopes of smoking them out, but it was no go, as they would bite us even after we got into the smoke. But as we could not stand the smoke, we had to back out to escape being smothered to death. Everything else failing we wrapped ourselves up in our blankets, leaving nothing but our eyes and nose exposed and stood it as best we could until daylight, when they retreated. They were the largest specimens I ever saw and the most blood thirsty as well.

Our watering place was a large pond of running
water that had been dammed off for running mills

While in this camp, our 1st Sergt. [George S. Lawyer] (or Sergt. dresser as the boys called him) showed his teeth by trying to humiliate me in the presence of the officers, but was himself brought to grass on the run. One morning about cleaning up time one of our sergeants who was a german [Gustavus Goetz], ordered me to clean up the company street, before cleaning my tent, and on trying to reason the matter with him as to the propriety of cleaning up the street before the debris from the tents had been swept out, was ordered to shut up, and do as ordered. Not complying with the order soon enough to suit his lord ship, he made a grab for me, which resulted in a tussel. Hard words followed from both sides, commenced by the sergeant. The result was, that his dignity was insulted besides having his coat torn.

He at once reported the fact to Sergt. dresser, who, instead of ordering me out at once for an example, waited until I had occasion to pass his tent, when he stopped me, and wanted to know what was the matter between myself and the sergt. Upon being told the circumstances, I was informed that in order to enforce disipline in the camp, I would have to carry a log for the rest of the day. Being duly armed with the new weapon, I was posted by dresser in front of the officers' tent, who were at the time at breakfast. Upon the completion of their meal, Lieut. Mitchell came out of the tent, and wished to know what I had that stick on my shoulder for. The whole circumstance was repeated to him. When he went off muttering to himself "I'll see about that" and sure enough he did, for in two or three minutes, Mr. Dresser came back with a very crest fallen look and told me that I could drop the log, and get ready for drill. I did as ordered, and that was the last exibition of airs that he put on while in company "C."

On the 4th our division was again on the move, this time for an advance movement. Leaving camp about 11 a.m. we marched past our cavalry pickets, and about 12 o'clock that night we went into bivouac. But instead of keeping this movement secret as was intended, Genl. Patterson blew his bugle for the line to halt and so let the rebels know we were coming. While drawn up in line previous to stacking arms the officers were ordered to the front and centre by the Genl. and in a short speech told them what he expected us to do, that we were going to have some fighting, and if any of them did not want to go they were at perfect liberty to return. Suffice it to say, that all were willing, and on hand when wanted.

Starting again next morning early we marched past Glendale where the Battle of June 30th was fought, and found ourselves in the rear of Malvern Hill. A few shots being fired by our cavalry at the rebel pickets gave us notice that we were near some rebs. Upon nearing the hill we saw the result of the cannonading on July 1st. Shot, shell, and fragments were scattered all over the ground. Trees had been cut completely off by shells, while branches were strewn in all directions.

When the head of our division got into the open field, clear of the woods, they were saluted with a shell thrown from a gun placed in position at Malvern Hill Tavern. Steps were quickened and in less time than it takes to write it, we were in line of battle ready for an advance. The 5th and 6th New Jersey were ordered to charge the battery, and away we went on the double time. Passing over a line of battle that lay in our front, we had no sooner got under way when two shells in quick succession came whistling over our heads just near enough to miss and bursting in the line we had just passed over. That was their last shot, for we were on them before they could get their pieces trained for another shot, owing to the rolling nature of the ground, being one minute on top of a knol, and the next down in a hollow.

Just as we were congratulating ourselves on the capture of the battery it was whisked out of sight over the hill, followed by their infantry. And when we reached the Tavern a moment after there was nothing to be seen but a few straglers, and one of their guns laying in a creek at the foot of the hill. The rebels in retreating had gone straight down the hill, which was very steep, not having time to take the road, and in making the turn to get into the river road had upset the gun into the creek and left it behind. Our division drew up in line on the brow of the hill, while the cavalry started after the flying rebs. At the foot of the hill was a larger wood, and here and there among the trees stragling rebs could be seen trying to make their escape. Some of our men having their blood up at fighting pitch, started down the hill after them. When the grey backs saw the jig was up, they came out into the road holding a handkerchief or rag on their gun as a token of surrender. Quite a number were captured in this manner, and when the cavalry returned after a sharp skirmish the number was considerable. One of the cavalry had his uniform and equipment cut by bullets in a dozen places, and his horse received one or two, but he himself was not scratched. Another one not quite so lucky was brought in laying across the saddle of his horse dead, and he was the first dead cavalry man we ever saw. Some of our infantry were killed, but none of our Regt. although we made the charge.

Two of the rebel gunners were left behind on their retreat. One of them was lying on his back, dead, with a shell in each hand, as he was in the act of supplying the guns with ammunition. A piece of shell had gone clean through his head. The other lay alongside of the Tavern, and had been hit with a solid shot or shell that was stil in his body. The ball struck him in the back and after penetrating his body staid there. He was alive when we arrived on the ground, groaning and begging of us to shoot him and put him out of his misery. It was hard to see him suffer so much agony, but none of us could muster up courage enough to kill him in cold blood, although we knew it would have been a blessing to him. After lingering in agony for some time, death put an end to his misery.

From our position on the hill we had a splendid view of the country. In front of us was the James River winding through the hills and meadows like a big snake, upon whose waters a few gun boats were running up and down awaiting the arrival of a transport that was expected from Richmond with parolled prisoners. Woods extended as far as the eye could reach while away off to our right, in the direction of Richmond, a large rebel camp could be plainly seen as it was situated on a large hill, and dotted over with white tents. From that camp trouble was expected so soon as the fleeing rebels got the news to them.

Little Mac appearing on the ground, a consultation was held in the Tavern, and as a result we were sent out on picket, as it was decided to hold the ground for a time at least. After the pickets had been posted we who were in the reserve had the pleasure of a bath, to take off some of the dust, after which we took a row on a large pond that belonged to a rebel gent's mansion. A large mansion that stood outside of our picket lines was burnt to the ground by the general's orders, as it had been used by the rebel sharp shooters and might be used for the same purpose again.

Ascertaining on the 7th that a large force of the enemy were advancing towards us, it was deemed advisable to retreat, as our force was not strong enough to oppose them. Leaving the hill before daylight, we took the river road and arrived safe at our camp about reveille. After the rebels retreated on the 5th, Genl. Patterson was driven up to our lines in an ambulance

Another one not quite so lucky was brought in laying across the saddle of his horse dead

having again been taken sick or incapacitated in some way, and this after his speech on the night of the 4th did not look very well.

On the 8th a little excitement was created in our Regt. by Co. "A" having lost their captain by resignation the company was ordered to be disbanded and the men distributed amongst the rest of the companys. Upon enforcing the order, a mutiny was the consequence. The men refusing to obey were placed under arrest. The mutineers were ordered to walk up and down on the rifle works with a log of wood on their shoulder as punishment and Co. "C" was detailed as a guard to see that they kept on the go. Sticking it out as long as they could, they had to give in, and were distributed through the Regt. This consolidation was condemned by the rest of the Regt. but orders were orders and had to be obeyed or take the consequence.

As another change of base was contemplated orders were issued to pack knapsacks and keep nothing but blankets, overcoats and provisions. The knapsacks being packed were placed on board of a canal boat at Harrison's Landing for conveyance to Alexandria. That was the last we ever saw of them, as the boat sank carrying our traps with it. After being raised and unloaded, men were sent out of the diferent companys to dry them, but after reaching Alexandria they were condemned by a committee of officers who had been detailed to examine them. We afterwards had the pleasure of paying for a new rig. As I had received a box from home a few days before I also lost some of the contents, but a shirt that was in it I put on my back, while I put half of the tobacco in my haversack and so saved that much.

IX

Rations, Cookery & Utensils

OUR RATIONS WERE for the most part good and plenty of it. Consisting of hard tac (that is square biscuit) that sometimes had to be broken with your heel or musket. Soft bread when in a permanent camp. Fresh beef. Salt junk (pork). Salt horse (beef). Peas. Beans. Potatoes. Desecated vegetables. Rice etc.

The following bill of fare taken at random for 9 days while we lay in Washington will answer for the rest of the time, as it was about the same, only that we sometimes had vegetable soup and occasionally tea instead of coffee. Our breakfast and supper always consisted of bread and coffee unles we were saving enough to reserve some meat. Here it is.

Nov. 19, 1861 "Dinner"
Salt Beef and Potatoes.
 20th Fresh Beef and Rice Soup.
  21st Salt Pork and Bean soup.
   22nd Fresh Beef and Pea Soup.
    23rd Salt Beef.
     24th Fresh Beef and Rice with raisons.

25th Salt Pork and Pea Soup.
26th Salt Pork and Bean Soup.
and 27th Salt Beef and Pea Soup.

The raisons mentioned, were bought out of the company funds and had nothing to do with Uncle Sam. The desacated vegetables were all kinds of green stuf pressed into a square cake, and when we wanted any soup a piece of it was broken off and put in the pot, when it would swell out and make a very nice soup. The bean soup was good, but with some cooks it was made so thin that the boys used to say that there was one bean to a quart of water. Our coffee when we first went out was issued to us green, so that we had to roast and grind it, which was not always a success, some of it being burnt, while some would be almost green. In roasting it we put a quantity of it in a mess pan, and placing the pan over the fire would have to keep stirring it round with a stick in order to have it roasted as evenly as possible.

These mess pans were used to fry our pork in and also as a wash bason. Our soup, coffee and meat were boiled in camp kettles suspended over the fire as in the sketch, which were also used for boiling our dirty clothes. Not a very nice thing for a soup pot, especially when they were full of vermin, as they were most of the time when on active service. Our stomachs were strong enough however to stand it, and our appetites did not suffer on that account.

Fresh beef was taken along with us on the march, the cattle following in the rear of the army to be killed when wanted. When the quartermaster wanted some fresh beef, some of the men who were good shots would go with the butchers to the drove, and having selected the oxen, a ball would be fired into his head, and as soon as he was down, his throat was cut by the butcher, after which the carcas was cut up, and issued to the companys. On one of the hot days at Fair Oaks, the meat when issued to us was fly blown, and the maggots had to be scraped off before it was put into the pot, although the

Our soup, coffee and meat were boiled in camp kettles suspended over the fire as in the sketch

beef was just killed and was yet warm when I carried some of it to the cooks. The salt junk as we called our pork was sometimes alive with worms, as was also an occasional box of crackers, but that did not happen very often. Instead of having our pork boiled, we sometimes had it fried and in order to do it up quick, we had a large square frying pan made in Washington that would fry enough at once to furnish the entire company.

When on the march we had to do our own cooking as the rations were issued out to last 3 days. The pork we fried on a pan of our own construction consisting of half a canteen and a stick, or else broiled it on our home made toasting fork. Coffee and sugar we kept in a bag mixed together, and when we wanted a cup of coffee we put two tablespoons full of the mixture in a pint cup of water and placing the cup on two sticks with some hot coals beneath let it boil. And it often happened that just as the coffee was about boiled enough some one in lighting his pipe at the fire would touch one of the sticks with his foot and over went the coffee, when we had to do without or else use up more of our supply of coffee. Our crackers we used to fry, to make them more palatable soaking them an hour or two to make them soft. We fried them in pork fat and made a tasty meal. The bread we fixed in the same way. Whenever flour was issued out as rations we made what was called slapjacks, that is flour and water made into a batter with a little salt and fried in our frying pans. They were not very light of course, but still it was a change. We had flour dealt out to us at Harrison's Landing but had no canteen to fry it in, so it was of no use until I found an old broken shovel. This was cleaned and cooked the slapjacks for the company.

As forraging was strictly forbidden in general orders, we could not do much of that but still managed to get a little on the sly. I know one day we passed a corn field, when some of the men went after some. As they were

The balloon was used as means of finding out what the rebels were doing

121

This tree was one of many at Harrison's Landing that was marked for the use of the gun boats. The bark had been cut off in strips as a range for their guns

busy filling their haversacks the old farmer came across his farm with a gun and big dog, to frighten us off I suppose, but when he saw we were armed and not disposed to go, he took the hint and went himself. The corn was roasted over the fire without taking off any of the husk, and it was a great deal better than boiled corn, as it retained all of its flavor. Potatoes were roasted or baked in the live coals, while all game was rolled in mud and baked. Chickens and ducks are all game in war times.

One of our dishes was composed of anything that we could get hold of. Pork or beef, salt or fresh, was cut up with potatoes, tomatoes, crackers, and garlic, seasoned with pepper and salt, and stewed. This we called Hish and Hash or Hell fired stew. If we wanted something extra, we pounded our crackers into fine pieces, mixed it up with sugar, raisons and water, and boiled it in our tin cups. This we called a pudding.

The country through which we marched was for the most part woody with large wheat and corn fields between. The roads being either very muddy or very dusty, as it happened to be rainy or dry weather. In some parts we have marched all day and did not see a stone big enough to kill a bird with, being mostly sand. The cre[e]ks or brooks are not bridged over and so [we] had to wade through. Even the Chickahominy River had to be bridged before we could get over, as it had been swollen by the rain to about a half a mile wide, although I think it is only about 50 feet wide generally. Hills were plenty. For some days we were marching up and down hill all day. We no sooner got to the bottom of one than the road run over another one. The woods were for the most part pine, with an occasional lot of oak and chestnut. Good springs of cool water were found here and there, and when we did come across one, it was immediately surrounded by a crowd, all anxious to fill their canteens first.

The balloon was used as means of finding out what the rebels were doing, how many troops they had, and what kind of fortifications they had ready for us. The rebels fired at it on several occasions but did not succeed in hitting it. When the balloon was in the air, it was held by men holding on to the ropes so that it could be moved from one place to the other. I do not know that it did us much good, although it might. The gas used in the balloon was made on the field by machines the balloonist carried with him.

X

Reinforcing Pope

WHILE McCLELLAN WAS *on the Peninsula, President Lincoln decided to regroup the other Union forces in Northern Virginia, and he entrusted command of the new army to General John Pope, a braggart who had won minor victories in the West. The new commander announced that his headquarters would be in the saddle — a remark that led to indelicate jokes about a commander who put his headquarters where his hindquarters ought to be — and he promised to be constantly on the offensive. Pope and his staff gave the impression that they had come from the rugged West to show the effete Easterners how to fight.*

To meet this new threat, Lee detached Jackson's troops from his army before Richmond. On August 9, charging into Jackson's force on Cedar Mountain, Pope showed that his eagerness to fight was genuine. What remained doubtful was his ability to handle an army. The events of the next three weeks would decide that question definitively.

Correctly judging that McClellan, still at Harrison's Landing, would undertake no offensive action against Richmond, Lee sent more and more of his troops north in the hope of overwhelming Pope. Sensing the danger, Lincoln overruled McClellan's wishes, withdrew the Army of the Potomac from the Peninsula, and ordered it to speed to Pope's assistance. Some of McClellan's lieutenants, devoted to that commander and his strategy, were slow in complying, but Heintzelman promptly despatched his III Corps, including Bellard's regiment. In the rush down the Peninsula Bellard understandably got his geography a little confused; after all, one obscure Virginia crossroads looked much like another.

———◆———

Orders were given to strike tents on the 11th of August but were afterwards countermanded and we did not get away from there until the 15th when we left our camp and marched about 8 miles, when we bivouaced for the night. Starting again on the 16th we made about seventeen miles, when we halted near the Chickahominy River, and bivouacked in the same field that Jackson's Corps occupied when he got into our rear during the Seven Days battle. The remains of his camp fires being in plenty all round.

Marching again on the morning of the 17th we crossed the river at Jones Ford on a pontoon bridge that had been built for our accomidation, and was taken up as soon as we crossed. A gun boat lay there to protect it. After traveling about eighteen miles we halted for the night at the West Point cross roads, passing through on our way, a place called Charles City, that was composed of some half a dozen houses. The marching was very bad, on account of the dust that was some four inches deep so much so that while the Regt. was on the move, we could hardly see the company ahead of us. And to make matters worse water was very scarce, there being none to be had, except what was found in cow paths through the woods or in the ponds that were found in the roads. The latter was very thick with mud on account of the cavalry wading through them to water their horses.

Starting again about 7 a.m. on the 18th we marched about eighteen miles and camped in a field on the outskirts of Williamsburg, about 3 o'clock p.m., the boys being pretty well fagged out. During our march from Harrison's Landing strict orders were issued prohibiting forraging, and although we passed some very fine corn fields, we could only get a supply by running the guards, who were always posted to prevent it whenever we happened to halt near a farm.

Leaving camp about 10 a.m. on the 19th we marched through the city of Williamsburg (that was now guarded by a regt. of cavalry) passing over the old battle field on our way. We halted about two miles from Yorktown, having made about twelve miles. As we were encamped in a peach orchard, a great deal of the fruit disapeared, although they were as green as grass and hard as stones, but anything for a change was our mottoe just then. In the woods a short distance from camp a bee tree had been found by some of the boys, who at once proceeded to get at the sweets. But the bees objected to the intrusion and came out in a body, soon routing the blue coats and sent them back to camp pell mell.

Taking shank's mare again the next morning we passed through the fortifications of Yorktown, and bivouacked in the lower breastworks facing the York River. The works had been turned since we left them, the guns now pointing towards Williamsburgh instead of Fortress Monroe. The 8th N.Y. Volls. and a Regt. called the Lost Children were doing the guard duty, and a lost looking lot they were. Desertions were going on every day but when you take into consideration that they were the dregs of New York City, it need not be wondered at. On the side of a hill could still be seen the remains of one of the old earthworks that had been used during the Revolutionary War, but was now so overgrown with shrubs and weeds as to be hardly discernable.

There being a splendid beach for bathing, a squad of us were soon in the river washing off some of the sacred soil of Virginia, that had been accumilating on our persons for five days. When I got through and was dressing myself, I found that some one had been through my clothes and helped themselves to two dollars which had been in my pants pocket. As that was all I was worth it saved me the trouble of carrying it about with me, or burning a hole in my pocket. The ammount was not much but before we got another pay I missed it especially when I wanted some tobacco.

On the 21st we went through the ancient village of Yorktown and embarked on board of the steamer Baltic, five of our decimated Regts. being taken on without being packed. Laying at the warf until evening she dropped down stream. By daylight of the 22nd we were fairly on our way for Alexandria to reenforce Pope, who, in his general orders, said that his head quarters were in the saddle, so we expected some lively work. It commenced to rain about 8 in the morning and kept it up till one in the afternoon, making our sail up the bay very cold and disagreeable as we were out on the deck.

On the trip, some of the boys thinking that the army grub was not good enough managed to help themselves to some roast chicken that was intended for the officers' table. Over the cooking range of the steamer was an open place in the deck enclosed by a railing. We had gathered around the railing to get a smell of the good things that were being prepared by the cooks, and seeing a roast fowl on top of the range, that had been placed there to keep warm for dinner, a plan was set on foot to seize it. A rifle was brought into requisition, a bayonette attached and after a few vigorous thrusts, up came Mr. Fowl. It was hauled on deck amid a shower of hot water sent after it by the exasperated cooks. In a few minutes there was nothing left of it but the bones, and as no more oppertunitys were given us, we contented ourselves with hard tac and pork.

About 4 o'clock in the afternoon the Baltic being a large ocean steamer ran aground on a sand bar, a little below Aquia Creek. All attempts to get her off were useless, and we stuck there until night when we were transferred to the river steamer New York. Starting again at half past three in the morning we went as far as Aquia Creek for orders. Receiving them we were sent on to Alexandria, where we arrived safe and sound at noon on the 23rd.

Fresh grub was also stolen on this boat by placing a screw wormer on the end of a ramrod. It made a very good and long fork. This was run through the window of the mess room, screwed into the eatables laying on the tables, and being drawn out it vanished as if by magic. The worst feature of our sail was the scarcity of good water, there being none on board but condensed sea water, that was very warm and brackish nearly making us sick to drink it. This gave out at last as the condensor could not make it fast enough. And from morning till night a string of men were waiting their turn for a cup of water.

Upon reaching the city, the Regt. disembarked and marched to the outskirts of the city and encamped on a square. We had been so long away from any city that the boys very naturally had an inclination to enjoy themselves, and in a short time nearly half of the Regt. were reeling round the streets drunk. The Col. in order to stop it had double guards put on to keep the boys in camp, but it was of no use, for as fast as one came in, two would slip out between the guards, and were soon as lively as the rest. The next morning soldiers could be seen laying on the stoops with the pocket cut clean out of their pants, and the money gone of course. Upon coming to their sences, they returned to their regts. without a cent, besides having a beautiful swelled head on them to remind them of their liquod potations.

Eager to reinforce Pope, Heintzelman rushed his troops south on the Orange & Alexandria Railroad, the main supply line of the Union army. Before they could reach the front they learned on August 27 that Jackson, by a circuitous march, had interposed his army between Pope and Washington. While some of Jackson's men tore up the railroad, others raided the main Union supply depot at Manassas Junction, seizing whatever they could and destroying the rest. Heintzelman ordered his Third Brigade, which included the Fifth New Jersey Infantry, to turn back toward Wash-

ington, in the hope of capturing or driving off the Confederate marauders. In a nasty little engagement at Kettle Run they ran the Confederates out of Bristoe Station, but by the time they reached the smoldering depots at Manassas Junction, Jackson's force had already withdrawn.

———◆———

When the Regt. had got together, we marched about three miles from the city and camped alongside of the Orange and Alexandria R.R. to await transportation to the front. While waiting, I washed my shirt in the ditch that ran along the railroad track and went without one while it dried. On the 26th we got on board a train of cattle cars and left for Warrenton Junction. Being on guard over the quartermaster's stores, we got aboard about noon taking our stores with us. After riding about 45 miles we got out of the cars about a mile past the junction and commenced unloading the stores. After finishing the job we bivouaced in the fields.

The next morning we were routed out before daylight, as it was reported that the rebels had got in our rear and were destroying things generally. By daylight we were on the back track for Manassas Junction. At a farm house on the road we saw as we were passing, a lot of bushwhackers under guard. They had been captured during the night prowling round our camp. They were a hard looking set both in person and dress and looked every inch the cut throat. Passing Warrenton Junction we passed a wagon train that had just come in, and upon questioning the drivers we learned that Stonewall Jackson had destroyed the R.R. bridge and trains near Manassas.

About 3 p.m. we neared Bristoe Station where we expected to meet with some opposition. The brigade was formed in line of battle and advanced to the edge of a wood that extended on both sides of the railroad. Our advance was made over a clover field that stood up about 18 inches besides being mixed in with brambles. This made the marching very unsteady and laborious causing several of the men to stumble besides tiring us out before we got into the fight. Getting through at last our Regt. was deployed out on the right of the R.R. and advanced into the woods, skirmishers being deployed in advance. We were now worse off than when we were in clover, for filling up the spaces between the trees were any quantity of scrub pines that were about the height of a man and sent their branches out in all directions. No matter what way you went a branch was sure either to swing back and give you a whack over the face or else some of the spruce leaves would get into your eye. Working our way through the best we could, we got into a sort of ravine that ran through the wood and at once formed line. This was free from scrubs.

Up to this time not a shot had been fired from either side, but no sooner had we got into line than we were saluted with a volley of musketry that rattled through the leaves like hail. No one was hurt however as they went over our heads. But some one seemed to be excited, for we were ordered by the right flank double quick, and after going a short distance, were ordered back again, but this time not to stop. The rebels by this time had a battery in position and gave us a few shells, while the bullets flew thick and fast. Advancing by the left flank the head of our column soon came to the railroad. But the instant the rebels saw us come out of the woods, they gave us a volley and took to their heels. We returned the fire with double interest, but as they had the start and we were tired out, they got off in safety, excepting a few who were laid out at the first fire.

As our Regt. was charging after them along the railroad, a new regt. belonging to our brigade (the 115 Pen. Vols.) who held a position on the other side of the R.R. and being under fire for the first time, got excited and not seeming to know that the rebels had left gave us the benefit of their bullets. Our color bearer was ordered to raise our flag over the bank which was done. The firing did not cease however until the flag had been shown two or three times, and their officers told them repeatedly that they were firing on their own men. The result of that fusilade was one man killed, one or two wounded, and gave the rebels a chance to get clear out of range before it was stoped. Our color bearer had a very narrow escape while he stood half way up the bank with the flag raised. A ball struck the flag staff cutting it half off and ca[u]sing him to beat a hasty retreat.

While halting waiting for orders, Genl. Hooker mounted on his white charger, rode out to a little hill that was in front of our position to take a look at the rebel battery, that was in plain sight at the edge of a wood. At a motion from the General our battery was planted where he wanted it, and shell number one was sent after the Johnys. Bursting directly over their guns it had the effect of clearing them out, for before the smoke from the shell had cleared away the horses had been attached and the battery whisked out of sight into the woods. That was the last we saw of them for that day.

In marching over the field we picked up several prisoners who were hiding in the grass. One of them who was lying along side of the road, waiting as we supposed for a chance to pop off some of our generals when they should come in range, when ordered to get up said he was wounded, but when the boys found out there was nothing the matter with him, knocked him over. Another one was found lying down in the grass by one of our drummers and marched off a prisoner.

The rebels must have been enjoying themselves hughely [hugely] when we surprised them for all over the field were scattered the carcasses of dead cattle. Some were just skinned, others cut up in pieces ready for the pot, while others lay just as they had been shot. Finding plenty of meat frying in their pans, we helped ourselves and with the biscuits that they had left in their hurry we made a very substantial meal, and we did good justice to it, as we had not eaten anything since the night before. Being ordered to form line, we had no time to fill our haversacks, but only took what we could grab as we marched along.

Marching to the right a short distance, we halted. While resting, one of the Regt. who was fooling with his rifle, pulled the trigger in some way, and received an ugly wound in his leg for his foolishness. The report of his piece

The tracks had been torn up and destroyed . . .

brought the Regt. to their feet thinking that we were attacked. Towards night we were ordered to the left of our line for picket duty, and during the night we captured about 20 of Jackson's men, who had been unable to keep up with their regts. and had hid in the woods. Amongst them was an old man and a mere boy, neither of whom were fit to carry a musket, but who had been pressed into the service, according to their own statement.

We started again on the 28th and marched down the railroad track to Manassas. The bridge at Bristoe had been cut through so that when a train came along the weight of the locomotive broke it down, and it went down with the bridge, and lay in the creek at the bottom when we passed. Upon nearing Manassas Junction we came across the remains of a train that had

. . . by burning the rails and twisting them round a tree

been burnt. Nothing was left of it but the iron work and charred wood. Horse shoes, the iron tripods of tent poles, and other scraps were lying on the road bed in heaps. The tracks had been torn up and destroyed, by burning the rails and twisting them round a tree, and [the Confederates] finished their work by setting fire to the buildings.

Passing by Manassas Junction, we halted for the night at Bull Run creek, close by the bridge that leads to Centreville. This had been the rebels' winter quarters. Their huts were still there. The huts had been built in

The huts had been built in regular streets

regular streets and were made of narrow strips of wood about four feet long, and had a shingle roof. We went into bivouac in the streets between the houses and tearing down the shantys used them for fuel. After posting guards, we rolled ourselves up in our blankets and with our feet to the fire, and soon forgot our fatigue in sleep.

———————◆———————

Finally ascertaining that Jackson had withdrawn from Manassas Junction to Stony Ridge, which overlooked the battlefield of Bull Run, where the Union army had been trounced in July 1861, Pope began to concentrate all his forces for an assault. Apparently he forgot or ignored reports that an even larger part of Lee's army, under General James Long-street, was rapidly approaching from the west. By the time Bellard's regi-ment arrived on August 29, the Union attack on Stony Ridge had already begun. General Franz Sigel's troops, which had helped make the initial assault, were now nearly exhausted, and Bellard's regiment was rushed to the front to take their place. The Fifth Jersey entered action that day with 350 men. By nightfall 48 of them were casualties.

Because Bellard's regiment suffered such heavy losses, it took little part in the second day of fighting (August 30). Late in the day it was sent to the left wing of the Union army to support an artillery battery, but before it could reach this position Longstreet's men had burst through Thoroughfare Gap and were driving the entire Union army back. The sec-ond battle of Bull Run had turned into as much of a disaster as the first, and Bellard's commander could take comfort only in the fact that his men "marched in perfect order" on their retreat.

Headed back toward Washington, Heintzelman's soldiers had one more brush with the Confederates, near Chantilly (September 1). Jackson made a surprise attack on the retreating Union column and for a time threatened to capture its supply train. Finally the Confederates were beaten off, but the sharp engagement cost the lives of two promising Union generals, Philip Kearny and Isaac Stevens.

———◆———

In the morning reveille sounded at 3 o'clock and by 4 we took up our line of march. Crossing the bridge, we had an up hill job until we got near Centreville, when we halted to make some coffee and get our breakfast. While we were resting, the 2nd Battle of Bull Run commenced, and from our position the smoke from the shells could be plainly seen as they burst in the air over the tops of the trees. After we had lunched, the march was again commenced and passing through the village of Centreville we started for Bull Run, crossing over the stone bridge where the fight took place in July [1861]. On the march we passed another lot of shantys that were in a wood and built the same as the others. We could now hear the artilery and musketry quite plain, and we knew from former experience, that before many hours would elapse, our corps would have a chance to distinguish themselves, besides extinguishing some of its members.

In fording Bull Run creek, just before going into battle, some of Pope's officers who were waiting there on horseback, thinking perhaps that we were not crossing quick enough to suit them or were shirking our duty, told us that if we did not cross they would shoot us, at the same time pulling out a revolver. One of our men who had got over told the officer, that if he shot any one he would be shot himself, at the same time bringing his piece down for action, informing them at the same time that we belonged to the Army of the Potomac, and were not used to running away or be shot down either. This had the desired effect and we heard no more about shooting.

Halting in the open field we rested. In front of us was a thick wood in which Kearny's Division of our corps were already engaged. When we had rested about an hour an aid de camp came galloping up to our Col. and at 2 o'clock p.m. we were ordered to advance our Regt. as skirmishers for the brigade. Deploying out in the field, we advanced to the edge of the wood in which the rebels and our skirmish line were popping away at each other. Jumping over a fence that was in our way, we found ourselves in the rear of Sigel's men whom we were to relieve. Marching beyond their position we halted and took up our position, Sigel's men falling to the rear as soon as we got into line. When we had got to our posts, two or three men who were out in front of our Regt. dressed in the uniform of Uncle Sam said they were some of our men, but some of our men did not believe them, and taking them for rebs in disguise, ordered them to fall back. But instead of doing so [the men] started for their lines on the double quick, having their steps hastened by a few ounces of lead.

Directly in our front was the Manassas Gap railroad that formed a good line of defence for the rebels, and between that and our line was their skirmish line, about 15 yards away from us. They soon commenced to pop at us, and the compliment being returned, popping became general. Our orders were to fire away wither [whether] we saw an enemy or not, so as to make as much noise as possible. There was no need to waste powder however as their troops could be seen marching up and down in front of us all the time, nearly all of them going to our left preparing for a flank movement that was executed the next day.

I believe we did more execution that day as a single Regt. than at any other battle either before or after. At one time the rebels were getting their men ready for a charge, the orders of their officers being plainly heard as the line was being formed. Word was passed from one skirmisher to another to be ready and give them a volley as soon as the order to move was given. At last the order was given by the commanding officer (to charge) and every gun in the 5th blazed away in that direction. We gave them such a dose of lead that it must have broken their line, for no rebel was seen, nor any other order heard.

The position that I held in the fight was anything but pleasant, as I was unable to find a tree as is the case in bushwhacking, and so had to content myself with a low bush as the next best thing I could find in the way of cover. When kneeling or laying down it screened me from the view of the rebel skirmishers but was no protection from bullets. In a line with my bush was a large tree and behind it was one of the butternuts, who seemed to take a pride in seeing how near he could come to me without hitting me. As the branches were clipped off close to my head several times, I did not relish it quite as much as Mr. Reb, who got behind his tree whenever I fired at him. A little stratagem was used to good effect, and we fixed him, getting one of the

When he fired the last shot, my comrade on my left made his Austrian speak, and there was one less in the Confederate Army

men on my left to cooperate with me by watching his chance of plugging him when he poked his head out from behind his tree to give me a dose. Loading up my rifle I looked for Mr. Reb but he was not ready yet for a shot. So aiming my piece so that the ball would clip the bark from the tree that he was behind and go into the line of battle to the rear, I let drive.

Looking over the bush to see what effect my shot had on Johny I was saluted with the barrell of his gun pointed directly towards me. Dodging on the instant, I escaped the ball that flew past me, and so saved my bacon. But Mr. Reb was not so lucky, for when he fired the last shot, my comrade on my left made his Austrian speak, and there was one less in the Confederate Army. Clapping his hand on his boddy he rolled over, and after that I received no special favors but was treated like the rest.

Our Captain Woolsey was wounded early in the fight, receiving a ball in the groin. Another one Mr. Healey was shot in the body and was taken to the field hospital that was just in the rear of our line, and when the army fell back, he was captured, as was also his brother Ben, who was stopping with him. He must have died on the field as he was never heard of afterwards. Another of the men Ed. Peale [Peel] got a bullet in the fleshy part of his arm, after which it went into the canteen of Corpl. Castro, and made such a loud whistling noise as it spun round in the water, that he got scared and made him jump around as if he was shot. One ball struck a cartridge box going completely through mashing the ammunition and raising a welt on the man's body.

As our ammunition was nearly run out we were ordered to fall back. Our guns had become so fouled with burnt powder that we had to jam the rammer against a tree to drive the ball home. When we had fallen back to the edge of the wood we met the 2nd Maryland going in to take our place. One of them as they passed our Regt. raised his hand and said "There's your good Maryland blood," but it proved that time to be inferior to Virginia blood, for they were driven out shortly after they went in and brought our Regt. into the muss again.

When the Regt. had reformed on the edge of the wood, we received some cartridges from the color company that had not been engaged, having been kept in reserve in charge of the colors. Marching to our right into an open field, arms were stacked and ranks broken, Myself and two other men were then detailed to fill the canteens of company with water. Loading ourselves with canteens we started for the spring about 3/4 of a mile to the rear, everything being quiet. While we were at the spring filling the can-

Loading ourselves with canteens we started for the spring

Carrying Water,

teens the fight broke out afresh, and we could see by the flashes that it was close to our Regt. As it lasted only a few minutes we filled the canteens and started back. It was now so dark that we could hardly tell where we were going and so struck out on guess work. We were shortly hailed by one of our company who told us that the Regt. had fallen back and were resting in the wood to our right. Going in we found them just as the sergeant was calling the roll.

After answering to our names, the canteens were distributed, and we proceeded to get some thing to eat, while listening to the account of the last fight. It seems that about as quick as we left, the 2nd Maryland came running out of the woods pell mell with the Johny after them. Waiting until our men had got out of the way, the 5th commenced firing and had quite a lively skirmish when the artilery opened on them and soon sent them back into the woods. One of them who was more daring than the rest stood in the field alone after his regt. had gone back into the woods and kept firing at our men as cool as a cucumber. But as the bullets got too thick he too disapeared. One of our company received a ball in the shin that left him on the field. What was curious (or a coincidence as some would have it) was, that this and another got into a dispute as we were crossing the fence just before the fight and had nearly come to blows, when the captain told them that they would have fighting enough before they were done without fighting between themselves. And so it proved, for one of them was shot in the body and died on the field, while the other got a ball on the shin, that disabled him from further active service.

After dark the rebels opened fire on some of our men, and going into the road to see what was the matter, we saw a splendid show of fireworks. On the edge of the woods where our men were posted a continuous stream of fire seemed to shoot into the woods accompanyed by the roar of musketry, while a stray flash was seen in the woods, wherever the trees or bushes were rather thin. In a few minutes it died away and everything was quiet for the night.

The next morning it was rumoured about that the rebels had left, and as no firing was heard, we took it for granted that it was so. As there was no quarter master waggons with us, and consequently no grub, two of us started out on an expedition for grub from the rebel haversacks. Going direct to the front, we soon reached the woods where the fight of the day before took place, but could find no haversacks with anything in them. Going further in we came across an officer and two men of our army who

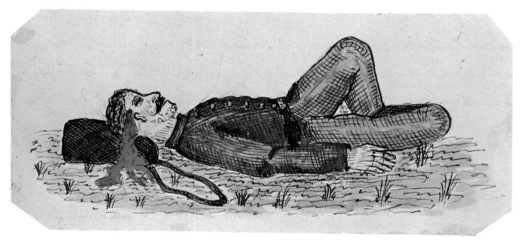

One in particular was lying under the head of a Union soldier who had been shot in the head and was a horrible sight

acted as if they were looking for game. When we got up to them they were standing behind a tree with rifles in their hands, firing into the woods as if they saw something. The officer soon put the gun to his shoulder, and taking steady aim "fired." He had no sooner done so, when two reports rang out from the oppisite direction and two balls ploughed up the ground at our feet, but luckily without doing any damage. Being convinced that the rebels had not all left, we took our departure in a hurry, leaving the glory of being shot at to any other who might hanker after military ambition.

Getting out again into the open field, we were more successful in our grub hunt, and found several haversacks that were pretty well filled, their owners having been shot early in the action. One in particular was lying under the head of a Union soldier who had been shot in the head and was a horrible sight to look at being covered with blood and dust. We were not very squeamish however and soon had the straps cut and the haversack pulled from under the head. We found in it apples, potatoes, and crackers being quite bulky, besides a cup, knife, fork and spoon. The grub we divided and the cutlery I kept while I was in the army. On another part of the field we found a mail bag that had been dropped by some one in their hurry to get away. The bag had been opened and the letters scattered all over, some of them being opened. Picking up the letters and placing them in the bag, we carried them to the Regt. and turned them over to the Adjutant, who I believe had them sent to their destination.

In the afternoon the artilery opened fire and in a short time the infantry got at it. And it was not long before the battle became fast and furious, the rebels trying to flank us on the left, and our men trying to stop them. About 4 o'clock our quarter master succeeded in getting some fresh beef. While the cook was in the act of cutting it up, and before we could be served, the order was given to fall in, and off we went on the double quick, grabbing a piece of raw meat as we went past the cook's box.

Marching to the right of our army, we had a good view of the battle without much actual danger. In our front, the artilery was consolidated, with the 6th N.J. as support. On their left, our infantry were in line fighting steadily, while on the hills, towards our left and in plain view, could be seen the rebel artilery taking up their position to cut off our retreat. The infantry seemed to fire by batallion, as it was a continual roll of musketry, the men standing in the ranks as if on dress parade, while every now and then a vacant space would be seen, where some poor fellow had met his fate. His place was quickly filled, and the fight went on. One of the shells or solid shot that was fired at our artilery missed its mark and came bounding over the field like a rubber ball, and just cleared the heads of the 2nd N.Y. who were on our right, spinning between their heads and bayonettes, as they were kneeling down. After passing the line it plunged into the ground, a little to our rear, in the wood w[h]ere our General and staff were standing.

As the rebels were driving our men steadily back on the left, we were ordered to their support on the double quick. We had not gone very far, when the rebels captured some of the guns that had been in front of our former position, and turning them round commenced firing into our rear with our own guns and ammunition, and [we] found ourselves under a cross fire of artilery. Running along a narrow road as fast as we could, we were saluted with a shower of shot and shell that made some of the men fairly bewildered. One of the shells that came from our right flank struck the bank on one side of the Regt. and sent a shower of small stones and pebbles through our ranks. But strange to say only one man (George Curtis) was struck, and he received a flesh wound in the arm. Giving a yell, like a Comanche Indian, he started on a run up the hill in the exact range of the rebel fire and between the rebel guns and our own. The shell that did the damage must have bounced over our heads or have went into the ground for it struck no one.

When we got to the left of our army, we formed line in the rear of our men, but could see nothing but a sheet of fire, as they were pegging away at each other at short range. The rebels getting more artilery to bear on us we were forced to fall back again, this time not to stop, until we reached Centreville.

Upon falling back we found the road blocked up with straglers, waggons and artilery, making it look very much like Bull Run the 1st. Not being able to march on the road we took to the woods, and made a path for ourselves. In crossing Bull Run Creek, we waded in water waist deep, holding up our cartridge box and haversack with one hand and the gun in the other to keep them dry. It was a very easy matter to get into the creek, but not so easy getting out as the bank was about 2 or 3 feet above the water,

143

and rather steep and slipery. One of the officers in order to get out as easy as possible, got hold of my coat-tail, but one of my heels comming near his face in my efforts to climb the bank, he let go and shifted for himself the best way he could.

In crossing Bull Run Creek, we waded in water waist deep

When we got safely over, we soon struck the main road and found it filled with men of all regts. who were making their way to the rear on their own hook. Stopping at a brook that crossed the road to replenish our stock of water we were unable to catch up to our Regt. and plodded along in the dark with the crowd and finally reached the heights of Centreville about midnight. As we could not find our Regt. we got some supper, and laying down by a large fire, slept soundly until morning, only to find when daylight made its appearance that we had slept next to our Regt. all night. And so ended the 2nd Battle of Bull Run.

As we had nothing to do the next morning and having a curiosity to see the wounded, I paid a visit to a church that was used for a hospital, a little way from our camp. The building was filled with wounded, and as I got there, our regimental surgeon was just finishing the amputation of a victim's arm, and was engaged in tying up the arteries and sewing the flaps of flesh together. A continous stream of ambulances were going towards Alexandria all day long, loaded with the wounded.

Towards evening our brigade marched to the rear of the town and bivouacked. We had now plenty of fresh beef, for all we had to do was to cut off as much as we wanted from freshly killed cattle that had been shot during the day by some of our men who had been on a foraging expedition. In visiting a farm house a short distance from camp we found plenty of tobacco in the shape of the raw material in a dry house. We of course helped ourselves to a few bunches of them and also laid in a stock of apples at the same time, which were found in abundance.

At 5 o'clock in the morning of Sept. 1st we left camp as guard over the waggon train with Kearny's Division in the advance. The roads were ankle deep in mud, and the clouds that had been very threatening now broke loose in a regular rain storm that drenched us to the skin in short order. When we had reached a place called Chantilly, we were surprised at hearing a volley of musketry fired in the woods to our left. Hastily forming the Regt. we were advanced in line of battle and halted in rear of Kearny's Division who were posted behind a fence and hard at work. After firing at each other for some time, it gradually ceased, as neither party could see the other on account of the darkness. Our train was saved but with the loss of Generals Kearny and Stevens, who were killed. Genl. Kearny went to the front of his men to reconnoiter and getting close to the enemy's lines was ordered to halt, but instead of doing so turned his horse and tried to reach our lines, but was shot dead. The rebels knew him and sent his body into our lines together with his equipments.

In the woods close to our line was a large fire, toward which all the wounded who could walk came expecting to find the surgeon and get their wounds dressed. No surgeon was there, and no one knew where to find them. One man came along while I was standing there to warm myself who was shot in the head, and the blood was still running down his face. Finding no one there to attend to him, he traveled off in the rain.

The rebs having fallen back we took the road again and reached Fairfax Court House at sun rise. Marching into an open field outside of the town, we halted for a rest. After stacking arms and throwing off our baggage, we captured all the fence rails we could find to boil our coffee. The rails soon giving out, the boys turned their attention to a house that stood close by, and getting to work with a will, soon had one side of the kitchen pulled down before the officers found it out and put a stop to it. After breakfast, we rested till noon, when we started again and marched through Fairfax. At the centre of the village, stood some army waggons loaded with fresh bread, and as we marched past every man was handed a loaf. This we understood was sent out by the ladies of Alexandria for Hooker's Division.

Taking the Alexandria road, we reached Fairfax Station on the railroad at 4 o'clock in the afternoon. Here we halted for a short time and saw some surgeons opperating on wounded men who were to be sent on to Alex-[andria]. by train. One of them had his leg cut off above the knee, and when we arrived the surgeon was tying up the arteries. The stump looked like a piece of raw beef. The other man had a part of his foot taken off. Neither of them seemed to be under the influence of cloreform, but were held down by some four men, while nothing but a groan escaped them, as the operation proceeded.

Leaving this impromtu hospital behind, we crossed the railroad and went some 3 miles further and bivouacked for the night. No sooner had the ranks been broken than foraging expeditions started out to find some provender. As there was a farm house with a garden attached close to us, we went for it, and the corn and potatoes soon found their way into our haversacks, so that by the time the officers came along and cleared us out for the purpose of getting something for themselves, there was not much left. Returning to camp we threw the corn and potatoes into the fire and in a short time [they] were nicely roasted. We then sat or laid down to a good supper of fried pork, soft bread, roast corn and potatoes.

After supper I was detailed to go on picket as the rebs were expected to pay us a visit before morning. Going away from camp about half a mile, we crawled into the bushes alongside of the road. We were out of sight of anyone who might be passing along the road, and [it] was a good spot for an ambush. We neither saw nor heard anything during the night with the exception of one of our men who had fallen asleep soon after being posted. Waking up rather suddenly, he yelled out that a rabbit had jumped down his throat. This set the boys roaring and more so, because the man actually thought that such was the case. Towards daylight we returned to the Regt. where the rabbit story was pretty well circulated amongst the rest of the boys, and when any of us wished to make him mad, all we had to do was to sing out "who swallowed the rabbit."

Leaving camp after breakfast, we marched about 20 miles and camped at Fort Lyons near Alexandria, about 4 o'clock in the afternoon pretty well tired out and ragged. Our uniforms at this time would have disgraced a beggar. Our pants had worn away so much that they hardly reached the knee, and the bottoms were in tatters. Our overcoats were not much better being burnt here and there in the skirts, by laying too near the fire. The whole uniform being pretty well stained up with mud and ashes. The shirt that I had on had seen active service for some 3 or 4 weeks and needed washing.

As our corps was the only one from the Army of the Potomac that took part in the Bull Run battle, we were left behind to guard the defences of

Alexandria and Washington, while the rest went on to Maryland. On the
4th we moved about a quarter of a mile to get a better camp ground, but saw
no grub, but plenty of promises.

After Bull Run.

*Our uniforms at this
time would have
disgraced a beggar*

XI

Defenses of Washington

THE MONTHS OF *September and October 1862 were among the most tranquil that Bellard spent in the army. Too depleted and exhausted after the second battle of Bull Run for further active campaigning, the Fifth New Jersey Infantry remained idle near Washington during Lee's invasion of Maryland. Bellard's memoir makes no mention of the bloody battle of Antietam (September 17), when McClellan checked Lee's advance. Despite repeated prodding from Washington, McClellan remained idle for a month after the battle, claiming that his army needed to recover from its recent losses. Finally, in late October, after a series of elaborate reviews, which as Bellard noted usually preceded a new campaign, the Army of the Potomac began slowly to advance.*

Bellard's memoir also fails to refer to President Lincoln's preliminary Emancipation Proclamation, issued after the Union success at Antietam. Doubtless Bellard disapproved of it, for, like most white Union soldiers, he was intensely prejudiced, and he usually referred to Negroes as "darkeys," "contrabands," or "cullud gemmens." He and other members of his all-white company considered it perfectly legitimate to steal the food and supplies of Negro troops.

Union soldiers now also considered it fair to seize the food and other belongings of white Southerners, whom they derisively called "butternuts." Early in the war Union generals had set guards to protect the cornfields of Southern civilians, but by the end of 1862 Federal officers ostentatiously turned their backs so as not to witness the foraging of their soldiers.

———◆———

I was detailed on the 8th for picket duty, and at 5 p.m. we went about two miles from camp, where myself and two others were posted after dark on the main road to the city, to look after straglers. We had nothing to do all night but tell stories or sleep until about 4 o'clock in the morning when the farmers' waggons arrived on their way to town, with produce for the markets. We halted each one and examined their passes to see if all was right. If it was, they were allowed to pass on, but not before we had secured some of their stock for private use. At daylight we were relieved and joined the reserve. After getting breakfast a few of us started to pick up what we could find and by dinner time had secured some fresh pork, as well as corn and potatoes. We spent the rest of the day in cooking and eating. About 6 p.m. we were relieved and ordered to camp.

On the 12th we moved camp about a half mile and pitched our tents on a hill that commanded a good view of the cities of Alexandria and Washington. We stopped there until the 15th when we went a mile further and camped on the right of Fort Lyons. Towards evening 100 men were detailed for picket from our Regt. myself amongst the rest. So buckling on our rations and ammunition, we soon found the picket line and at once took possession. On being relieved next morning, I carried back to camp a lot of mushrooms and potatoes, the spoils taken on picket.

On the 19th ten men of each company were detailed as a special guard to go 13 miles out on the Orange and Alexandria Railroad. We packed up our duds, and marched down to the depot under command of Captain Gamble. After waiting round the depot some time, we marched back to camp as no transportation had been provided for us. Before dismissing the squad, the Captain informed us that he wanted the same detail to be ready the next morning to go with him. As we expected a good time, we were on hand early, and marching down to the depot took the train, and were soon on our way to Burke's Station. We arrived there safe and sound, and found that we were the advance guard of the U.S. Army. As we had only 100 men, we of course had no drill, but plenty of outpost picket duty. The government had sent a lot of contrabands with us to fell trees and cut them into cord wood, which were afterwards sent by rail to the city to furnish fuel for the army during the winter. Pitching our tents, we were divided off in squads, I being on the reserve.

On the 21st I was on outpost picket with two others, and having nothing to do visited a farm house to get some peaches. Walking up to an old mill that looked as if it had not been worked since the war began, I came across some 2 or 3 homespun butternuts, who were standing there. When I told them that I would like some peaches, they said that we could help ourselves to all we wanted. So the tree was climbed, and in a few minutes [we] had our haversacks and caps full of fine ripe peaches. Thanking the butternuts for their kindness we returned to our post and demolished the fruit, making ourselves nearly sick by eating too many. The night being cold we built a good fire and while one stood guard the others lay down by the fire and passed the time away in conversation or story telling. In this way the night slipped away without our knowing it or feeling the least sleepy. As the pickets were drawn in during the day, our turn only came on about every 5th day, so we had plenty of time for sleep before we went on again.

On the 22nd a first squad of "cullud gemmens" [colored gentlemen] arrived bringing with them a good stock of fresh bread and provisions. As it happened, our own grub had not arrived, so the darkeys had to suffer. While one man would offer his services to help them carry the bread to their commissary tent, two more would act together, and before the one who was carrying the bread got half way to the tent, it was knocked out of his arms and vanished in a moment. When the darkeys found out the dodge they carried it themselves. But one or two of them lost their bread also before they got to the tent. The stealing did not end there, for during the night some one cut a hole in the tent and carried off quite a lot of provisions. After that, some one slept in the tent every night to prevent any more depredations.

The next day our own rations came up, and we were all right once more. During the day three of us went into the woods a short distance from camp and came back with a load of wild grapes, both green and blue. As I was acting as cook for that day, I treated the boys to some stewed grapes for supper, and it was well received.

Hearing from some of the boys that there was some fine apples at Widdow Burke's, a few of us went there one day to get some. Meeting the lady of the house, we asked her if we could have some apples and peaches. She said yes of course, and pointing to an orchard at some distance from the house, told us to take what we wanted. We found when we got there, that the apples were small and the peaches not much better. We filled our haversacks with them in case there was nothing better. As we were returning to camp we thought that we might as well see what she had in the rear garden. When we got back of the house we found an apple tree that was loaded with large fruit, and up I went into the tree and commenced to shake them off. The widow, who had come out on the back stoop, stood looking at me but said nothing. When we had got enough, each of us had our haversacks full, as well as the pocket. Besides the orchard the widow had quite a farm. One large field being covered with broom corn that grows something like Indian corn but instead of soft flowers, has a sort of brush standing out on top.

152

On the 26th we received another 3 days rations of grub and at night went on picket in the woods. When we got to the post, we found the men whom we were to relieve very bussy in frying beef steaks that had been cut from a quarter of beef that lay alongside of them behind a log. When they had finished eating, they packed up their traps and returned to camp, taking a few pounds of the meat with them, but leaving us the frying pan and the rest of the beef. Posting one of our men on guard we went into the meat bussines and during the night managed to put away several meals. Being relieved next morning we returned to camp with beef enough in our haversacks to last the day, and left the ballance and the frying pan for our successors.

During the day a secesh gentleman came into camp looking for his cow, that he believed had been shot by one of our men. It happened to be his favorite and had a bell on its neck to act as leader for the herd. He said that he heard the bell when the cows were coming home, but before they got their [there], he heard a shot and had not seen the cow since. The captain turned to the men who were standing round and told them in the presence of old

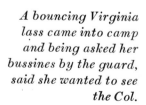

A bouncing Virginia lass came into camp and being asked her bussines by the guard, said she wanted to see the Col.

153

Virginia, that he would shoot the first man whom he found killing anything belonging to the farmers. This satisfied the old gent and he went off. When he had gone the Capt. turned to the men, and remarked that it was rather rough on the old man, but so long as he did not see it done it was all right.

At another time the men had been pretty successful on a duck hunt and presented the captain with a pair of them for his supper. But before he had the chance to get them cooked, a bouncing Virginia lass came into camp and being asked her bussines by the guard, said she wanted to see the Col. Being directed to the Capt's. tent, she made for it and informed him that some of his men had stolen her ducks. When he heard ducks, he stood in the flap of the tent so that she could not look in, for fear that she would see a pair of them that lay under his bunk in plain sight. After satisfying the lady that if his men took them it was not to his knowledge and against his orders, she left and the Capt. had his roast duck for supper.

We arrested a citizen on the 28th for having government property in his possession. After turning the same over to us, we let him go and he went on his way rejoicing. On the 29th I was detailed for picket with Buck and another man, and took up our post at an old shanty, kept by one Mrs. Murphy. During the day we got quite a lot of potatoes from a farmer who lived near there and borrowing some stew pans from Mrs. Murphy we proceeded to make ourselves comfortable. Buck acted as cook and made a very good dinner of beef steak, with flour gravy and as many baked and boiled potatoes as we could get away with.

On being relieved next day, myself and Buck started out on a tour of observation about half a mile from camp. The country road that we took was completely hedged in with a nut-bearing shrub called "chincopins" [chinquapins]. They have the appearance of a chestnut both as to tree and nut but [are] a great deal smaller and very sweet. The nuts were so thick that we could lay under one almost anywhere and pick as many as we wanted to eat.

Passing along this road we came across a large farm house, and upon nearing it were surprised to hear some one playing the Star Spangdled Banner upon a piano. Not knowing there was any lover of the starry banner in that region, we took the liberty of walking up the window to liston. While there the owner Dr. Holsopple came out of the house and seeing two of Uncle Sam's soldiers standing there requested us to walk in. After some little persuasion we did so, and were introduced to his wife and daughter, the latter being the performer. Seating ourselves at his invitation, he informed us that he was a native of New York but having a farm there, he did not like to leave it, although he had been threatened with a halter by rabid secesh before our troops came up. After quite a talk about old times and the war, Mrs. Holsopple served up dinner to which we were invited. Being old soldiers the second invitation was not required, so we sat down with the family and did justice to the best meal we had eaton since leaving home. As Buck was well up in chin music, conversation was carried on to season the vituals. After dinner the young lady played a few pieces on the piano for our benefit. As it was now time to return to camp, the Doctor showed us round his farm and in his potatoe field we saw plain evidence where some of our boys had made free with them. The Doctor said that if any of them came and asked him for any he would give them all they wanted, but he did not like to have them stolen. He wanted us to take a mess, but we thanked him and declined. When we left, a pressing invitation was extended to us to call again whenever we were near, either during the war or after. From there we went to another northern family, who treated us very cordially and they also offered us some vegetables to take with us to camp, but we refused.

The next morning about half a dozen of us took our rifles and started on a tour amongst the secesh for forage. Comming up to a farm house at some distance from the Doctor's, we found a peach orchard laden with fruit and a young native engaged in shaking them down previous to doing them up for winter. Asking permission to take some, it was granted, and we jumped the fence to pick up a few to eat. We had no sooner got in, than the lady of the house came out and ordered us about our bussines, calling us northern thieves and such like. Upon trying to reason with the woman she got mad and called for the dogs, threatening to set them on us. As we did not relish the idea of being bit by a dog, we started up the road. We soon came across a potatoe patch and made up our minds that we would have some potatoes if we could not have peaches. So while two of us sat on the fence with rifles ready in case of dogs, the rest jumped over the fence and began digging up spuds, using their bayonettes for a spade. In a few minutes some one yelled out that the northern sogers were digging the potatoes, and up she came as mad as a March hare, with a stone in each hand. She stamped and raved, telling the men to get out, but instead of paying any attention to her they kept on digging away, putting the spuds in haversacks as soon as dug out. At last her Virginia blood got up, and raising her hand, [she] said she would dash out his brains. The man merely pointed his bayonette at her, and said he guessed she had better not try it, and again got to work on the potatoes.

Finding that she could not scare us, she called for a horse, to go and see the Col. It was now high time for us to git, and we did so, taking the shortest road to camp. In going through a wood, the sound of her horse's feet came to our ears, and not wishing to be seen by the excited damsel, we struck off through the fields, and by a short cut reached camp before her. We had no sooner reached camp, and got rid of our foraging proceeds, when in rode the lady astride of her horse, and proceeded at once to the Captain, to whom she related her grievances. As luck would have it, while we were absent the 29th N.Y. Infantry, a German regt. from Segills [Sigel's] Division had arrived to relieve us. This was fortunate for us. The Captain ordered the company to fall in for inspection, and when they were drawn up in line, the lady was asked to point out the foragers. This of course she could not do as the delinquents lay in their tents, or mingled with the other regt. Not being able to pick any of them out, the Captain informed her that the 29th was in charge and it must have been some of their men and not his, and so sent her off to see the Col. commanding. As he was a German she got no satisfaction from him and had to return home without seeing the marauders punished.

That afternoon we packed up our baggage and taking the train arrived at Alexandria that night. Our division had been reviewed that day by Genl. Heintzelman and staff, which according to previous experience looked like a move. The next day the 3rd, our Regt. went on picket outside the city, but as for myself [I] was on camp guard, which is not so pleasant, their [there] being no chance for foraging.

On the 5th we struck tents and marched about a mile to our first line of entrenchments. Here we laid out a new camp called Camp Kearny. This was afterwards changed to Van Lear, as there was another camp of the same name. Our time was now pretty well taken up between camp guard, picket, drill, and building fortifications. The brigade had a drill every day, and as for duty, when the men came back from picket or entrenchment duty, say today, they would go on fatigue duty tomorrow, and the detail from camp

*There was no rest for
the wicked*

157

guard go on water police, who had to carry all the water for the cooks. So there was no rest for the wicked.

On the 8th, Mr. F. F. Paterson came to our Regt. as sutler and was hailed with delight by the boys, who could now hang him up for sundrys etc. that we would have had to do without any other way. Having no cash of course we had to pay rather dear for the accomidation. Only 10 cents for a paper of chewing tobacco, $1.50 for a plug of navy tobacco, 10 cents for smoking, 60 cents for a dozen eggs, 60 cents for a pound of butter, 25 cents for a sole leather, pie, and all else in proportion. I received a box from home on the 9th containing cakes, pickles, tobacco, pipes, etc. They came in good time, as I was out of the weed, with no cash to replenish. A soldier would almost as soon do without his dinner as his chew.

On the 11th we marched out of camp for inspection and review by Genl. Sickles, who was now in command of our division. It commenced to rain very hard and we were ordered back to camp on the run. We were not at all sorry as we had got pretty well tired of reviews and parades.

Since the arrival of the sutler, individual cooking was the order of the day and was going on from morning until night, and all conceivable dishes from toasting bread, making a beef pot pie or mutton chop, the boys indulged in. My own dinner consisted of fried sausage, and for supper fried sausage and onions with a cup of coffee.

Our Captain who was wounded at the Battle of Bull Run, came back to us again and took command, having recovered from his wound. Lieut. Hill who was our second Lieutenant and left us at Williamsburg, was now Captain, and act[ing]. Asst. Adjt. Genl. of our Brigade. Genl. Patterson who came back and took command, having so far recovered from his sprained ancle that he received at Malvern Hill, that he could take command on horseback, although on foot he had to use crutches.

About this time Col. Starr left us to go back to the regular cavalry, taking with him a company made up of volunteers from our Regt., 10 men of each company being transferred to serve out the ballance of their term. By taking this 100 men from us, it made our Regt. rather small in numbers, but the men were so eager to join the cavalry and ride on a horse, that applications were made by men of all the Regts. guarding the city, as well as the men in the convelesant camp. But orders were orders and the men of our Regt. were the only ones taken.

Rumors were now flying round that the rebels were marching on the city, and that 10,000 cavalry were expected to make an attack at any time. An order was at once issued that we were to be ready to fall in at a moment's notice. Belts were to be kept on at all times night or day, and [we were] to fall in at all roll calls with arms in our hands.

On the 16th our Brigade was drilled and inspected by Genl Sickles. The 20th found me detailed for picket outside the city, and posted on a high hill, that was named by the pickets Point Look Out. It was a round hill commanding a good view of the surrounding country, and on the top of it, we had built a little shed with a fire place in it, so that we could have a fire on cold nights to make us comfortable. In the morning I took a strol among the fields and comming across some mushrooms (that I am very fond of) I picked up an old cavalryman's hat that would hold about a half peck, and in a short time filled it. Returning with these to my post, I made a very good breakfast having what we call in the Army a hish & hash, consisting of pork, tomatoes, potatoes, crackers and mushrooms all stewed together and seasoned with a little salt and pepper. This dish was considered a great luxury by the soldiers, but at the present time would probably be thrown to the dogs.

The 22nd our division was reviewed in a large open field about a mile or so from camp by President Lincoln, and Genls. Banks and Heintzelman with their staffs, who made quite a show in themselves. It was a grand sight, as the infantry, artilery and the ambulance corps of our division were

Shouldering our picks, axes, and spades,
we took our place at the head of the line

reviewed. I was detailed as a pioneer for the occasion, and shouldering our picks, axes, and spades, we took our place at the head of the line. The review must have been a splendid sight to anyone who was looking on but was not so much so for those who took part, as we had to march division front (that is two companys) in an open field, without any land marks except stones that happened to lay on the ground, at the same time keeping our front like a chalk line. We could do it however, and make as fine an appearance in regard to marching as any regt. I have ever seen in N.Y. City, where the curb stone is the guide. The 7th Regt. not eccepted.

We had now plenty of duty to perform in picket, campguard, guarding parolled prisoners and in the trenches. Entrenchments were being dug on all the hills round the city, while more forts were to be put up during the winter. At this time we were building a large fort near Fort Lyons.

On the 25th I was again on picket, but this time in the open field without shelter. As it was rather cold, we built a fire of fence rails, and managed to make ourselves comfortable. In the afternoon I took a strol through the farms to pick up a few ears of corn for a roast (cabbaged of course) when I came across one of our picket posts stationed near a farm,

The members of which were enjoying themselves with the contents of the spring house

161

the members of which were enjoying themselves with the contents of the spring house. Stopping a short time with them, I continued my stroll, when I run across some more pickets who were out for pork, having their guns with them. Two or three porkers were running round loose trying to get out of the way. One of them failed and his carcas was put into the cook's kettle to furnish meat for the boys.

That night it commenced to rain and kept it up for two days, sending us back to camp soaked to the skin. It cleared up on the afternoon of the 27th but was very windy and cold.

On the 29th we were engaged in building a fort on the site of our old camp. The fort or earthwork was a very large one with a ditch or moat all round it. This was filled with water. The outside of the forts were sodded. In building these works the engineers first built a light frame of wood the size and shape that is wanted, and when it is fixed to suit them with the necessary angles, etc. the men are put to work with pick and shovel and digging from the outside throw the dirt between the frame work until it is filled up, some of the men being on the pile to spread the dirt. When it has been graded over nicely, it is covered over with sods. The ditch soon fills with water from the many rain storms, and after the Chevaux de Frisse is staked down, it only needs the guns to complete it. The Chevaux de Frisse that we employed were large branches of trees pinned to the ground, with the brush outward. The ends of the branches were then cut off and sharpened, and it would have bothered man or horse to get over it.

The numbers of the Regt. who had been transferred to the Cavalry left camp on the 30th with Col. Starr to proceed to Carlisle Barracks, Penn. to be mounted and drilled.

The 31st we were again on picket for the last time round Alexandria, as we were ordered in at daylight next morning, a new regt. the 120 N.Y. taking our place. While we were halted by the road side, leaning against a fence waiting for the order to march, the new regt. made a break for the fence to build their fires with and commenced tearing it down. They were ordered to stop by the members of our Regt. as we had not been relieved as yet, and had of course full charge. They did not feel inclined to do so, and as their regt. was about 3 times as strong as ours, they had an idea that numbers would do it, and proposed to drive us out. Their officers however thought diferent, and ordered them into line. If a fight had taken place, I think the new recruits would have been driven off the field at the point of bayonette, as they were fresh and knew very little about disipline, while we were old hands at the bussines. The dutys being at last turned over to our successors, we started for camp, and had no sooner got into the road, leaving the fence clear, when a grand rush was made for it and it was soon carried over entire and used for fuel.

The men are put to work with pick and shovel and digging from the outside throw the dirt between the frame work until it is filled up

XII

On the March

On NOVEMBER 7, 1862, after McClellan had begun shifting troops in preparation for a new campaign, President Lincoln removed the general from command and put Ambrose E. Burnside at the head of the Army of the Potomac. Many Union soldiers deeply regretted McClellan's departure, for the general, with all his faults, had tried to keep his men well equipped and had seen that they were not needlessly exposed in battle.

If the new commander of the Army of the Potomac had reservations about his abilities, so did his men. Having witnessed numerous previous reorganizations of the army, they were not much impressed by Burnside's decision to group his corps into three "Grand Divisions." Assigned to the Center Grand Division, members of the Fifth New Jersey Infantry were pleased to learn that its commander was a man they knew and respected, General Joseph Hooker, now recovered from the wound he had received at Antietam. Bellard and his friends were less happy to hear that General Sickles was commander of their division in the III Corps, which was part of Hooker's Grand Center Division. Notorious for having killed his wife's lover in cold blood, Sickles was considered a bully and a glory-seeker careless of his men's lives.

Before the month was over, the Fifth New Jersey had fresh reason to distrust Sickles, who accused their brigade commander, General Francis E. Patterson, of cowardice in ordering a retreat from Warrenton Junction. Though Patterson had, in fact, been conspicuously absent, claiming illness, whenever his brigade was under heavy fire, his men had a certain loyalty to him, and they were shocked to learn that, faced with Sickles's charge and a court-martial, he committed suicide on November 22.

Even while Burnside was reorganizing the army he was developing a new strategy. Proposing to make his main supply base on Aquia Creek, he planned to push south along the line of the Richmond, Fredericksburg & Potomac Railroad. His first step was to shift the army southeast to Falmouth, on the north bank of the Rappahannock River. Then, using pontoon bridges, he intended to cross the river, seize Fredericksburg, and advance upon the Confederate capital. Requesting approval from Washington, Burnside on November 14 was informed: "The President has just assented to your plan. He thinks it will succeed if you move rapidly; otherwise not."

———◆———

We struck tents upon reaching camp, and in the afternoon we marched out, the band playing The Girl I Left Behind Me, as a number of the men's wives had come out to see them, while stationed near the city. There was a great deal of crying and wringing of hands as the Regt. marched past them on our way to the front. A number of whom were destined never to return. I suppose the men and their wives thought of this when the band struck up and so made the scene worse. We were soon out of camp however and saw no more of them. When we had marched about six miles we bivouacked for the night.

In the morning we started about daylight and passing through Fairfax and Centreville, we bivouacked at Bull Run Creek between the same shantys that we had occupied in August. Tearing down what was left of them, we built fires and laying down beside them were soon fast asleep. In the morning we got up about daylight, and getting our breakfast were on the road again. Passing through Manassas, we encamped about half a mile from the Junction. As soon as we halted, our company was sent out as pickets. During the day the grass, that was very dry, caught on fire and there was some lively jumping round, before it was put out. No damage was done, as our tents had not been put up. The next morning we were called in from picket, and starting early, marched to Bristoe Station, where we bivouacked in the woods. Stacking arms, the boys armed themselves with sticks and commenced hunting rabbits, the woods being alive with them. As soon as a rabbit ran past one of the men in his hurry to get away he was knocked over with a stick.

We lay here until the 6th when we had orders to move again. Leaving camp about one o'clock we marched up the Orange and Alexandria Railroad, to within 3 miles of Warrenton Junction, where we went into bivouac. Pickets were posted to give the alarm in case of an attack. As the night was bitter cold, we proceeded to make ourselves as comfortable as possible. Some of the boys had found a hand car on the road and it was pressed into the service, to bring logs for the fires. When the boys had got it loaded with railroad sleepers, it was run up oppisite our camp, where the sleepers were dumped, and the car sent after another load. Each company helped themselves to the sleepers, and piling up 8 or 10 of them, the fire was started. After it had got into a good blaze, the beds were made. Our rubber blankets were placed on the ground to keep out the dampness (in a circle round the fire) with some of the woolen blankets over them to keep us warmer. We then lay down spoon fashion, with our feet to the fire, and after covering ourselves with the balance of the rubber and woolen blankets where [were] fixed for the night. Although it was a terrible cold night, we slept very comfortable. The only trouble with the spoon fashion of sleeping being that when one man wanted to turn over, all the rest had to turn with him, or else loose our covering.

The scouts that had been sent out by Genl. Patterson reported that 10,000 rebel cavalry were at Warrenton, and as our brigade only numbered about 920 men, it was decided to turn back. We did so, but in such a hurry that we left our pickets behind, and they came stragling in the next day. We were routed out at one o'clock in the morning and got ready to march, which we did about 5 o'clock, and reached our camp at half past six o'clock, and remained there til night. It began to snow about seven o'clock and kept it up all day. As I was placed on guard over the Col's. tent as soon as we reached camp, I did not have a very pleasant time of it. About seven p.m. orders came to move again, and we marched as far as Manassas Junction, where we bivouacked. In the morning we pitched our shelter tents and got under cover. A tents had been sent for our use, but as yet had not been unloaded.

While out for a walk, looking at the sights, I met an old friend from New York (a plate printer) who was an officer in one of the N.Y. Regts. but had resigned and was on his way home, with another officer. He was glad to see me and after inquirys had been made of friends etc. he asked me where we could get something to drink. I informed him and was asked to go and partake, but the shoulder strap who was with him objecting on account of my rank, I was left out in the cold (so much for red tape) as my room was better than my company. I bade him good bye and we parted never to meet again. Loosing the drink did not make much diference, as we received a ration of whiskey and quinine the same day.

On the 10th we pitched our new A tents and were quite comfortable, four men occupy[ing] each tent, two on each side. We laid a floor of boards, over which we put plenty of hay or straw, and so slept quite warm. The first train went over the bridge at Brístoe today, it having been repaired by the troops. It had been partially destroyed by the rebels before the Battle of

"A" Tent.

*On the 10th we pitched
our new A tents*

Bristoe. Each one of the upright timbers had been cut through, as well as the braces, and then set on fire, but was not burnt very bad. When the first train came along, after it had been cut, it of course went to the bottom as soon as it struck the bridge, where it lay when we passed. The tracks were covered with burnt cars, guns, pans, kettles, tent tripods, horse shoes and everything made of iron that is used in an army, and would not burn.

During our march from Bristoe to Manassas, we passed Genl. Sickles with the other two brigades of our division going to the front as we supposed. His own brigade (Excelsior) were so drunk that nothing could be done with them and they returned to camp. While they were marching past, our boys struck up "Johnny stole a Ham, and Sickles killed a Man" but no notice was taken of it.

Genl. McClellan being relieved from the command of the army of the Potomac about this time, our division on the 11th was drawn up in line of battle alongside of the railroad to salute him when he passed on his way to Washington. In the afternoon a gun was fired, as a signal that he was comming. Forming in line at a carry arms, we soon saw a train approaching, with the stars and stripes floating over it, and as it passed, we saw little Mac standing on the platform of the car, waving his cap to us. As we presented arms, the artilery also gave him a salute of 15 guns. Soon after he had passed, another train came along from Washington on board of which was our old Genl. Hooker on his way to the front. As the train came in sight, the battery fired a salute of 15 guns, and as soon as the first gun was fired, we came to a present [arms]. When he had passed we came to a carry [arms], and gave him 3 rousing cheers, which he returned by waving his hat. After he had gone we passed in review by column of company, and returned to camp. We had been under arms from 8 a.m. to 3 p.m.

While waiting for the trains to come along, the boys had a little fun with a sutler who had come on the ground to make some money. As the boys seemed inclined to help themselves from his waggon without the cash, he started to drive them off, when some of them upset a barrell of cakes from his waggon and went for the cheese, but a nigger who was with him, held on too tight. Soldiers are down on the sutlers and take any chance they have of getting square with them. As to the right or wrong of the question, it is something they do not bother their brains about. The reason was, I suppose, on account of the exorbitant prices that we had to pay for anything we got from them. For instance, a 3 cent paper of tobacco 10 cents. A paper of pins 5 cents. A small loaf of bread 10 cents, and everything else in proportion.

Another move being contemplated, we were ordered to strike our A tents and place them on the cars, after which we pitched our shelter tents, and awaited further orders. All the military stores were packed up, and placed on the cars, ready for removal, so that it looked like a move. I was detailed for fatigue duty on the railroad to pack up, but not being wanted, I returned to camp and laid off. On the 19th a fight took place at the station between some of Sickles's men and the guard, and during the meelee, one of the men received a bayonette thrust, that laid him up for repairs (cause

John Barleycorn). The last train left for Alexandria the same day, leaving us alone in our glory.

The next morning we struck tents about 8 o'clock, and after setting fire to the depot, water tank and other railroad buildings, we marched from Manassas, taking the road to Centreville, over Bull Run Creek. We passed through Centreville, and halted about a mile from Fairfax Court House. When we had got a short distance from Manassas, it commenced to rain and kept it up all night, so that by the time we halted we were wet through and very uncomfortable, it being in November. The ranks being broken, fires were started, and the fences were soon cleared and burnt up. In the morning we started again, and passing through Fairfax took the Dumfries road. After marching about six miles we went into camp near Wolf Run ford.

During our stay at this camp Genl. Patterson of our brigade shot and killed himself. It was reported at the time, that he killed himself because Genl. Sickles called him a coward for his conduct at Warrenton Junction. His body was taken away from camp on the 24th, the artilery firing a salute. The body was taken to his home in Pa. under the escort of Capt. Hill the Asst. Adjut. Genl. Col. Revere of the 7th being senior col. now took command of the brigade.

At 8 o'clock on the morning of the 25th we broke camp, at Wolf Run and after a short march we came to a ford of that name. Taking off our shoes and stockings and rolling up our pants, we plunged through the icy water, and took the road for Dumfries. The water in Wolf Run was cold as ice, and the stones at the bottom so sharp that besides having our feet and legs almost frozen with the icy water, they were hurt by the sharp stones. To make matters still worse it commenced to rain, and kept it up all night. Our blankets and uniforms were soaked through and when we halted at 8 o'clock that night we had to sleep in our wet clothes. It was not very pleasant, but we passed the night as comfortable as possible under the circumstances. We started again on the morning of the 26th for a march through the mud, which in this part of the country is more like glue than anything else. When you put your foot down it sinks in over your shoe tops, and they must be well fastened on or they would be left behind in the mud. The rocks around Dumfries Creek along which we marched had a very black appearance, as if they were seamed with coal.

Passing through the town of Dumfries, we went into camp about 8 miles beyond. While we were passing through the town, some of the boys went into a variety store that we passed to purchase some tobacco, but the proprietor said that he had none, and would not sell any for our money, if he had. Some sharp eyed blue coat however spied a barrel of it in the cellar, and on its being noised around a grand rush was made for that barrell. And it was not long before Mr. Reb had none in reality, and with none of our cash for it either. I managed to fill my pockets with it, so that I was fixed. The tobacco question being disposed of, attention was paid to the ballance of his stock in trade. Dry goods were thrown down from the shelves, on to the counter, and were soon converted into gun rags by as many men as could crowd into the store. Ladies' crinoline were strewn around, and in fact everything that was in the store was torn up, carried away, or distroyed, even to his cash box. When the sacking became general, the proprietor got afraid of his life and left to find the Genl. While he was gone the stable was opened, his saddle was brought out and given to one of our officers, who rode off with it. The horse was next trotted out, and would have been trotted out of reach in a few minutes had not the Genl. appeared just as we got him out of the stable, and ordered us to return it. We did so, but that was all he did get back that was of any value. I rather think that when U.S. troops passed his way again he was more obliging and so save[d] his reputation and his goods at the same time.

We started again on the 27th with our brigade as rear guard. We had a very easy march as we could take our own time to it, as we had to drive before us all stragglers who were resting in the woods (coffee coolers) for this purpose. One company was deployed out as skirmishers on either side of the road in the woods, and all men found laying off in the woods or straggling along the road were picked up and taken along with us. We fared well as to grub on this march, for the roads were so heavy for the teams that they could not pull their loads, and they had to be lightened, by taking out some of the provisions. This was piled up alongside of the road to be called for later. Of course when we came across any of these piles, we were not backward in helping ourselves, and so had a good supply of tack, pork and coffee for emergencys.

While halted for dinner, the boys started for the woods after persimmons which seemed by the trees around to be plentiful. But a soldier who was on picket and belonged to some new regt. objected to our going and said we had no bussines there. We being on the march took no notice of him, only to inform him that if he attempted to shoot, as he had threatened to do, he would get a bayonette rammed into him. That settled him, and we went into the woods and had a good feast of them. Persimmons are very sweet when fully ripe and touched with the frost, but before that will pucker up your mouth like so much allum.

Returning to our Regt. we had our dinner and started off again. (From our halting place which was on a hill, several camps could be seen, showing us that we were nearing the front once more.) When we reached the foot of the hill, we found the road lined with crowds of soldiers, who had come down from their camps to see if they could find any friends amongst the new arrivals. I met quite a number of friends among the crowd who belonged to the 21st N.J. and came from Hudson City. After a shake hands, I was requested to spend the night with them at their camp, which was about two miles away. I promised to do so if I could get leave from the officers.

A short distance from the foot of the hill ran Aquia Creek. It was rather wide and deep, and not being fordable for infantry was bridged over by a single tree. And as the first man over continued on the same gait, upon reaching the other side, the last man over had a good running match before he caught up to his regt.

Marching about two miles past the creek we bivouacked for the night. After roll had been called, I asked for and received permission to visit the 21st and with a companion we struck out through the woods, mud and darkness to find our friends at Sleepy Hollow (that being the name of their camp). After floundering through the mud for some time, we found them, and were shown around the camp by some of the boys. After a supper of fried pork and hard tack, we had a chat and smoke with several of them. They all seemed to be tired of the war and wished they were safe home. After a good sleep under canvas we bade the boys of the 21st good bye and returned to our Regt.

When after dispatching our breakfast we started off for a twelve mile march over the worst road I think I ever traveled on. Up hill and down hill. Through mud, slush, water and sand, and passing lots of baggage waggons

It was rather wide and deep, and not being fordable for infantry was bridged over by a single tree

The worst road I think I ever traveled on

that were stuck in the mud. And all the swearing of the teamsters and the clubbing [of the horses] over the head could not pull them out. On the march we saw several Hudson City boys who belonged to Hexamer's Battery from Hoboken. Passing through the Stafford Court House on the way, we went into camp about a mile from Hooker's head quarters at Falmouth on the Rappahannock River and directly oppisite Fredericksburg.

XIII

―◆―

Fredericksburg

I F BURNSIDE'S STRATEGY *was to succeed, speed was essential. The general moved his army with great expedition to Falmouth and was ready to cross the Rappahannock before Lee guessed his plan. But the railroad bridge at Fredericksburg had been burned, and the supply authorities in Washington failed to heed the urgency of Burnside's request for pontoons. By the time Bellard's regiment, a part of the rear guard of the Union army, reached Falmouth, virtually all of Lee's forces were in position south of the river, waiting for the Federals to advance.*

Although all elements of surprise had now been lost, Burnside adhered to his original plan. He ordered General Edwin V. Sumner's Right Grand Division to cross the river at Fredericksburg and attack the Confederate entrenchments on top of Marye's Heights. General William B. Franklin's Left Grand Division was to cross the river farther down and turn thé Confederate right flank. Bellard was fortunate to be in Hooker's Grand Center Division, which was held in reserve.

On December 12 Sumner's and Franklin's grand divisions crossed the Rappahannock. The next morning Franklin's troops opened the attack upon the Confederates, who were posted on hills overlooking the river. During the first few hours of the fight it seemed possible that the Union soldiers might break the Confederate line. By 1:30 P.M., however, a furious counter-attack drove Franklin's men back, and he called for reinforcements.

While this fighting was going on, Bellard's regiment, in reserve, had nothing to do, and the men watched as spectators the gallant but disastrous attempt of Sumner's men to storm Marye's Heights. Then, summoned to support Franklin's crumbling line, they rushed across the river in time to help blunt the Confederate offensive.

For the next two days the Fifth New Jersey Infantry remained on the battlefield while Burnside made up his mind to accept the obvious necessity of withdrawing across the river. During much of that time there was little firing, for, as Colonel Sewell reported, an informal cease-fire prevailed "through some arrangement of the pickets themselves."

Thoroughly defeated again, the Union army on the night of December 15 began to retreat across the Rappahannock. Not until 3:30 the next morning was Bellard's regiment, one of the last to recross the pontoon bridges, safe again on the northern bank.

———◆———

The camp was regulated on the 29th and we proceeded to make ourselves as comfortable as possible. We were well enough off as regards shelter, but could not get any grub, as the waggons could not reach us on account of the mud. A new company was added to our Regt. the same day that took the letter of the company that had been consolidated [Company A]. A good commencement for them, with nothing to eat in camp. Our encampment was on the side of a hill, beautifully situated for drainage but not very easy to climb, when ice had formed on it. At the foot of the hill was a forrest of pine and oak trees, with a good spring of clear water. My tent being on left of the company was near the top of the hill, while the officers were quartered at the foot on the edge of the woods and out of the way of the wind. The next day being Sunday, we had Regt. inspection in the morning and dress parade in the evening, but with nothing to eat until one o'clock when the waggons arrived. We were rather hungry by this time and did full justice to Uncle Sam's pies and pork.

Dec. 1st I was on fatigue duty, digging sinks and [building] brush houses for the guard, and wound up the day with dress parade. We were now getting our rations regularly with an allowance of fresh beef two or three times a week, and we felt as happy as a clam at high water. On the 2nd the new company were put through a course of sprouts and the usual parade of the Regt. took place. The weather was very fine but cold.

Having nothing to do on the 3rd I took a stroll down to the Rappahannock River oppisite Fredericksburg to see what it looked like. It was quite a large city and had several churches in it. There was one thing I remarked that was diferent from our experience on the Peninsular Campaign. The people were walking round the streets and the pickets were also promenading up and down in plain sight, but not a shot was fired on either side. Back of the city was a range of hills that were thickly wooded and on the crest of the hills at the edge of the woods was their fortifications, well armed and manned, as we found to our cost later on. The railroad bridge that had spanned the river was now in ruins, having been burnt, and nothing remained of it but two or three stone pillars.

Genl. Sickles at this time issued an order that we should have 3 drills each day, so we were not to be kept in idleness. On the 4th we were reviewed by our old Commander Hooker, who was now in command of the centre grand division. As he passed by, each regt. gave him 3 cheers. The old man was held in as high esteem as ever by the boys. It commenced to rain on the 5th but late in the day turned to snow, which it kept up and being very cold in the bargain, we had only one drill.

The 10th we had nothing but drills, dress parade and very cold weather, but on that day matters began to look serious. An order was issued that we were to be ready to move an hour after sunrise, with four days' rations of tack, meat and coffee and also 60 rounds of leadon pills. While engaged in cooking my breakfast at half past four o'clock in the morning of

Indulging in Luxuries, An army shave

the 11th two signal guns were fired by one of our batteries, and in a short time after two more. This opened the ball and the firing became lively. It was nearly all artilery, which continued at intervals all day.

While this was going on the 15th N.Y. Engineers were trying to build a pontoon bridge across the river. But the fire was so hot from sharpshooters stationed in the houses along the river bank that it had to be abandoned. Volunteers were called for to cross the river in boats and drive the rebels out. This was done, and while the boats were being rowed over, our artilery opened on the houses with shells and soon set fire to several of them, which drove the rebels out. When the boats reached the shore the men jumped out, and after a little skirmish the rebels were cleaned out, and the bridge laid. Our troops occupied the city that night.

Before we left camp that morning, the members of the new company were distributed amongst the rest of the companys in the Regt. and put through a drill in loading and firing. When they had been instructed in this most important part of their military education, we left camp about six o'clock and marching about a mile halted for the night. As my feet were on the ground and no shoes to be had, I did not relish this short march as it was very cold, besides having a slight sprinkling of snow on the ground. During the afternoon the quarter master came along with a supply of clothing, and I drew a pair of shoes and felt quite comfortable.

The morning of the 12th we started at seven o'clock and after marching about a half mile we halted. The firing commenced again and lasted about an hour when it ceased. It started again about 2 o'clock in the afternoon but did not last long. About 3 o'clock we moved to the rear and halted in the woods. Having been ordered to the left grand division under Franklin, we took up our line of march again, and after a tramp of about four miles we bivouacked for the night. The roads were in a horrible condition, being nothing but a mass of mud that was over our shoe tops and as the night was dark we floundered through it not knowing where we were going.

Sometimes we would run up against a stump, or stumbling into a ditch would find ourselves up to our knees in water. That night we slept in the woods without tents. In the morning (13th) we moved about a quarter of a mile nearer the river and halted in a wood to draw rations and await our turn to cross the river.

At this time our troops were advancing from Fredericksburg to storm St. Marys [Marye's] Heights that was in plain sight of our position. So I went over to one of our batteries that were hard at work to look at them. The guns of our heavy artilery were planted on the edge of the hill all along our front and were pegging away at the rebel batterys on the heights over the river, to cover our men, who were charging up the hills to drive the rebel infantry away from a stone wall that was about half way up, and used by them as a breastwork. In front of where I stood, rebel infantry occupied one hollow and our men another, and they fired away at each other as fast as they could load and fire. While another brigade was advancing to support them, one of the shells that was intended for the rebels fell short and, as I could follow it with the eye from the time it left the gun until it burst, I saw it explode right in the rear of of our men but w[h]ether it killed anyone or not we could not see, but rather think it did. On the right of these troops and directly in rear of the city, 3 lines of our troops charged up to the stone wall on the double quick, with the shot and shell flying round them like hail stones. It was of no use. They would get close to the stone wall, when they received such a volley of small arms in their faces that they had to fall back, leaving half of their number dead and wounded on the field. On the left of the line our artilery fired by battery and drove them back about half a mile into the woods.

About 3 o'clock in the afternoon we started for the front and crossing the river on a pontoon bridge we took up our possition. The river was crossed by 3 bridges. One for infantry. One for cavalry and artilery and one for waggons. When marching over these bridges we had to break step, or else break the bridge. The 1st and 2nd brigades took the advance lines, while the 3rd held the reserve in the rear. We had not been there long when the rebels opened on us with artilery, and one of the shells went screaming over the Col's. head. As this was too close for him, he ordered us to fall back about 10 feet and take our position in a road that had been the rebels' first line of battle, but [they] had been driven out by our artilery. Here we were sheltered from the stray shots, as a bank had been thrown up on each side of the road forming a regular breastwork. The skirmishing was kept up pretty much all night. The 21st N.J. being on our right on the other side of the road several of us went over to see them, but as their col. had his men laying down, and ordered us to do the same or leave, we left. A few bullets were dropping amongst them but they were thrown there by some of our men for a joke.

On the morning of the 14th skirmishing commenced about 4 o'clock and continued til 4 in the afternoon, at which time it was stopped by mutual consent. Under a flag of truce the wounded were collected and the dead burried. Before the truce was ordered, one of our Jersey batterys that was planted in the open field did a little good practice. One of the officers saw a group of mounted rebel officers under some trees, and judging from the number of horses that they were of some consequence, ordered his gunners to fire into them. Taking careful aim he fired, and with such good effect that a scattering took place, leaving some of their number dead behind them. As it was afterwards learned one of their generals was killed and others wounded. In the skirmishing the 1st Brigade lost about 100 men, the 2nd a good many more, while the 3rd had only one man killed and none wounded (except myself, who had a bloody nose while on the march. When the boys saw it they sang out "There's one man wounded, see the blood?")

The 15th our brigade was sent out to the front line to relieve the 1st who had been there for two nights and a day. Taking our position, a com-

Pantoon Bridge

The river was crossed by 3 bridges. One for infantry. One for cavalry and artilery and one for waggons

pany was sent out as skirmishers to relieve a company of the 1st who were then on duty. No firing took place, and one of our officers and one of the rebs met half way and had a friendly chat. While we lay here, the boys amused themselves by playing cards, while one of the recruits who was a good singer gave us some songs.

Towards dark our company was sent out on picket, and on arriving at our posts witch [which] was about 30 yards from the rebs, I was surprised to see them walking about without arms in their hands. We received orders to lay ours down also, and were not to fire at them unles they advanced. So throwing my knapsack on the ground I placed my rifle on top of it and had leasure to look around. On our left was a pile of dead men that had been collected previous to burrial. The wounded were being conveyed to the Lacy house, that was in our rear near the river and was used for a hospital (it was afterwards burnt down). In our front was the rebel pickets, with our officers and theirs talking together, while on the hill back of them and a little to our right was an ugly looking brass battery that we had not seen before, all ready to lay us out on the morrow. All that night we could hear the rebels singing and laughing, while chopping was going on in the woods, showing that they were making their defences as strong as possible.

About 11 o'clock that night we got orders to put on our knapsacks and to keep very still, which we did until about 2 o'clock in the morning of the 16th when Major Ramsey of our Regt. came along and ordered us to fall back. We did so, marching off in a stooping posture, getting down as low as

signalling

The signal officer's flag could be seen waving

possible, so as not to be seen by the rebels. As a large black cloud hung over us at the time it helped us a great deal. When we had got to a safe distance from the line we straightened up and continued our march in good order. Upon reaching the river, we found a brigade drawn up in line of battle to cover our retreat. (The rest of the army being already across the river.) Forming the company, we marched over the bridge and rejoined our Regt. which then marched about a half mile from the river and halted for the night. After we had got comfortably laid down for a few hours sleep, it commenced to rain, and when I woke up in the morning I found myself laying in a puddle of water.

The morning found our entire army across the river, having been favored by black clouds that prevented the rebels from seeing what was going on. So that when they were ready to give us a dose in the morning they found nothing but open fields in front of them, with our army safe and sound on our side of the river and the bridges taken down. When I got up, the rebel cavalry were scouting over the ground we had left. After resting nearly all day we returned to camp that night.

While the city was being bombarded, one of the houses fell in burrying some of the rebels with it. As soon as the city was taken, our boys went through it taking all the tobacco they could find and selling it to those who were not fortunate enough to get there. One of them comming to our Regt. with a bag full, met with bad luck as the boys took the bag away from him, and divided the spoils amongst the company. While on the march I had received a letter from home with two plugs in it, so that I was fixed. Some of the boys also went into the houses, and thinking perhaps of the men who were killed while attempting to build the pontoon bridge, threw the furniture out of the windows and anything else they could lay their hands on. During the battle one of the church steeples was made use of as a signal station, and the signal officer's flag could be seen waving from one of the windows all through the engagement. The rebel signal flag could also be

Fredericksburg

Captain Gould of Co. E had two
of his men tied up by their thumbs

seen flying at one of their forts as they signalled from one part of the field to another.

A little excitement was caused in the camp on the 19th by the actions of one of our captains. For some cause or other Captain Gould of Co. E had two of his men tied up by their thumbs to trees, so that their toes would just touch the ground. As the captain was noted as a tyrant, and not liked by any of the Regt. some of the boys untied them. This brought out the noble

187

capt. who cut one of the boys over the head with his sword. He had no sooner done so, when the rest of the Regt. turned out and there was every appearance of a riot. The guard was turned out and ordered to quell the disturbance, but just then Col. Sewell arrived on the scene and demanded the reasons for the row. When he was told, he ordered the men to their quarters, and as we knew that he would do what was proper in the case besides having a great regard for him as a man, we retired. One man however of Co. "B" was not inclined to go until he had satisfaction out of the Capt. The Col. told him to go to his quarters and pushed him, upon which the man said that if he (the Col) did not have on the shoulder straps he would not do it. The Col. informed him that he would take his straps off and lick him. Before it went any further the man was hustled off by his comrades. Capt. Gould never tied up a man after that and shortly after resigned. It was such officers as that who received a stray ball occasionly on the field of battle.

During the winter it had been our custom when we wanted a change of grub to go over to our brigade slaughter house, that was over at head quarters, and buy from one of the butchers who belonged to our company, some tripe, head cheese, or brains, as the fancy took us. So on Saturday the 20th we went over to get some head cheese for supper and Sunday's breakfast. On getting back to camp we fell to and made a hearty meal. It was not long before one of the men said that he felt sick and started for the rear. He had not gone far before he commenced to cast up accounts. Another one soon went the same road. As none of us knew what to make of it, we began to laugh at them, but the laugh was soon turned the other way. Feeling a little squamish myself, I started for the rear and was soon as sick as any of them. Every man who had eaton any of the stuf was laid up, and what with the heaving up and the back door trot, we had a sorry time of it. Poor Crowell the butcher who was the inocent cause of all this sickness was sent for by the Col. of the 7th or 8th N.J. (I forget which) for some of his men were sick from the same cause. The Col. told him that he ought to be shot. He was placed under arrest and relieved from butchering at head quarters. It came out afterwards that some one who had a grudge against him had dosed the kettles in which he made his cheese so that the inocent suffered for the guilty.

On the 23rd orders were issued to make ourselves as comfortable as possible, as we were likely to stay for the winter. Accordingly we commenced the next day to raise our shelter tents into more of the dignity of a house. I had to leave the job shortly after to attend the funeral of Private Wm. Newell as pall bearer. This man had the consumption and was in the hospital before the battle of Fredericksburg, but had been sent to his company for duty by order of the doctor and went with us. While on the skirmish line the night that we retreated, he was coughing all night long and could hardly keep up with us when we fell back. Upon our return he was at once sent back to the hospital and remained there until his death seven days later. Old Pill Garlic as we called our surgeon did not seem to have much judgment as my own case showed later on.

On Christmas eve we were regaled with a ration of whiskey and dried apples, and on Christmas day we took possession of our new hotel and passed a very comfortable night in it. Up to this time we had nothing to keep out the wind, snow or rain, but the shelter tents, and had to lay on the ground. We built a wall of pine logs, about 4 feet high, with a log chimney on one side, and over the walls we had stretched and buttoned 4 shelter tents. This when closed for the night made us as snug as possible. Inside we had built 2 bunks of pine sticks and over this we spread spruce pine leaves. This made a bed almost equal to a straw tick, and when our blankets were spread over and under us we had a very nice and comfortable abode. We named it Hotel on the Hill, kept by Bellard, Larkins and Heatl[e]y. Owing to some defect in our chimney, it caught fire one night, and was not put out without some trouble. No lives lost however. When the men had got their tents to rights, we had to build one for the captain and were all day at it.

———◆———

Improbably enough, Burnside was not disheartened by his fiasco at Fredericksburg. Though it was now midwinter, he wanted to keep on the offensive. "I am not disposed to go into winter quarters," he wrote the authorities in Washington, and the Union war office promptly agreed: "It will not do to keep your large army inactive."

Since advance was impossible and retreat was ruled out, Burnside decided to move his army sideways up the Rappahannock, in the hope of making a crossing that would allow him to flank Lee's army at Fredericksburg and to cut its communications with Richmond. Though all Burnside's major subordinates thought the plan impracticable in view of the weather and doubted his ability to execute it whatever the weather, the general persisted. Day after day he sent out small detachments, to ascertain the best roads in the vicinity and to determine the position of Lee's cavalry. Finally, by mid-January 1863, all was in readiness, and on January 20 the Army of the Potomac began its celebrated "Mud March."

———◆———

On the 28th we had orders to move in the morning with one day's rations in haversacks and in light marching order. Being on water police, I had to turn out at 11 o'clock that night to bring water for the cooks to boil the rations with. The men were out early, and after getting breakfast, line was formed about 8 o'clock, consisting of the 5th and 6th N.J. and the 2nd N.Y. Leaving camp we marched about 3 miles to the railroad station where the commissary stores were kept and stacked arms to await further orders. After waiting for some time we were ordered back to camp.

Genl. Mott our old Lieut. Col. had been placed in command of our brigade. When we reached camp we had dress parade, and an order was read off, ordering Genl. Mott to detail the 3 most efficient regts. in his brigade for special duty, and to report to Genl. Averell commanding cavalry. The Regts. selected were the 5th and 6th N.J. and the 2nd N.Y. Volls. Next morning we left camp about 7 o'clock in light marching order (that is overcoats on your back and blankets slung over the shoulder) 3 days' rations in your haversacks, and the usual dose of leadon pills in cartridge box (40 ounce balls). Marching to Hartwood Church we came to halt to allow the column to form, consisting of a detail of picked men from every cavalry company in the Army of the Potomac, and a battery of flying artilery, every man being mounted, except the dough boys or infantry who had to foot it.

As we had to wait about two hours, I paid a visit to the church. Upon going inside, the first thing that caught my eye was a large charcoal drawing right over the pulpit, of a cavalry charge on the rebel infantry with artilery in the distance. It was well drawn and never done by an amateur. The walls wer[e] covered in places with other pictures and names. It was here that some of our cavalry were captured not long before and perhaps the artist with them.

The column having formed the cavalry took the lead up the Warrenton road, the artilery followed suit and the dough boys brought up the rear. Marching until near midnight, we bivouacked near the artilery, whom we had to support pretty well tired out, having marched some 20 miles. About 6 o'clock next morning we were up again, and after getting outside of our breakfast we started gradually breaking to the left towards the river, through woods and bye roads, up hill and down, passing through the village of Morrisville on the way. As we found no rebel cavalry, we took the back track and halted about 3 miles from Hartwood Church. The cavalry and artilery had left us to continue the scout on their own hook.

The Regt. had no sooner halted when a farmer steped up to the Col.

and requested him to send a safe guard to his house and another to a neighbor's to keep our soldiers from destroying his property. Accordingly

We had orders to move in the morning with one day's rations in haversacks and in light marching order

myself and one of my comrades were detailed from our company by the Col. to look after the farmer's interests and see that no prowler took any of his stray chicks. On the way to the house the old man told my comrade about his sons and daughters, and my bold comrade having an eye to the female portion of the secesh asked me if I would as leave stay at the first house with the old lady, while he went with the gent. I said certainly, as it made no diference to me w[h]ether I guarded an old woman's house or an old man's. So when we got to the first farm, I bade him good night and reported myself to the lady of the house informing her what I had come for.

I was well received and invited in, but instead of the old lady being the only occupant, I found the lady's four daughters and two sons, besides the old gent's daughter, whom my comrade was so anxious to meet. The old lady's husband had been arrested that day by our troops on suspicion of being a bushwhacker and taken to head quarters, hence the reason of no man in the house. After being introduced to the young ladies, I was asked to lay aside my gun and equipments and join them in supper. This I did, as I had no time to get my own in the camp, and was glad of the invitation. For a supper we had corn cake, bread, coffee, butter, meat and peaches. A very good one I should say for people in the line of army, who generally help themselves without being asked w[h]ether friend or foe. The only thing they were short of was coffee and salt. As I had a good stock I gave it to them, and it was thankfully received.

Supper being over, I was handed a lot of nuts to crack for pastime, while we talked about Secesh and the War. They seemed to have no idea of the number of people in the Northern states and were astonished when I told them about New York City and the number of people who were passing along Broadway. One of the young ladies had three brothers in the rebel army, one of whom was wounded on the retreat from Fair Oaks, and was now at home to recover. (My chum had the pleasure of his company instead of the girls'.)

As the back log in the fireplace had nearly burnt out, the old lady asked me if I would go out with the girls to the wood pile and bring one in. Of course I would. Why not. Before leaving the house I was warned by the old lady not to make the girls laugh. I said no of course, and off we started for the back log. On our way over the fields, the girls said they were taking me out to the rebel lines and would have me taken prisoner and all that, for a joke. I said all right, if I was taken prisoner they would have to go with me. Having found the wood pile, we got a log that suited, and having two smal saplings under it to carry it by, the oldest girl took hold in front, while I took the rear and started for the house. The girls got laughing about something, perhaps at having a Northern soldier to help them with the log, when the first thing I knew down went the log. Just then the old lady stepped into view saying, Didn't I tell you not to make them laugh. She of course knew them better than I did, but I could not see anything very wrong in having a laugh. As she was our escort to the house, very little was said, and the back log was duly planted in the fire place which was about 6 feet wide. After some light stuf had been put on we soon had a rousing fire. The lady having given me some leaf tobacco, and their [there] being no objections to my smoking, I lit my pipe to have a smoke before retiring. Just before bed time the old lady immagined that some one was out in the stable trying to steal the horse or cow, so picking up my rifle I went out to the barn with her but everything was quiet.

At ten o'clock I was shown a room that I was to occupy for the night and as the ladies wished to go to bed and had to go through that room to get there, I placed my arms and equipments within easy reach and retired. Some time afterwards the light was turned down, and I could just see a shadowy outline going up the step ladder that was at the foot of the bed. As this was the only bed in the house that I could see, I protested against occupying it, as I could sleep on the floor just as well, and perhaps better, as I was more used to it. It was no use. To bed I had to go, and a feather one at that. I found that same feeling in other cases amongst the poor white trash as they are called by their slave owning neighbors.

When I got up next morning I found that all hands were ahead of me and were ready for breakfast, but I could not stay as the Regt. was getting ready to march. So to make up for it they put some cake and meat in my haversack to help me along on the road, at the same time giving me an invitation to call and see them whenever I had a chance, w[h]ether during the war or after. After kissing the girls all round, I bade them good bye and that was the last I saw of them, although we passed through there once afterwards. When I left the house my comrade made his appearance and was very much down in the mouth about the swop he had made, more especially when he saw me kissing the young lady, whom he supposed he would have for company.

Getting back to the Regt. we started about 8 o'clock, passed by Hartwood Church and marching through woods and fields, struck the rear of our camp about one o'clock on New Year's day 1863, pretty well played out after a three days' march of between 50 and 60 miles, after Stuart's Cavalry. In the way of spoils, we had captured some 3 or 4 rebels, one sutler's waggon and a lot of chickens from the farmers on the road. Upon reaching camp we were given a New Year's treat of two loaves of fresh bread and a ration of whiskey and quinine.

The Col. inspected the Regt. on the 4th after which I paid a visit to the 21st N.J. and Hexamer's Battery to see the boys from Hudson City, who were all in good health and spirits. On the 5th our division was reviewed by Genls. Burnside, Stoneman, and Sickles. As the weather was very cold it was not at all pleasant to stand under arms for some 3 or 4 hours, waiting for the commanding officer to make his appearance. We were reviewed and inspected again on the 9th, this time by Genl. Mott our Brigade Commander.

The 2nd Dragoons passed our camp at this time, Col. Starr with his company of volunteers from our Regt. being with them. The boys were well pleased at being mounted, but for myself I prefer shank's mare. I remember my first attempt to ride a cavalry horse. One of the 2nd [Dragoons] came to our camp one day, and leaving his horse standing by my tent, I thought I would have a ride. So I mounted the horse and got hold of the bridel telling him to git up, and git up he did with a vengeance. Raising up on his hind leggs he let me slide down his back very easily. Mounting him again, I let him go his own gait and he took me straight towards the officers' stables. As I could not stop him, he went straight through the opening that was left in the brush wood, just high enough to clear a horse's back, and so instead of sliding down to the ground as in the first instance, I was sweft off his back by the brush wood, and landed sprawling on the ground. I took no more interest in horse flesh after that.

On the 15th we had a brigade inspection by Genl. Stoneman commanding division, and a grand guard mount at head quarters. As all these inspections and reviews were the forerunner of some move, we were not surprised when at dress parade on the 18th, the orders were read off that we were to be ready to move at one o'clock. The order was afterwards changed to 24 hours.

On the morning of the 20th our Regt. was formed in line as for dress parade, and the adjutant taking his place in the front and centre read the following order from Genl. Burnside: That the Army of the Potomac was about to meet the enemy once more. That the enemy was weakened. And by the help of providence we would be able to strike a death blow to the Rebellion (but providence didn't help worth a cent). Accordingly at 10 o'clock we left camp in heavy marching order and going some 2 miles we halted for further orders. After dark it commenced to rain and we were ordered back to camp.

Horses, waggons, pontoons and guns were spread
round in all directions, stuck so fast in the mud

*All the fence rails we could lay hands on were confiscated and
planted in the mud*

We were up again by daylight next morning with our house and furniture on our backs ready for a march through mud and rain. Leaving camp
at 7 a.m. we commenced our march through mud that was so deep that my
coat-tails dragged in it as we went along. Horses, waggons, pontoons and
guns were spread round in all directions, stuck so fast in the mud that roads
had to be built to get them out. Halting in a pine wood we rested until
morning, still raining and wet through.

It having stopped raining in the afternoon our brigade was sent out
about 2 miles from our bivouac to build roads, so that the guns, waggons

etc. could be got back to camp. Trees were cut down and laid in the mud. All the fence rails we could lay hands on were confiscated and planted in the mud, and over all was laid brush wood. This made a pretty good foundation and answered the purpose. One gun and caison that I saw close by us had ten horses attached and it took all their strength to move it. The horses were in mud up to their bellies and the wheels of the gun up to the hub. About dark we started back to camp, but loosing our way in the attempt, we had considerable floundering through the mud before we found it.

The brigade was sent out again the next morning on the same duty, but as I was lame, [I] remained in camp. They returned about 10 o'clock, when we struck tents and returned to camp, reaching there about dark, and so ended the stick in the mud march (so called by the men).

A great many men from the diferent regts. took advantage of this mud march to desert or attempt to do so, for they were nearly all brought back by the cavalry scouts, who caught them making their way to the Potomac river. The woods were full of them. The mud I suppose sickened them. Hundreds of horses and mules were also lost. It was reported by some of the men who had got as far as the Rappahannock River that the rebs had the head of a flour barrell nailed to a post on their side of the river upon which they had painted "Burnside stuck in the mud." Some 3 or 4 of our company, who undertook to take french leave on this march, were brought back and slapped in the guard house as deserters, but were not brought to trial.

On the 25th we left camp for outside picket duty. Starting in the morning we waded through the mud and water until about noon when we reached the picket line. The pickets being posted, our company was placed in the woods as reserve. It had rained just enough in the morning to make it very disagreable traveling, but cleared up in the afternoon and remained clear until the 27th when it commenced again and continued all night, wetting us through to the skin, having no tents to shelter us. Before daylight of the 28th it began to snow and came down in a good old fashioned style. The

18th Mass. having come out to relieve us, the outside pickets were called in and we started for camp. This was anything but a pleasant trip, as the snow blew in our faces, while the mud was simply horrible, being more like a mixture of glue and paste than water and soil. We finally reached camp tired out and wet through. The snow ceased the next morning, and the weather getting warmer it soon made the foot of snow that fell a mass of slush.

From this time until the 5th of February, we had nothing to do but build a log house for the use of the camp guard, and the usual dose of camp guard, fatigue duty and so on.

So ended the stick in the mud march

XIV

Chancellorsville

O N JANUARY 25, 1863, *President Lincoln named Joseph Hooker to succeed Burnside as commander of the Army of the Potomac. Resisting pressure from Washington to undertake an immediate advance, Hooker attempted first to improve the organization of his army and to boost his soldiers' morale. He did away with Burnside's "Grand Divisions," which had proved cumbersome and ineffectual at Fredericksburg, and reverted to the earlier system of army corps, whose commanders reported directly to him. Sickles continued in command of III Corps, to which Bellard's regiment belonged. Hooker also consolidated the previously scattered Union cavalry units into a single corps under General George Stoneman.*

Finding the soldiers "disheartened and almost sulky" when he took command, Hooker took pains to improve their health and spirits. He ordered that they receive "a diet which in quantity, quality and variety are captivating, appetizing and nutritious." He saw that they were paid regularly. Over the opposition of Washington officials, he introduced a regular system of furloughs. To strengthen morale he devised a set of brightly colored shoulder patches to identify members of the different corps. Stress-

ing cleanliness in the camp, Hooker through repeated inspections and drills compelled the men to keep their uniforms and weapons in prime condition.

During February and March both Union and Confederate cavalrymen became increasingly active. Both forces explored the fords for crossing the Rappahannock above Fredericksburg, and each sought to get in the rear of the opposing army so as to garner information and to cut lines of communication. During this period Bellard's regiment was sent to Kelly's Ford and to Hartwood Church in support of Union cavalry operations.

By the end of April Hooker felt ready to start a general offensive. Having overwhelming numerical superiority, he planned to catch Lee's army between the jaws of a giant pincer. General John Sedgwick's VI Corps was to hold Lee's army in place by recrossing the Rappahannock below Fredericksburg, while Hooker would lead his main force up the river and, crossing at easy fords, would attack Lee from the rear. The initial stages of Hooker's plan worked beautifully. By April 29 he had a large force safely south of the Rappahannock, and Sickles's III Corps came up the next day to guard the fords behind them. About this time, however, Hooker lost his nerve and ordered his troops south of the river to pull back to defensive positions before Chancellorsville, a "town" consisting of one farmhouse at a crossroads.

When Hooker paused, Lee took the offensive. Bringing up reinforcements, he decided to take a gamble in the face of still greatly superior Union force by dividing his army. On May 2, having moved 28,000 men across the Union front by a concealed route, "Stonewall" Jackson launched a devastating surprise attack upon the exposed Union right flank and sent General Oliver Otis Howard's XI Corps reeling in demoralized retreat back to the fords of the Rappahannock.

At this point, Bellard's regiment was rushed to the front in order to support General Henry W. Slocum's XII Corps, which was now under attack from the main body of Lee's army. The New Jersey men arrived just in time, for early the next morning they were needed to replace the 114th Pennsylvania Infantry, a Zouave regiment that broke and ran under Confederate attack.

————◆————

On the 5th we left camp at 7 o'clock in the morning with 3 days rations in our haversacks for a reconoisance in force. Marching past Hartwood Church we went into bivouac in the snow. Next morning we were off again at 8 and reaching the Rappahannock river, crossed over at Kelly's ford and halted about 2 miles beyond. At 11 o'clock after a short rest we moved again and went about 9 miles further, when we were ordered to turn back. Recrossing the river we marched to Hartwood Church and halted for the night. In the morning we left early and passing the church took the road to camp, which we reached in the afternoon.

As my foot was quite lame, I reported to the doctor, and asked for some linemint to rub it with. On the 1st day he gave me a dose of castor oil to be taken on the spot, and a box of pills that were to be taken during the days, but no linemint. I took my physic and was relieved from duty for the day. The pills of course opperated and made me sick in ernest. Going to him next morning, he said that medicine was no good for me and gave me some linement to rub my foot with, at the same time reporting me fit for duty. The officers knew that I was not fit for duty, so did the best they could under the circumstances. As we were fixing up the officers' quarters by bunking dirt around them to keep out the cold, I was detailed to fill up the boxes with dirt, while the other men carried them and banked it up around the tent. I could rest myself and at the same time was doing duty without hurting my foot. The officers on the 2nd day's march saw that I was lame and had informed the adjutant of the fact, so that when I got to the bivouac that night, I was some distance behind the Regt. not being able to keep up on account of my foot. I reported to the adjutant, as all stragglers had to do, but instead of being put on extra duty, as is the rule in such cases, I was told it was all right, and to go to my company.

As fresh bread was rather scarce, we had commenced to build a bakery for the brigade close to our camp so as to bake it ourselves, having plenty of bakers in our ranks. As we were to be inspected by the Col. of the 2nd N.Y. Volls. on the 14th, we spent the day before in cleaning up, so that we would make as good an appearance as possible. And to such good purpose did we clean that our company was complimented by the Col. for their clean equipments and neat appearence generally. The 15th I paid a visit to the 21st N.J. and Hexamer's Battery to see the Hudson City boys. The roads were in a very bad state, for when we happened to step off the corduroy road, we went into the mud over our shoe tops.

From this time until March 3rd our time was occupied with company and battalion drills, dress parades, and building corduroy roads. I was generally armed with an ax, being rather proficient in the use of it. As our bakery was now finished, we soon had fresh bread 3 or 4 times a week. Feb. 22nd Washington's Birthday, the artilery fired a salute in honor of the day.

March 3rd as our turn for picket had arrived again, we left camp and marched some six miles in a snow storm, and halted at the same spot where we got stuck in the mud. Our Regt. being on the reserve, we lay quiet having nothing to do, but enjoy ourselves as best we could. Next morning we were sent out on outpost picket and found ourselves on the same ground that Stewart [J. E. B. Stuart] held during his last raid in our rear. I and two others were stationed at a cross road, and about a hundred yards in advance of us stood a cavalry vedette mounted. During the night we captured two citizens and soldier who were taking a waggon through the lines in which they had a boat. As they could not give a good account of themselves as to what they were doing there at that time of night we arrested them, sending

Our orders in regard to challenging
mounted men were very strict

the prisoners to head quarters under guard, while the waggon and boat was sent to our lines.

Our orders in regard to challenging mounted men were very strict, they being obliged to dismount before giving the countersign. Some time during the night one of our officers (who I believe was the field officer of the day) came along and was ordered to halt, who comes there. Upon answering who he was, he was ordered to dismount, advance, and give the countersign. It being very muddy at the time, he did not relish the idea, but orders are orders, and he had to get off from his horse, and walk up to the picket on foot before he would take the countersign. The countersign being correct, he was allowed to go about his bussines.

The next morning we were relieved from outpost duty and joined the reserve, and staid there until relieved by another brigade, when we took up our line of march for camp, making the six miles in 2 hours and 5 minutes. I was detailed with a squad on the 9th to build roads about 6½ miles from camp, while another squad went to Stoneman's Switch on the railroad to unload cars.

At dress parade that night an order was read off from the division headquarters, that as the 5th and 6th N.J. and the 1st Mass. Regts. made the best appearence on inspection, their furloughs should be lengthened to 15 days and that 3 men should go out of each hundred. This was a very fine thing but did not do me any good, as of the first two men who went from our company, one overstaid his time, while the other did not go back until taken back under guard. This upset all my calculations, and I got no furlough.

Rebel Pipe Bowl.

I sent home by one of the men a pipe bowl made out of laurel root

I sent home by one of the men a pipe bowl made out of laurel root upon which was carved a heart and hand, meaning I suppose that he was heart and hand in the service of his country. It was made by a rebel soldier and was picked up at Yorktown by one of our men. Another pipe found there had the owner's name, co. and regt. carved on it, and it was very well done.

Quite an unusual event took place in camp on the 12th being the marriage of an officer of the 7th N.J. From the road to the camp an arch had been built out of the branches of pine trees. This answered for the triumphal arch. The bands played all day, and at night we had a display of fireworks. This was an unlooked for event and created quite a stir about camp.

On the 17th two men were drummed out of the 2nd N.Y. and the next day the Jersey boys had a little variation of the same kind. The brigade marched out to a large field some distance from our camp, and having formed 3 sides of a square, we thought that some poor fellow was about to be shot for desertion, but instead of that it was one of the 8th N.J. who was to be drummed out of camp. After resting on our arms for some time, the command "Attention" was given, and a guard who had passed by our rear was marched past us going to the centre of the square where the general and his staff had taken position. The culprit had the cape of his overcoat over his head when he first passed us, so that we saw nothing peculiar about him. When the squad arrived opposite the Genl. the prisoner was ordered to uncover his head, and there he was, with his head as bald as a razor could make it, and not a button on his coat. The march past the brigade was made in the following order. First came the drummers playing the Rouges [Rogues'] March then two men with arms at a reverse, next the prisoner who was followed by two more men with arms at a secure, so that he could go neither backwards nor forwards without coming in contact with a bayonette. He was as brazen as you please and held his head up as if he enjoyed it. When he had passed in review, he was taken to the rail-road station and set adrift to shift for himself.

On the 26th we had more variation from the usual routine of camp life. A horse race between a woman and young girl which took place about a mile from camp and was largely attended by the shoulder straps.

Picket duty having come along again, we left camp on the 30th in light marching order, and went some 8 miles from camp in a snow storm, halting near the Rappahannock river. I and two more men were posted near the river and had a good view of the Johnys on the other side. Some of them were sitting round the picket fire while others were strolling along the bank, but no firing took place. One of the rebels saluted Sergt. Austin who was on post with us by raising his hat, and the compliment was returned. In the afternoon some of our officers came down to the river to take a look at the butternuts when one of them turned up his posterior to the shoulder strap and slapped it 3 times. I do not think they relished the situation, as they went off vowing vengeance on the rebels, whenever they caught them. At this part of the river a dam had been built across, to turn the water into a creek that supplied some of the mills near the city with water power. Dame rumor had it that the rebels were advancing, but all was quiet on the Rappahannock. Berdan's sharpshooters relieved us on the 2nd of April, and we returned to camp.

On the 4th we were detailed for grand guard at head quarters, but as it snowed all night with a strong wind in the bargain, we did not have a very pleasant time of it. Prest. Lincoln, Genls. Hooker and Stoneman with their respective staffs reviewed the cavalry and flying artilery. It was a splendid sight to see the cavalry march past in company front at a trot with sabres drawn and equipments jingling. After them came the artilery, and flying was a good name for them as they went past on the gallop. The next day our turn came. After inspection in the morning, we stacked arms and waited for the reviewing officers, who at length made their appearance, and reviewed us after being under arms from 8 in the morning until 4 in the afternoon. The next day we had another review this time with the 11th corps. It was a splendid sight. The regts. marched past the President in column of division (2 companys front). The front was well kept with one exception. When we were passing the reviewing officer, one of the staff

Some of them were sitting round the picket fire

officers' horses commenced to prance around and backing into our division, who had the lead, broke us up. As soon as the regt. passed the Prest. it took the double time, so as to get out of the way of the troops in the rear, and returned to camp.

As all these reviews meant something, we expected a move in a short

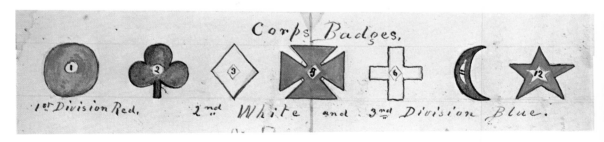

Each corps should wear a badge to distinguish one corps from another

time. Genl. Hooker, being now in command of the army, issued an order that each corps should wear a badge to distinguish one corps from another. The 1st Division to be red, the 2nd white and the 3rd blue. The 9th had a shield with an anchor and cannon crossed to represent the army and navy.

On the 10th we marched about half a mile from camp and forming lines we gave the President 3 cheers as he passed us on his way back to Washington. On the 13th the cavalry left camp to invade the enemy's country and destroy their communications, and on the 14th we were ordered to turn in everything, but one shirt, one pair of socks in knapsacks and blanket, and

On the morning of the first of May we took up our baggage and started again

Before the Battle, 8 Days Rations.

that we were to move soon with 8 days' rations in our haversacks and knapsacks. Paying a visit to the 21st N.J. I found that they had the same orders, but as their time was nearly out, they were very much down in the mouth about it. The 15th it rained heavy, making the roads soft so that they would not hurt our feet, but making marching a burden.

On the 17th a detail was sent to Stoneman's Switch to load our surplus stores on cars ready for removal. As our expected move did not take place, base ball matches were played to keep up a little excitement. The 20th 9 officers of the 5th played 9 from the rest of the brigade, and the 5th got left. The next day the 2nd N.Y. tried their hand with the brigade and got left also. On the 26th we were reviewed by Gov. Parker of N.J. and the same day got our extra blankets back as we were not ready to move yet. On the 27th we were reviewed by Genl. Hooker in the morning and in the afternoon went on picket, our Regt. being on the reserve.

The 2nd corps passed us on the 28th on their way to the front, and at 3 o'clock in the afternoon we returned to camp and packed up. Having a presentment or something of the kind that I would be shot, I provided myself with lint and bandages, so that I might be able to help myself in case of need, but although wounded, had no occasion to use them. The next morning we left camp with our house and furniture on our backs, along with 8 days' rations of grub, and 60 rounds of leaden pills. Taking the road to the left of our line, we halted opposite the place that we had crossed on the previous fight, and lay there waiting for further orders. To prevent the rebels from seeing us, no fires were allowed, so that we eat our pork raw and having no coffee to wash it down.

It was reported that Kearny's Division of our corps was already across the river. The 20th N.Y. believing that their time of service had expired, refused to go to the front and were placed under arrest, and when I saw them, were guarded by the 21st N.J. (They afterwards altered their minds and went into the battle.) As our move to the left was only a feint to mask our real advance in another direction, we were ordered to move about 10 o'clock on the 30th, and passing through our old camp we halted about midnight on the right of our army.

On the morning of the first of May we took up our baggage and started again. On the road we passed 3 batches of prisoners who had been captured and were on their way to the rear. Crossing over the Rappahannock at the U.S. ford on a pontoon bridge, we passed through the rebel works that lined the banks and halted for a short time to rest and receive further orders. We were soon ordered back again and went on picket. The mule train that was used in lieu of the regular waggon train to carry our provisions passed us on their way to the front. In the afternoon we were called in from picket and crossing the river for the second time (this time at Kelly's ford) we took up our position in rear of a battery of artilery as a guard over the pontoon bridge. The 11th corps marched past us on their way to the front.

In the early part of the night word was passed round that if any man wished to write home, he had about ten minutes to do it in, as the mail carrier would be around about that time to take them. As this would probably be the last time that I would have a chance to write, as a big battle was expected, I threw myself flat on the gras and wrote a short letter home by the light of the moon, getting it finished just as the letter carrier came round.

About 3 o'clock in the afternoon of the 2nd May we went on picket about a mile up the river, near an old saw mill, and as I was hungry, [I] was preparing myself a good dinner of fried pork, when the orders came to fall in. The 11th corps had broke and run, and Hooker had called for his old division to check the rebel advance. Stowing my half cooked grub in my haversack, I joined the Regt. and we marched out to the road. Here we came acros the 11th corps, who were rushing from the front pell mell and so blocked up the road that we could not advance. Turning to our left, we crossed over some fields and soon came up to the rest of our brigade, the battle flag of our brigade showing their position.

Taking the Richmond plank road, we arrived at the front somewhere

*The mule train
that was used in
lieu of the regular
waggon train*

about nine o'clock just as the last volley was fired. Forming in column of
battalions we halted and stacked arms, after which we hunted for water. As
it was dark, we could not see what we were drinking, so got plenty of mud
with it, but it was better than none so we drank it down and getting out our
half cooked pork we got something to eat, after which we lay down by the
stacked muskets to get some sleep. But it was rather disturbed, for all night
long chopping was going on in our front.

*I threw my-
self flat on the
gras and
wrote a short
letter home by
the light of
the moon . . .*

212

*. . . getting it finished just as the letter carrier
came round*

In the morning we saw what the chopping was about, for all along our front was a low line of breastworks that were held by the 12th corps. The muss commenced at once, and the skirmishers had no sooner fallen back than the whole line was engaged. Before long a regt. of Red Legged Zouaves who were on the left of the first line broke, and running past our Regt. their officers called upon us to fire into them. We did not obey the order. The Red Leggs started the rest, and soon after all the troops on our left had fallen back thus leaving us in a bad position. The bullets were now flying round us like hail, and one of our men named Flick was struck in the shoulder by a minnie ball. This made him yel so with pain that the Capt. ordered some one to take him to the rear, which was done.

As the rebels were getting the best of the men in our front, our Col. gave the command to charge. We did not get very far before the rebels fell back and we halted. In front of us was a piece of woods in which the rebels were stationed and as it was low ground on their side we could not see them until they were close to us. At the edge of this wood was our first line of battle.

The rebels came out again shortly and commenced firing into us, when we were ordered to charge again. Running down the hill with a yel, we jumped the ditch that was in our way and halted in rear of the 12th corps, that lay behind the breastworks, just as the rebels fell back. When we halted, a piece of shell, that had exploded close to us struck the knapsack of Corpl. Deary [Deery] on the corner near his shoulder, with such force as to turn him round. Thinking that he was shot, he dug out for the rear, but soon came back, as he found that the missile had only bruised his skin and torn his blouse. The men of the 12th corps were laying huddled up behind the breastwork, looking to their own safety and taking no notice of their wounded. One of whom being shot in the head was a pitiful sight, he lay there moaning with his brains oozing out with every breath.

The rebels did not give us much time to think over these matters, for they soon came out again in our front while another line were marching in column of fours towards our left, with the intention of flanking us. We commenced firing at the line in our front and the 7th N.J. who were on our left started out to flank the flankers. As soon as the 7th had fairly started, Col. Sewell gave the order to charge and over the breast works we went, driving the rebels back in short order and capturing some seven stands of colors, besides a lot of prisoners. One of the colors was captured by the 7th N.J. after a knock down argument. The color bearer would not give up the standard until he was knocked down by the but of a musket and the flag wrested from his grasp. A rebel col. having been cut off from his men, was ordered to halt and surrender, but as he would do neither was shot from his horse. The woods were strewn with dead and wounded rebels with an odd one of our own. Having no support, we fell back to the works and found when we got there that the 12th corps had skipped out, leaving our brigade alone without any support but a battery of artilery that was posted on top of the mound in our rear.

The rebels soon made their appearence again, advancing in a solid body of about twelve deep and not a musket to be seen. One of our officers (Lieut. Lawyer) told us not to fire as they were comming in to surrender. No notice was taken of such orders however, and we blazed away until they were close to us. All at once their guns came from behind their backs, and they let us have it in good earnest. This was too hot for us and we had to fall back under a heavy fire. The rebels came up to our works, and poured lead into us like hail, but came no further.

Soon after we left the works I received a wound in the legg that prevented me from keeping up with the Regt. and I had to paddle my own canoe. There being a ditch in front of me which I had to cross and not knowing wither [whether] I was badly wounded or not, I took it into my head to jump over and if my legg would stand that, to go on my way to the rear. But if not, I made up my mind to lay down in the ditch and take my chances of being captured (quite a number of men were laying in this ditch but wither [whether] wounded or not I did not know). Jumping over I found to my satisfaction that my leg would stand it and started after the regt. as near as I could guess, for they were nowhere to be seen. Shot and shell were ploughing up the ground in all directions, while the bullets whistled past my ears in dangerous proximity.

Throwing my gun away to lighten my load, I went over the field the

We commenced firing at the line in our front

I received a wound in the legg that prevented me from keeping up with the Regt. and I had to paddle my own canoe

The color bearer would not give up the standard until he was knocked down

217

best I could, and not looking to see where I was going, I was brought to my sences by a command to lay down, and looking up found myself in front of a battery of artilery that was firing into the rebels and in between two guns that were about to fire. Throwing myself flat on my face, the guns were discharged the shells passing over me, while I was enveloped in smoke from the powder.

No damage was done, and getting up again, I wended my way past the Chancellorsville House, Hooker's head quarters. Old Joe himself was leaning against one of the pillars when I passed. (This was burnt down during the battle, as was also the woods around it, in which some of our wounded perished.) Being now out of the line of fire, I was met by the ambulance corps, who wanted to carry me off the field on a strecher, but being able to walk, while so many badly wounded lay on the field, I declined the invitation and told them to pick up some of the boys, who could not help themselves. This I believe they did not do, as they were anxious to keep out of the way of the bullets themselves.

As I was now out of immediate danger, I unslung my knapsack and taking out what rations I wanted to carry me along on the road, I threw it away, along with my equipments and started for the river. I had not gone far, when I ran against the cavalry, who were drawn up in line acros the road to drive back the straglers. I was halted by the officer in command, who asked me where I was going. I told him, "To the rear wounded," but as there was no blood on the leg of my pants, I had to roll my pants up and show him the wound before he would let me pass.

Traveling along slowly, I crossed the river and reaching the field hospital by dark, I lay down and went to sleep. The next morning I got some bandages from the hospital steward and dressed the wound myself, for I was afraid from the looks of the wound, which had turned black, that the doctors would want to experiment on it and perhaps cut it off altogether.

While we lay here, the rebels sent a few shells into us killing some two or three men. We left as quick as we could, but as it soon ceased, we went back again, and received some crackers and a bowl of soup, from a lady, who was connected with the sanitary commission. My leg had now got so stiff, that when I got up after laying down a short time it was like getting up on a wooden leg, no bend in it.

In the afternoon I went over to the corps field hospital, where the doctors were busy in probing for balls, binding up wounds, and in cutting off arms and legs, a pile of which lay under the table. One drummer boy was brought in to be operated upon, who had both hands shattered by the explosion of a gun barrell. He had picked up a gun barrel on the field, and was holding it in the fire to have a little fun, when it exploded. His hands were shattered all to pieces, saving nothing but a thumb on one hand, and a thumb and finger on the other. When the doctors had him on the table and under the influence of cloraform, they picked out the pieces of bone with their fingers. One of the men died at this hospital who had been shot through the breast and was held by a vivandiere of one of the regts. in her lap, until he was dead.

On the 5th the ambulance train began to carry away the badly wounded, all the men who could help themselves having to stay behind. When the last ambulance had gone, myself and another member of the Regt. who was hit in the leg the same as myself took up our quarters on the door steps of a house, with the raining pouring down and wet to the skin. About 12 o'clock at night we were awakened by the doctors who had returned with the ambulances and were told that we would be taken away. As we could hobble along, we started to go ourselves, but two of the doctors got hold of each of us and carrying us to the ambulance put us in. We were now out of the rain and felt quite comfortable, although wet through. My friend, who always had the cleanest rifle in the Regt. had brought it off the field with him intending to carry it along. He was ordered to throw it away by the doctors, and much against his will, it was left behind. In the ambulance with

I declined the invitation and told them to pick up some of the boys, who could not help themselves

One of the men died at this hospital who had been shot through the breast and was held by a vivandiere of one of the Regts. in her lap, until he was dead

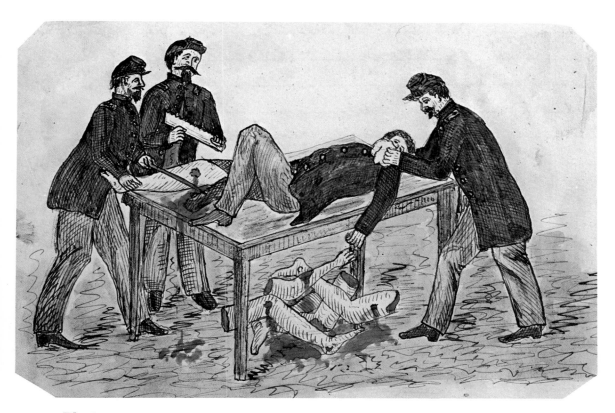

The doctors were busy in probing for balls, binding up wounds, and in cutting off arms and legs, a pile of which lay under the table

us was a badly wounded man, who lay on a bed, and every jolt of the ambulance over the corduroy road would make him cry out with pain. As we had an all night ride over corduroy roads and stumps of trees, it was not very pleasant even for me.

The Army Telegraph line for head-quarters

XV

———◆———

Hospitals

BELLARD'S WOUND PREVENTED *him from witnessing the outcome of the battle of Chancellorsville. Hopelessly confused by the way the fighting developed and more befuddled than usual from the concussion of a shell that landed near him, Hooker pulled his troops back from Chancellorsville to a strong defensive position and then, on May 6, withdrew his army north of the Rappahannock. Meanwhile Lee also drove Sedgwick's troops back across the river near Fredericksburg.*

For the Fifth New Jersey Infantry the Chancellorsville battle proved costly. Bellard's reckoning of casualties is slightly inaccurate; the regiment actually suffered 121 casualties — 13 officers and men killed, 102 wounded, and 6 missing in action.

Hospitalized during the summer of 1863, Bellard took no part in the Gettysburg campaign. Nor was he able to participate in putting down the draft riots in New York (July 13–16), which broke out in protest against the new Union policy of conscription.

By fall, however, he was well enough to serve in the Invalid Corps, which had been established in April 1863 to permit officers and men unfit for full combat duty to perform limited infantry service. The first battalion of the Invalid Corps consisted of those who could handle a weapon. The second battalion received the worst crippled, who were used as nurses and cooks around hospitals. By December 1863 the corps numbered 20,000 men.

We arrived at Potomac Creek Hospital at noon on the 6th, wet through and hungry, but after getting something to eat I felt better. In the tent were men with their legs off, some with arms off, and men with all kinds of wounds. The most cheerful one of the lot was a man with his hand cut off at the wrist. As it had commenced to superate [suppurate], of course it did not smel very sweet, and every little while he would poke it under some one's nose, and tel[l] him to smel of that.

On the 7th our brigade got back to camp, bringing in with them seven stand of colors captured from the rebels in the last engagement. The 5th Regt. taking the battle flag of the 19th N.C., the body of which was a brownish red, and the stripes blue, with the names of 8 battles painted on one side and 4 on the other. The loss to our Regt. was 105 wounded, 13 killed and 8 missing. Of the last named, the chances were that they were killed, making a total of 126 officers and men out of a Regt. that mustered previus to the battle 315 all told. My company was represented by wounded only, to wit. Corpl. Rapp severe in shin, Privates Austin, bruised by a piece of shell on the breast, Bellard, slight in knee, musket ball, Dugan, severe in groin, piece of shell, Flick, severe in shoulder, musket ball, Heslin [Heslen], severe in leg, musket ball, Heatl[e]y, slight in finger, musket ball, Reilly [Riely], slight in leg, musket ball, Robinson, severe in knee, musket ball, Sweitzer [Switzer], slight in thigh, musket ball, and VanBuskirk, slight in arm musket ball with Fenton, missing.

On the 8th a lot of wounded were sent off to Washington. Col. Sewell

Hospital tents

and Capt. Woolsey came to the hospital to see how we were getting along. The Capt. came again the next day along with the orderly and gave us some tobacco, etc.

On the next bed to me lay a man who was badly wounded in the side, having a hole in his body that you could almost run your hand in, besides being shot in the thumb. The doctor amputated the thumb on[e] day, by nipping it off with an instrument that looked like a pair of pincers. The chaplain of his regt. in passing through the tent told him that his wound would be something to show his grandchildren when he got home. The poor fellow never got there, however, for I was awakened one morning with the attendents carrying him out, as he had died during the night.

It was reported on the 12th that Richmond was taken, but as dame rumor was always prolific with reports, no particular notice was taken of it. The wounded were still coming in from the late battle fields, some of them having lain where they fell for 11 days, without medical aid and very little to eat. Amongst them was Lieut. Lawyer, who had been shot through the lungs, by one of his own regt. at about the same time that I was. After laying on the field for 3 days, he was picked up by the rebel surgeons and cared for as well as their limited medicine chest would allow.

On the 18th the Capt. and Lieut. came to the hospital to see the boys, and the Capt. wanted to know very badly how soon I would get back to the Regt. but as my leg was so stif at the time that I could not bend it, I could give him no satisfaction. Genl. Hooker also passed through the tents looking after the welfare of his wounded. The Genl. asked us how we were getting along, and wanted to know if there was anything he could do for us. (Of course there was.) Some of the boys said they would like to go home to be cured, and he told them that the doctors would get us away as soon as they could. We also complained of being kept on short rations. This he attended to, and we had plenty while we staid there. Genl. Carr of our division also paid us a visit.

About the 23rd bunks were put up in our tents and we were more comfortable. Our names were also taken down for furloughs, which were filled out but never issued. Heavy firing was going on at Fredericksburg on the 5th of June between the artilery, and our infantry crossed the river. All the sick men who were not able to march from the diferent regts. were sent to the general hospital, as the army had orders to move at a moment's notice, with 5 days' ration in haversacks.

At this hospital, funerals were of every day occurence. One poor boy who was shot through the lungs died in his mother's arms, who had come to the hospital for the purpose of taking him home. Matters were made worse for her by the actions of one of the officers, who tried to commit an assault on her. He was at once arrested and placed under guard, and I hope got his dissert.

On the 19th the medical director of the army passed through our tent examining the wounded. On comming to mine and examining it for some time, he said, Young man, you have had a very narrow escape, as a quarter of an inch further to the right, you would have bled to death, and a quarter of an inch to the left, your leg would have had to come off. So as it was, I considered myself a lucky dog. The weather being hot, one of the nurses poured some kind of liquor on the wound, and running in at one hole, and out of the other, it made it smart, but I said nothing. An old man on the bunk opposite to me, and who was wounded in the fleshy part of the leg, yelled as if he was getting killed when it was poured on him, and because I did not kick up a rumpus, he would have it, that it was water and not liquor that was poured on mine.

These military hospitals were a fine field for young M.D.'s to practice in. While limping round amongst the tents with two sticks to keep me up, I came across the tent were operations were performed. Stretched on a table inside was a man under the influence of chloreform who had been shot in the knee, in about the same place as myself, only that the ball penetrated the bone. While I stood there, the doctors were running their fingers in the wound, probing and cutting trying to find the ball. After working in that way for some time with no success, they finally cut off the leg, and wound up the job.

A short distance from the hospital in a hollow was Potomac Creek, where the boys who were able went for a bath or to fish. This creek was spanned by a trestle railroad bridge that [had] been built by our men. It was rather clumsy in looks but was strong enough to carry heavy trains. The former bridge had been burnt.

On the 13th the 6th corps hospital, that was close to us moved, and we were ordered to pack up and be ready to leave. Before daylight on the 14th we left the hospital, and those who could walk went to the rail-road station. We had to wait there nearly an hour, when a train came along and we got into it. After a short ride we got out at Aquia Creek, where we found the river steamer Hero in waiting. After all the wounded had been put on board, she started for Alexandria. All the men who could help themselves went around the boat looking for a place to sit down and rest. But as the entire deck and saloon were covered with mattrases upon which lay the badly wound soldiers we had to be very careful to avoid stepping on any of them.

This creek was spanned by a trestle railroad bridge
that [had] been built by our men

On passing Shipping Point, that was opposite our old camp ground on the lower Potomac, we saw a large camp of troops, and between that and Aquia Creek long waggon trains were wending their way amongst the hills, throwing up clouds of dust. After a pleasant sail up the river we arrived at Alexandria, when all the men who were able to walk, were formed in squads and marched to the diferent hospitals round the city, I being sent to Washington Hall, cor. of King and Washington Streets.

The 15th was a great day for the colored people, as the 1st Regt. Va. Col. Volls. [Virginia Colored Volunteers] passed through the city. They marched through the principal streets and made a very good appearance. They had a band of four pieces and were officered by white men. They marched without colors. The sidewalks were lined with "cullud pussons" who were laughing, chatting and shaking hands with their military friends. The city was guarded by the Pa. Reserves.

Our quarters were very pleasant, having plenty of room, good beds and plenty to eat. We could also go round the city as much as we liked, providing we kept sober. Our furloughs from Potomac Creek had been forwarded to this place by the division doctor, who was also in the city trying to make some arrangements to send us off. All the men who were so far recovered from their wounds or sicknes as to be fit for active service were sent to the convelesent camp every day, from there to be returned to their regts. The 21st N.J. passed through the city on their way home and a happy lot they were, as they had been tired of soldiering long since.

At eight o'clock on the morning of the 17th we were put into ambulances and driven to the depot, where we boarded the train and crossing over the Long Bridge were soon in Washington. Here we changed cars for the Baltimore and Ohio railroad, and starting again, we finally reached Balti-points of interest. I was one of the detail, but being a bashful young man, were off again, and went along at a ratling speed, until we reached Havre de Grace, where we crossed over on a ferry boat. We passed the 7th N.Y. militia here, who had enlisted for thirty days to repel the invaders from Penn. Some of them wanted to know what brigade that was on the train. One of the cripples sung out "The Cripple Brigade" but the 7th didn't seem to understand.

At Wilmington, Del. we stopped about half an hour to take in wood and water, after which we went on to Philadelphia, reaching there about noon. On this trip, I had a narrow escape from being killed, or badly crippled. The train being composed of freight and platform cars, the badly wounded were placed on beds that were laid on the floor, while the others who could walk or help themselves, took the top of the cars. On the way, I fell asleep lying on the platform that runs on top of the cars for the use of the breakman, and had rolled so far off that my legs hung over the edge of the car. One of the boys happened to see me, and catching me by the slack of the breeches, pulled me out of danger. It is needles[s] to say that I did not fall asleep again during the remainder of the trip.

On getting out of the cars at Philadelphia, we were marched into the Citizens' Volunteer Hospital, where we had a good wash, to get rid of the Virginia mud, after which we had a good dinner. It had been generally understood when we started that we were to be sent to our own state for treatment, but we were doomed to disapointment, for after resting about two hours, ambulances were driven up to the door and we were told to get into them. We did so, but instead of taking us to the Penn. R.R. to take train for Jersey City we were driven through the city to the depot of the Chestnut Hill Railroad. These ambulances were owned by the several fire companys in the city and were got up in style, being trimmed in all the colors of the rainbow. While on the way to the depot, we saw the 23rd Brooklyn Regt. marching through the city on their way to the front. As soon as the train was loaded we started, and arrived at the hospital in about an hour, where our knapsacks, haversacks, canteens etc had been put away in charge of the quarter-master's dept. We were weighed, and our descriptive lists made out, after which we were assigned to wards.

The hospital was a very large one, being built of wood in the shape of a hollow square. It had about fifty wards, and each ward or building held about sixty patients. In the centre of building and occupying one half of it, were the doctors' quarters, dispensary, cook house, reading-room and library, besides a cell or two for prisoners. The other half was used as a parade ground for the guard and had a music stand in the centre.

The guard was composed of three companys, two of whom were drafted men and one of veteran reserve corps, who spent their time in drilling, guarding the hospital and having a dress parade every morning. On the 23rd the guard was presented with a new set of colors, and they made as much noise over it as if they had won a great victory over the rebels. The band gave a concert every day for the benefit of the wounded, which livened them up considerable. At the entrance to wards, and running the entire circuit of the building was a narrow rail-road track. Upon this run a small car, that carried the rations and distributed them to each ward. The hospital was well supplied with fire buckets, axes, hose, ladders etc. Fire allarms were all over. Hydrants with three lengths of hose attached were always in readiness in case of fire, while a hose carriage was in the centre of the building, ready to go to any part of the building when needed.

Wednesdays and Fridays being visiting days, we had plenty of the fair sex comming to see the wounded and sick soldiers. The visitor upon entering the gate was shown into the reception room, where all inquiries in relation to patients were made, as no one was allowed to enter the wards without the permission of the surgeon in charge, as lots of people came there out of mere curiosity to see the place and the patients. A squad of men had been detailed for the purpose of escorting them round and showing them the diferent points of interest. I was one of the detail, but being a bashful young man, I declined the honor, in favor of a gentleman who was more of a ladies' man than myself.

On the 29th the drafted men were drafted into the army w[h]ere they belonged. The 3rd of July I got a pass from the doctor and took a flying trip to Jersey City, and arrived there about five o'clock in the morning before anyone was out of bed. After spending a very pleasant day with the girls, etc. I took the 11:30 train back, and arrived at Philadelphia too soon for the train that was to take me to Chestnut Hill, so that I had the pleasure of laying round the depot, waiting for daylight and the train that took me back to the hospital.

Examinations were made every week by orders of the head surgeons for purpose of clearing out the hospitals. The well men were sent to their regts., while all those who were fit to do duty round the hospitals, but not fit for a march, were transferred to the Invalid Corps. I was examined with the rest, but no decision was reached in my case.

At the time the riots took place in New York, all the boys in the hospital who could walk, volunteered to form a company or regt. and proceed to New York, but were not allowed to do so by the doctors. The verdict of the soldiers were that whenever one of them was caught, to string him up at once and be done with it.

I took a trip to the city [Philadelphia] the same day, but there was no signs of a disturbance there, everything going on peaceable and quiet. My father coming up to see me, I got a pass from the doctor and went off with him. After visiting the theatre, we put up at a hotel for the night, and the next morning took the little steamer Reindeer (a stern wheeler) that carried our mails while on the Potomac for a trip up the Schuylkill River as far as Mauch-Chauch, and also visited the Fairmount Waterworks.

As it was of no use to ask for a furlough and the men were leaving all the time, I determined to take the trip myself, the more so, as the ward-master told me that if I got back in fifteen days, nothing would be said about it. So on the 4th of August I asked for a pass and got it, allowing me to be out for twelve hours. With this in my pocket, I took the train for Philadelphia. As the train would not start from the Kensington depot until one o'clock, I took the Camden road that started at twelve, supposing that it would land me in New York one hour sooner. But in that I was sadly mistaken, for I had taken a way train that stopped at nearly all stations and switches, so that I did not reach Barclay St. N.Y. until seven o'clock that night, and finally reached home about eight. I had such a pleasant time of it home, that instead of going back in two weeks, I staid a month, and did not report myself to the hospital until the fourth of September.

Going to the ward that I had left I reported myself to the ward master, who informed me that I would have to report the doctor before I could be admitted. He went with me, and upon my reporting myself to him, was ordered to the guard-house for the night. I was introduced to a cell about four by six, after which the door was doubled locked and barred. For light and air, there was one small opening near the ceiling, about six inches wide by about a foot in heighth. While the furniture consisted of a single spittoon, neither a chair or bench being provided, so that you had either to stand up or lay on the floor. As I could not stand up all night and having no light, I lay down on the floor with the spittoon for my pillow and slept till morning.

After getting up, my breakfast was brought to me, consisting of a cup of coffee and a piece of bread. When I had demolished the grub, I was ushered into the presence of the court to be tried, said court being composed of the head doctor and him only. After he had asked me several questions, as to where I was, what I went for etc. I was declared guilty, and sentenced to three weeks in the prisoners' squad for punishment. Two other men who came back at the same time had taken the precaution to get a certificate from their family doctor, stating that their wounds would not allow them to travel. These men were let off not even being locked up in the guard-house. When I left the hospital, my wound was still running but while home I got some salve to use on it, so that when I went back it was all healed.

Going to the prisoners' quarters, I was assigned a bunk and started about my duties, which were to clean up the grounds and buildings and whitewash the foundation. We did white-wash it and no mistake. We slapped it on so thick that it all peeled off again. As the prisoners seemed to enjoy themselves too much, a guard was placed over us to prevent us from playing cards or cutting up shines. A crazy soldier who had been put in the guard-house for climbing out of the windows was no sooner released then he commenced the same thing over again.

Before my three weeks was up, I was ordered to report to my Regt. as my wound was well. In accordance with that order I was furnished with an order from the doctor, and getting my baggage from the quarter-master's dept. I with a lot more left the hospital on the 12th and reported ourselves at the provost-marshall's office in Philadelphia. Waiting there until five o'clock, we marched to the depot and took the six o'clock train for Baltimore. Arriving there at daybreak, getting out off the train we marched across the city to the Washington Depot. I had to march through the streets bare-headed as I had lost my cap out of the window on the road while I was asleep.

When I left the hospital I was handed a paper ordering me to report myself to my company, but on reaching the marshall's office, we were placed in charge of a squad of soldiers as a guard, who had eleven prisoners with them, who were being sent back to their regts. for desertion, all being hand-cuffed. One of them had deserted three times. This guard took us to the convelesant camp and turned us over to the officer in charge, so that reporting to my Regt. was out of the question. One of them a sergt. made himself very officious. When we were boarding the train that was to take us to Baltimore I stopped to look at something on the road, when this fellow hit me on the back with his sword to make me hurry into the train. He thought probably that I wanted to desert.

Getting our breakfast at the Baltimore depot, we took the ten o'clock for Washington and arrived there about three o'clock. Leaving the train, we went into the soldiers' retreat and staid there all night. The meals we had there were the same as we got when we first went out, that is dry bread, fat pork and greasy coffee. The next morning we marched to the Alexandria Rail-road depot and boarded a train waiting there. In a short time we started, and passing over the Long Bridge were soon at the convalescent camp.

Getting off the cars (platform cars) we were formed in line and examined by the doctors. Some were sent to the distribution camp to be returned to their regts. some to the hospital, while others were sent to the quarters for the Invalid Corps, myself amongst the rest. I went to the Jersey barracks, where I found lots of friends. This camp was quite a town in appearance, being laid out in streets, with barracks, sutler store, post office, library, barber's shop and photograph gallery. Its inhabitants were cripples, convalescents, paroled prisoners and prisoners not paroled (that is deserters) and men fit to go to their regts. There was also a fine brass band that gave us excellent music at headquarters every night, which never failed to draw a large and attentive audience. The forts which were all round were practicing every day with their big guns. It made it sound something like war, only that the whizing of the shells was not heard.

There were two boards of surgeons, whose duty it was to examine all the men as to their fitness for the service, w[h]ether for active service with their regts. in the field, and if not, but still able to do duty round hospitals or cities, to determine w[h]ether they should go into the first or second batalion of invalids, [and] if not fit for either, to grant their discharges. After being examined by the first board, I was sent back to my quarters as not being fit for active service, and on going before the second board, they had quite a discussion, w[h]ether to discharge me or not. They finally came to the conclusion to put me in the first batalion of invalids. Accordingly I changed my quarters to the invalid barracks, there to stay until the company was full.

Havelock worn by the troops in summer to keep the sun from the neck, they were uncomfortable and were soon discarded

XVI

———◆———

Veteran Reserve Corps

WHEN JOKESTERS BEGAN *to note that the initials of the Invalid Corps were the same as those used to stamp worn-out government equipment as "Inspected — Condemned," the name of the organization had to be changed, and it became the Veteran Reserve Corps. The change of name made no difference in Bellard's duties, which consisted primarily of guarding prisoners and deserters.*

The headquarters of the Army of the Potomac, which Bellard visited in December 1863, were near Culpeper, Virginia, where General George Gordon Meade had led his men into winter quarters after his failure to outmaneuver Lee in the Mine Run campaign (November 26–December 1). Bellard was in error in referring to prisoners captured by "Grant's Army" at this time, for Grant did not become general-in-chief of the armies until March 1864.

The Congressional debates, to which Bellard occasionally listened during the winter of 1863–1864, concerned proposals to increase the bounty offered for enlistment in the Union army and a bill, which was not adopted until June 1864, to raise the pay of privates.

———◆———

The company being full on the 14th of October, we received one day's rations of grub, and boarding the train at the camp we were soon on our way for Alexandria. Upon reaching there, we took another train that carried us to Washington, stopping at the end of the long bridge. Getting out of the cars, we marched up 14th street to Meridian Hill and took possession of some tents that were already there. As they were in a very dirty condi-

The next morning we received our arms and equipments, an extra pair of pants and the blue jacket of the Invalid Corps

Uniform. V. R. Corps

237

tion, we set to work and cleaned them out, after which we took it easy for the rest of the day. The next morning we received our arms and equipments, an extra pair of pants and the blue jacket of the Invalid Corps. The jacket was made of light blue cloth with black braid for trimmings and nine small brass buttons down the front. A camp guard being called for, I found myself detailed for the first time in five months, but as I had been there before it was like second nature to me.

As the corps was not organized into regts. as yet, our company was designated as the 97th company of the 1st Battalion of Invalids (or as the boys called us Condemned Yanks). Our captain in taking command of the company informed us that we were ordered to Washington to do provost duty, and he wanted every man to look neat and present a good appearance. After he had inspected the command, he declared himself as well pleased, having found everything to his satisfaction. There was nine companys stationed at the camp, and our routine of duty consisted of two drills during the day with dress parade in the evening, while every 3rd day we took our turn at guard duty. One night during a rain storm our tent came down and we got pretty wet before we could get it up again.

On the 18th a squad from our company was picked out by the captain to take some prisoners to Governor's Island N.Y. The men being picked out by the captain for their good appearance and discipline, fortunately I was one of the squad. This just suited me, as it gave me a chance to see the folks. Getting ourselves ready, we received one day's ration of grub, but no ammunition, and reported ourselves to the captain. When he had inspected the squad, he pronounced himself as well pleased with our appearance, and after he had given us a few parting remarks as to our behaviour during the trip we marched to the provost marshall's office, and took charge of our prisoners, fifteen altogether, who with the exception of 3 men, were chained in pairs.

Forming line on each side of them, we marched them down the avenue to the depot. While marching into the depot, some of the prisoners helped themselves to the apple woman's stock, who had a stand at the entrance. She demanded them back from the guard, but no notice was taken of her. Boarding the train, the prisoners were given seats at one end of the car, so as to keep them together, much to the disgust of some of the passengers who wanted the seats for themselves. But as Uncle Sam ran the road they had to stand up the same as the guard. After traveling some time and feeling tired, I rigged up a seat, by putting the bayonette point down on the floor, and placing my cartridge box on top. This made a pretty good seat, but I had to preserve my balance or else fall over.

Our prisoners were a hard lot, being for the most part deserters and bounty jumpers, who were on their way to a government fort for punishment. All went well with us until we passed Trenton, N.J. when most of us being tired fell asleep. The train was near Newark when the sergeant woke up just in time to see one of the men climbing out of the window. Grabbing him by the seat of his pants, the Sergt. hauled him back, and found that he had slipped his handcuffs. Placing them on his wrists again, he made sure of him by screwing them up so tight that the man complained of them hurting him, but he was fast this time, and it prevented the rest from trying the same game. By the time everything was quieted down the rest of us had woke up and the train ran into the depot at Jersey City.

Forming our squad, we passed over the river and took up our line of march for City Hall Park, where we had to report. We created quite a sensation on Broadway as we marched along with our linked prisoners. When we had arrived in front of St. Paul's Church I looked across the street for some face that I knew and saw my father, who had stopped to look at us, but had not recognized me as one of the squad. Crossing over, he knew me at once, and after a few words with him I rejoined the squad at the park. After a conference between the Sergt. and the officer in command, we were ordered to take the prisoners to Gove[r]nor's Island. Marching down B'way to the

Battery, we halted at the government boat house to wait for the propellor that was to take us over.

While waiting for the boat, an old gentleman came up and asked me if there was any of the 5th N.J. in that squad. I said yes, that I had belonged to that Regt. He then asked me if I knew his nephew who was an officer in that Regt. I said I did, and after telling him all that I knew about him, he asked me over to have a drink. As we had plenty of time, I thanked him and accepted the invitation, going into one of the hotels that were thick about that locality. I was treated to drinks and cigars, and was introduced to all hands as a soldier from his nephew's Regt. Bidding the old gentleman good bye at last, and promising to inform his nephew of my meeting with his uncle when I should see him, I started for the landing only to find that the sergt. and his squad were on board and the boat just starting out.

I told the sergt. that I would take a run home and meet him at the J[ersey]. C[ity]. Ferry that night. He said all right, and off I went. After paying a short visit to my father's shop and seeing some of the old friends there I went over to Hudson City. The folks were astonished to see me of course as they did not know I was comming. I passed a short but pleasant stay with them and after supper I left for the depot, where I found the rest of the squad.

The sergt. told me that when they got to the Island and the prisoners found out that our guns were not loaded and not a cartridge in the crowd, they were furious and declared that had they known it, not a man of them would have went to the Island, for they would have fixed us in the cars while asleep. But they thought we were loaded and were afraid to ta[c]kle us, for fear that if they had, it would have woke us up, and some of us would have given them a dose of cold lead.

Leaving Jersey City, we arrived at Philadelphia, too late for the Wash. train. So we went over to the Cooper Shop refreshment saloon. After getting away with a good supper, we went up stairs and turned in to

*After getting away with a good supper, we went up stairs
and turned in to sleep*

sleep. Getting up early next morning we washed ourselves and had a good breakfast, after which we took the 3:30 train for Baltimore, reaching there about 10 o'clock. Marching into the Volunteer Refreshment Saloon established in that city, we put away a substantial dinner, consisting of corn beef, potatoes and coffee with plenty of bread. Every one was satisfied except an Irishman of the squad, who growled because there was no cabbage. The Sergt. shut him up by saying that it was a blamed sight better dinner than he got when he was at home, but growlers are all over. About 4 p.m. we took the Wash. train and arrived there about 6. Marching to quarters, we reported to the Capt. and were dismissed.

About the 21st we had to leave our quarters to make room for the

241

178th N.Y. who were forming the regt. in a body preparitory to their going to the front. Some of their companys had been there before us, so that we had to vacate to make room for the rest who were comming. The rank and file of this regt. were for the most part made up of bounty jumpers and conscripts.

Leaving our quarters during a heavy rain storm, we marched through the city and took up our quarters in some negro shantys that stood on the top of Carroll Hill near the capitol grounds. The shantys stood six in a row, one story in height and went by the name of Sherburne Barracks. There was plenty of ventilation in these barracks, as the boards were not very well matched. The wind having full play, it would whistle through the cracks pretty lively and made them anything but warm. On 3 sides two tiers of bunks had been put up, each of which was occupied by two men. In the middle of the floor we had a small sheet iron wood stove, which helped to keep us warm.

One night as I was in bed my bunk mate gave me a kick that sent me out of the bed and landed me on top of the stove, knocking it over and nearly setting the shanty on fire. I jumped up quick as possible, and grabbing the fellow by his red beard I held on to him until he cried enough. This was last trouble with him. The next day I changed my bed fellow and had no more fights.

Nov. 12th we were packed up ready to move, but the orders were not issued. At this time we had been formed into regts. and we were now known as Co. C of the 1st Regt. Vet. Reserve Corps. As a large number of rebel prisoners were expected in Washington from Grant's Army, we were detailed along with the 157th Penn, 153rd N.Y. and the 14th New Hampshire Regts. to escort them from the train to the prison. Leaving our quarters at sundown we marched to the depot of the Alexandria R.R. where we formed in line and stacked arms to await their arrival. The weather being very cold, the boys seized some waggons that stood in front of a black-smith's shop and run them round to keep warm. Others took the wheels off and rolled them round but soon tiring of that, fires were started and it was not long before the wheels and waggon boddies were piled on to keep up the heat.

At last the trains commenced to arrive. The first ones to come in was loaded with wounded men from the 6th Corps. About half past two in the morning two large trains came slowly up the track, and stopped in front of us. These were filled with rebel prisoners, with one or two Zouaves in each car as a guard. The escort was now formed in two lines facing inward, and as each car door was opened, the rebels would give a yell and a jump, and start off on a run for the head of the column. It took some time for them to get out, as there was some 1700 of them. Nearly all of them were poorly clad, some without hats, some with no shoes to their feet, while others again had no coats. When they were going through the ranks, one of them sung out that they had taken Wash. at last. Well they had, but I should not have liked [so] to have taken Richmond. When the last of them had left the train, orders were given to march, the V[eteran]. R[eserve]. C[orps]. bringing up the rear. When we reached the old capitol prison, the line was halted, and the cripples sent back to quarters, tumbling into our bunks about five o'clock a.m. The next night the rebs were taken from the prison and marched on board of the steamer that was to take them to Point Lookout in Maryland. When they were marching away, they set up one of their yells that they generally gave when making a charge. It was kept up for some time and could be heard a long way off.

On the 14th we had another little trip, this time to take some prisoners to Genl. Meade's head-quarters at the front. Ten men of our company being detailed for this service with myself as a member under the command of our second lieutenant. Leaving our barrack with one day's rations in our haversacks, and ten rounds of ammunitions in our cartridge boxes, we marched to Forrest Hall, Georgetown, which was used for a military prison and halted in front of the door. After loading our pieces with buck and ball we received our charge of 21 deserters and marched them to the depot of the Orange and Ale[xandria]. R.R. outside the city. Boarding train, we took our position on the roofs of the cars, with our prisoners between us. We got started about 10 o'clock and after a long ride over a very uneven track we reached Warrenton Junction about 6 p.m.

As the track had not been repaired any further, we got off the train and started for a tramp of 16 miles. Soon after we left the cars, it commenced to rain and continued during the night. We had gone about 5 miles through mud and slush and [were] wet to the skin, when we espied a large fire in the woods. Going over to it, we found that a waggon train had halted for the night and we concluded to do the same, as we could not find our way in the dark, and the fire was too comfortable to leave. The teamsters having some coffee made, we roped ourselves in and got some of it, which made us feel more comfortable. The prisoners we let run where they liked, as they did not know the roads and were as anxious to make themselves comfortable as we were. They gave us no trouble, but helped the squad to gather fuel amongst the trees.

In the morning we were off again before daylight and marching along the rail-road track (or where it had been) through mud that was anckle deep, we came to a river. Crossing this on a pontoon bridge, we went about two and a half miles further when we reached Meade's head-quarters. Turning our prisoners over to Genl. Patrick, who was provost marshall of the army, we rested about an hour, and then started on the homeward track. I had intended to pay a visit to my Regt. from here but had no chance.

After marching a short distance we got on board of a gravel train that was going in our direction, and rode to Bealeton Station. We then had to get off and take shank's mare once more. Meeting with a baggage train on the road we took possesion and all went smooth until we came to a deep ditch, when the waggon that I was in, in trying to cross over, got one of its wheels on the bank, while the other was on the bottom of the creek. As a matter of course, it upset. When I tried to get out of the waggon as it was going over, I was thrown into the water on all fours, and got a thorough ducking. All hands who were in the waggon got wet, but I got the worst of it. Our guns and equipments with our haversacks, which were in the bottom of the waggon, came out of the water much the worse for wear. My bayonette was lost, while our grub was a regular mush. One of the boys who had some whiskey with him, gave me a swig at the canteen, as soon as I got out of the water, which helped to keep out the cold.

*I was thrown into the water on all fours, and got a
thorough ducking*

After righting the waggon and pulling it out of the creek we got in again and started off, but our troubles were not ended yet. When we arrived at Warrenton Junction, we found a train standing there, and most of the boys had got on when the train started but I with my wet clothes had not. The boys tried to pull me into the car but could not and let me go. As I did not want to be left alone all night in a strange country, I seized hold of the rails on each end of a freight car and tried to pull myself up so that I could get onto the platform. My clothes were so heavy however from the soaking I had got that I could make no headway. So swinging myself between the cars so as to give me force enough to throw myself clear of the wheels, I let go and landed on my back between the tracks, safe and sound.

I was as near Washington as the rest, however, for the rear of the train had only just passed me when it stopped with a jerk. The locomotive had jumped the track and lay over on its side. The tender and one car went with it. Men were set to work at once to repair damages and build a track around the locomotive, but it was not finished until next morning. In the mean time something had to be done to keep warm and dry my clothing. So looking round I saw a fire with some soldiers sitting round it, and went over to them. When I got there, I found my old Captain Woolsey and Corpl. Larkins to be of the party who were on their way home on recruiting service. So piling all the wood we could find on the fire, we sat there and chatted until morning.

All of the track from Manassas Junction to Rappahannock River had been torn up by the rebs. The ties had been piled up with the rails on top and set fire to. When the rails had become hot and soft they were twisted and bent so as to be of no further use. The rail-road bridge had been burnt, but our men had finished a new one, all but laying the rails. When we left, the track had all been relaid but as it was not solid on the road bed, no trains ran any further than the junction. In the morning the track being laid, we got off and riding around the fallen locomotive we reached Washington without any further mishaps, but very much fagged out. While we were at the front, we heard some artilery firing, but it was only a little skirmish and did not last long.

Veteran Reserve Corps

On the 17th three regts. of the Vet[eran]. Res[erve]. corps were reviewed by the Prest. After marching through the city we passed in review
through the White House grounds, and having a band with each regt. we
made a very creditable display, large numbers of citizens and soldiers looking on. When we got to camp after the review, the captain informed us, that
he was very proud of the company, that they had behaved like gentlemen,
and that the major in command said that we were the best company on the
ground. As we always got the praise when we paraded, for our appearance
and disipline, the boys made up their minds to keep it up and so we did.

On Christmas day the noise in Washington reminded one of the 4th of
July in the North, with the firing of guns and the small boy with his fire-
crackers. We had a double patrol out on that day, as there were so many
drunken soldiers in the city without passes, that they needed looking after.

The 157th Pen. Volls. having gone to the front, we cleaned out the
barracks and scrubbed them with the expectation of moving in, but were
informed that five companys of the 1st Regt. V[eteran]. R[eserve].
C[orps]. would occupy them. So we had our trouble for nothing. We now
had quite a large Regt. when we turned out for parade. The rest of the Regt.
did guard duty round the camp and took prisoners to the diferent camps
round the city, while our company had charge of the patrol bussines, which
was much the best, as we did not lose so much sleep at night, by being woke
up every time the relief guard went on duty. When our guard went on duty
we went in a body and came back the same way, unles some man was off with
a prisoner.

As Congress was in session I paid several visits to the Capitol when off
duty, to hear our law makers debate on a bill that was before them, to
increase the soldiers pay 50 pr ct. The bill was not passed, but was amended,
so as to give us 16 instead of 13 dollars per month. It was however good
wages for a soldier, and the only bad feature about it was that my time
being so short, it was not much benefit to me.

247

XVII

———◆———

Duties, Pleasures and Dangers
at Provost Marshal's Guard and Patrol

BELLARD SPENT *the final months of his three-year army enlistment in Washington. Still a member of the Veteran Reserve Corps, he had frequently to escort captured deserters to prison either at Forrest Hall, on Wisconsin Avenue in Georgetown, or at the Old Capitol, the brick building on First Street erected originally to house the Congress after the British burned the Capitol in 1815. He may well have seen Belle Boyd, the notorious Confederate spy, who until December 1, 1863, was confined in Carroll prison, an annex to the Old Capitol.*

The rest of the time Bellard and his companions served as military police. They had the responsibility for keeping drunken and rowdy soldiers from misbehaving in theaters and on the streets. Another of their duties was to keep soldiers out of off-limits saloons and the nearly five hundred houses of prostitution in the capital. These dens were located in noisome alleys on either side of Pennsylvania Avenue and were also concentrated in the Island, the sector of southwest Washington separated from the rest of the city by the odiferous Washington Canal.

In July 1864 Bellard came once more under enemy fire. Seeking to relieve the relentless pressure that Grant was exerting against Richmond, Lee despatched two divisions under Jubal A. Early down the Shenandoah Valley and into Maryland. Finding little resistance, Early pushed on toward Washington, which was defended only by a handful of Veteran Reserve Corps regiments, like Bellard's, and by some hastily mobilized government clerks. But just as the Confederates came within sight of the defenses of the capital at about noon on July 11, reinforcements began to arrive from Grant's army in Virginia.

During the next thirty-six hours, while the Confederates reconnoitered and engaged in some brisk skirmishing around Fort Stevens, President Lincoln, together with assorted cabinet members and Congressmen, repeatedly appeared on the parapet of the fort to observe the fighting. So fully did the tall President expose himself to enemy sniping that officers and even some enlisted men remonstrated with him; legend has it that young Oliver Wendell Holmes shouted, "Get down, you fool!" Though nearby, Bellard was apparently unaware of Lincoln's presence in the fort and made no reference to the incident.

During the night of July 12, sensing that he lacked strength for an assault, Early withdrew. Before leaving, his men set fire to the house of Postmaster General Montgomery Blair, whom they especially detested because, though a Southerner, he had entered Lincoln's cabinet. By the morning of July 13 the Confederate threat to Washington was gone, and Bellard's experience of war had ended.

———◆———

While on provost duty, it was our principle bussines to escort prisoners from the marshall's office to the diferent prisons round the city, and for that purpose one company was sent there every morning. As my company was only on for a short time, we did not have much of the dirty work to do, as it was not very pleasant to march a lot of deserters to the Old Capitol or Forrest Hall prisons, some of whom were perhaps destined to be shot, as soon as they reached the army.

Our company being on duty at the provost marshall's we were ordered to take a squad of prisoners to Forrest Hall in Georgetown, a suburb of Washington. Forming the squad of prisoners in two ranks, with the guard on the outside, we started off with fixed bayonettes but having no ammunition. We got along very well until we reached the bridge that connects the two cities, when one of our prisoners broke through the ranks and started on a run for liberty. The guard halted and one or two men started after the fugitive, but as he had the start and was not encumbered with a rifle, he got away, and the guard had to return without him. Starting off again, we reached the prison and halted in front of the door, while the sergeant went in to report. When the officer in command had been informed that one of the prisoners had escaped, he wanted to know why the devil we didn't shoot him, and he was very much surprised to hear that we had nothing to shoot with. When the papers had been examined and found correct, with this one exception, the squad fell in line and marched into prison. As I was the last man in the squad, I noticed one of them leaning over the railing that ran along the front of the building, as unconcerned as you please, and acting as if he was looking at the prisoners out of mere curiosity, and had nothing to do with the squad who were about disapearing behind the door. He evidently thought that the squad had all gone, and he was a free man, for when I touched him with the gun and told him to march, he gave a jump, and looking around he saw me in uniform, when without a word, he walked into the prison.

When the prisoners had answered to their names, the guard on duty there ushered them into the several rooms that they had been assigned to and a guard [was] placed over them. As we had nothing further to do with them, I went to one of the rooms to have a look at the prisoners. As soon as a new lot of prisoners made their appearance the old hands would yel out

"Fresh fish." At this signal the new ones were surrounded and a demand made for money or tobacco. If they were so unfortunate as to have neither, a blanket was soon procured and the old hands seizing hold of it, the new arrival was thrown in and tossed up to the ceiling, making him look more like a frog than anything else with his arms and legs spread out trying to catch the air. While I stood by the guard at the door, I saw an exibition of this kind of fun. One of the prisoners that we had just taken in was put in this room, and he was no sooner inside than he was seized by the crowd all yelling "Fresh fish." As he had nothing for them, he was tossed into the blanket. As many as could, got hold of it, and giving it a hoist up he went nearly touching the ceiling. He came down all right, without any damage, but the next toss he got was an extra one that sent him flying against the ceiling, striking it with his head. He fell back into the blanket unconcious. The boys, thinking perhaps that the man was badly stunned, took him out of the blanket and taking him over to the water troughs that were on one side of the room threw him in bodily clothes and all. The guard who stood at the door took no notice of it whatever, being I suppose used to it.

At the Old Capitol prison (at one time the capitol of U.S.) rebel soldiers were confined and also a female spy, who I believe was the notorious Belle Boyd. As this female had the free use of the jail corridor, the officers of the guard had quite a flirtation with her, and she could be seen walking up and [down] the corridor with them any day. Our orders were to see that none of the prisoners escaped, and if they tried it on to shoot them. Also to make them keep their heads in the window and not insult passers by. While I was on guard there, one of the rebs who was on the top floor persisted in thrusting his head through the window, and on being ordered to withdraw it, gave me some impudence. So I told him that if he did not draw his head in out of sight, I would put a ball through it. As I levelled my piece to enforce my demand, he drew back out of sight, and I had no further trouble with him.

As he had nothing for them, he was tossed into the blanket

As soldiers were apt to get drunk when ever they got a chance, orders were very strict in regard to selling it to us, but we managed to get it in some way. While out for a walk one afternoon, I stepped into a variety store, where everything was sold from a needle to a carcass of beef, boots, groceries, medicines, meats, dry goods, crockery, and in fact anything that you wanted, even whiskey, providing you knew the ropes. Asking the lady of the house if she would sell us some whiskey, she told us that she could not sell us any, as it was against the law, but that we could have some lemonade if we wanted it. Not being on the hunt for that kind of beverage, we left, but took notice before we left that two or three soldiers who came in asked for hot lemonade, and went into the back room. We afterwards learned that lemonade meant whiskey, but we were not initiated and got left for the time being. The only place w[h]ere a soldier could get what he asked for over the bar,

So I told him that if he did not draw his head in out of sight, I would put a ball through it

and no questions asked was in a deep cellar in Pen. Ave. that was partly under the sidewalk. We could step in there at any time and get what we called for. The place was well patronized by soldiers, who sat there smoking and drinking, without fear of the patrol.

A detail of two or four men were sent to each theatre every night to examine the passes of all soldiers and arrest all of those who had none. After standing guard at the entrance until the first act was well under way, we went inside and saw the ballance of the piece. In this way I visited all the theatres in the city. While on duty at Grover's Theatre one night, a government detective came up to us, and stated that there was two men in the theater whom he wished to arrest, and asked the officer in command for two men. I and another man were sent with him, and we followed him in. The detective led the way and after a short search found his men. Laying his hands on their shoulders, he told them they were wanted, and ordered us to take them to the central guard house. We did as ordered. The men protesting all the way to the guard house, that they were not the men and so it proved, for upon our arrival at the guard house, they proved to the satisfaction of the person in charge that they were government clerks, and were discharged. We were often called upon in this way to assist detectives, and in most cases got hold of the wrong men.

This [patrol] squad was composed of about 24 men, commanded by a commissioned officer, and our route was through Penn. Ave. and most of the cross streets, visiting the houses of ill fame on the look out for officers and soldiers who were not provided with passes. Twice a week an army surgeon went with us, and while he and the officer in command went through the houses, we *the guard* had to wait on the sidewalk until they came out. When snow was on the ground or [it was] raining fast, we did not have a very pleasant wait.

While out on this squad, I lost my first prisoner. We captured two men one night who were without passes, and myself and another were ordered to take them to the guard house. With our prisoners along side of us, we started but while going through a dark street near the guard house, and opposite an alley, the one I had charge of broke, and run up the alley, and I after him, calling upon him to halt or I would shoot. As there was no light, and he seemed to be acquainted with the place, I snapped the hammer of my gun to make out I was going to shoot, but as it was not loaded nor capped the fellow took no notice of it, but kept right on. Giving him up as a bad job, I returned to my partner and we took the remaining prisoner to the lock up. I received a reprimand for losing my prisoner, but as we were not allowed to shoot, it could not be helped.

During the time that the regts. who had reenlisted were on their way home, the city was full of soldiers, and as a number of them were on a good drunk, we had considerable trouble with them. It seemed to be a good joke for them to call us condemned yanks, and jeer at us while marching along the street.

Comming ácros some member of the 69th Pen. (an Irish Regt.) one day, they gave us a good deal of talk, and the Lieut. arrested one of them, the 1st Sergt. ordering two men to take him to the guard house. As they started with him, some one informed me that he had a revolver in his pocket. I told this to the Lieut. who ordered me to take it away from him. Telling the guard to halt, I asked the man for his revolver. Instead of doing so, he made me some surly answer, and made a motion as if to draw it. When I saw that I grabbed him by the neck and pinned him against the wall, while the other two tried to get it away from him. He fought so much that the Lieut. ordered them to stop and take him to the guard house, and told me to follow up in the rear, so that [if] he attempted any tricks, I could see him in time and stop him. On the way down he stopped several times and turning round to me threatened to blow my brains out. My bayonette was always down at a charge, however, ready to prod him at the first sign of treachery. At one time the guard had the but of his musket raised to crack his skull, when he was giving me an extra dose of his ill will. We got him to the guard house at last, when he was searched, and a loaded revolver was taken out of his pockets. He threatened to get square with me for what I had done, but as his regt. left the city the next day, I saw no more of him.

The Island Squad visited all the low places, that lay between Penn. Ave. and the river, and contained the worst places in the city. One called Tin Cup Alley was reached by going through an alley, when we came to a sort of a court surrounded by houses, that were occupied by white and black, all mixed up together, on the principle that you pays your money and takes your choice. Another one, a large brick house near the river, was named Castle Thunder. It was visited only in a body as it would not have been safe for any one man to go there. The stairs were winding and in one corner of the building, and a man thrown over the top would never stop until he struck the stone floor on the bottom. In one of our visits, men, women and children were there all mixed up together, and one of the men who was climbing the stairs at the time, stopped on one of the floors above and in plain view of the women and children, exposed his person and relieved himself. The place was evidently too dangerous for a soldier, as we never found one there.

Another notorious den was visited one night at 11 o'clock, and while the patrol stood in front of the door, I was sent round to the rear, to see that no one got out of the back window. As the shutters were not closed, I had a good view of the interior. In bed together were a man and woman. When the patrol commenced knocking on the door, I expected to see the man jump out of bed, and make a break for the window (as I supposed he was a soldier). But he did not. The woman got out of bed in her night dress and opened the door. The Sergeant went in and looked around, but seeing no uniforms retired. The woman locked the door and returned to bed. And as I left, they were hugging and kissing each other in plain view of anyone who might happen to pass by.

The worst place of all that we had to visit was a shanty that stood on the banks of the canal, close to the Capitol grounds, and was called the

Hospital. The building was occupied by the worst cases in town, and the stench that came from it was enough to turn our stomachs, whenever we halted in front of the door. We were always glad to get away as soon as possible. Bad as the place was, we once found a soldier there in bed with one of the women. (He must have had a cast iron stomach.)

One of our men went down to the Island one night to have a little fun with the girls, and he got it, being brought back to quarters on a shutter, with a bullet in his head, that he had received in a row, presumed to have been done by some jealous lover, whom he had had cut out from the affections of his darling. I had a little experience on the Island myself, that might have been a serious thing for me. As we were going our rounds one night with an officer in command [unusual]

---◆---

At this point one page has been carefully cut from Bellard's notebook. Obviously discretion triumphed over memory. The memoir then resumes:

---◆---

bussines, they got no satisfaction. Another one that we visited in 14th st. we found in an uproar one night. The women were running round wild, and a doctor being in the house. When we got inside we found one of the women laying on a lounge, pale as death and vomiting, while some of the other inmates were slapping her hands and patting her on the back, trying their best to rouse her from a stupor. The doctor told them at last to strip her for a bath. And as we had no further bussines there, we retired. It seems that she had taken a dose of laudanum to end her life, but having taken too much, it did not have the desired effect, but instead had made her deathly sick. The girl's mother and sister lived in the city, and were said to be very nice people. The mother had been trying to get her daughter to leave her evil ways and go home, but the other girls in the house said she would not go. On reflection, she had determined to end her life.

On New Year's day 1864, being with a squad that were taking a lot of prisoners from the marshall's office to the Old Capitol prison, one of the men suggested that we see the old year out and the new one in in a style befitting the occasion by having a little something hot. As the night was bitter cold, we all agreed. One of the men was relieved from duty, furnished with the necessary funds and told to get two canteens full of whiskey, and have some hot stuf ready for us by the time we got back to quarters. Transfering our prisoners to the Old Capitol, we returned to quarters and putting away our gun and equipments, each of us had a pint cup full of hot whiskey that our man had made up for us. We then got our supper, after which we had another dose of hot stuf. After giving it a little time to settle, myself and chum [Vail] went to bed. I dont know how long I had been there, when I was woke up by our mixer of drinks, and another pint cup of toddy was handed me. I drank it, turned in again, and went to sleep. I slept so sound that I did not remember getting up in the night and going outside. Although it was the coldest night that I experienced during my service, I got up with nothing on but my shirt and drawers, and opening the door, I stumbled and fell full length on the frosty ground outside and lay there. The wind, blowing in through the open door woke some of the boys up, who on getting up to shut the door found me laying on the ground. Picking me up, they put me back to bed again, and I knew nothing about it, until told by my chum next morning. (A pretty good drunk that.)

About the 1st of Feb. I received a ten days' furlough and went home. I enjoyed myself in fine style until it was time to go back, when I took the midnight train from Jersey City, and arrived in Wash. at noon next day. I took a little whiskey with me for the boys, with which they drank my health. On the same train were the 61st N.Y. Volls. on their way back from reenlistment furlough. Regts. were still passing through Wash. on their way home to spend their furlough and bounty money at the same time. During my absence, our company had been relieved from head quarters duty and returned to the patroll, which we liked better.

The 29th Lieut. Schafell [Schaffel] detailed myself and five others to attend a German ball, held at one of the halls, for the purpose of keeping order. We had a good supper and whenever any of the men were drinking at the barr, any soldier who happened to be near was asked to drink with them. During the eve. some citizen struck the Lieut. and as he only had one arm to defend himself with, he called for the guard to arrest them. As we got there one of them struck out again, but he had no sooner done so, then he got a thump under the ear that sent him head long down the stairs, through a swinging door, and landing him on the sidewalk, with two or three of us after him. When we got to him, he was on his feet, and proceeded to give us some chin. When ordered by the Lieut. who was now with us to take him in, the fellow ran away and I after him. As I got near him he made a backward slash at my face with a sword cane or something of the kind, that cut a slight gash in my nose. This made me so mad that I took the gun by the muzzle and swinging it round made a crack at his head with the butt. If it had hit him, there would have been no further bother with him, but missing my mark, the gun flew out of my hands, and by the time I had picked it up, he was out of my reach. The Lieut. told me to let him go, and I went back and found the other gent under guard. The Lieut. ordered him to the guard house, and while on the way there, the one I had been after tried to get him away by interfering with the guards. He was recognized and captured, and when they got to the guard house were treated to a shower both to cool off their temper.

At about daylight we found one of our men drunk in the water closet and were ordered to take him to the guard house. As the fellow was too drunk to walk we had to carry him. When we had seen him safe in the guard house, we returned to the hall, only to find the squad gone and our muskets with them. As we had nothing to do, we proposed before going to camp to

As the fellow was too drunk to walk we had to carry him

have a glass of whiskey at a saloon on the ave. that was kept by a New Yorker whom I had got acqua[i]nted with. We stepped in, but instead of one we had two or three, and this on top of the beer, put us in about the same condition as the man we had just taken to the lockup. We got into camp however by a little lying to the guard, and went to bed.

On the 20th of March we left Sherburne Barracks, and took up our quarters in the rear of the capitol grounds, known as Carroll Barracks. They were more roomy than those we had left, and at the same time were more bed buggy. There was bugs all over, in every crack and joint of the bunks, and they defied our efforts to get rid of them. On the 21st a heavy snow storm visited us, the snow being five inches deep on a level, but did not last long as the sun was now too hot for it.

We now had patrol duty every day, going out at 2 p.m. and returning at 4. After supper we had a rest, and turned out again at 7, when we paraded round the streets until 11, at which time we returned to our barracks. We then got a bite to eat, after which we turned in to sleep. Reveille was beaton at 5 a.m. to call out the men, but the night patrol slept until 6, at which time we had to get up or lose our breakfast. The Capitol grounds were now quite green, with new grass, and the flower beds presented a gay appearance, being covered with white, purple and yellow crocuses. These grounds were a favorite place for the soldiers to lounge in, as there was plenty of fine shade trees around. April 3rd our Regt. was marched to

Franklin Square on 14th street for dress parade, and some two or three thousand people witnessed the show.

Our company was again relieved from patrol duty, and put on guard over prisoners. We thought our good job was gone, but our captain was not satisfied, and besides there was so much dissatisfaction amongst the citizens that we were sent back again.

The 4th we moved quarters again this time to the rear of the War Dept. in some new barracks called Post Rush, named after Col. Rush formerly in command of Rush's Lancers, but now in command of our Regt. We were now under strict military rule not being allowed to wear anything that was not issued by the government, even to our shoes. When out on pass, we must have our jackets buttoned up to our chin, waist belt on and also white gloves. Our major, who was an officer of the regular army, and had but one eye, tried to make himself very conspicuous. While I was walking along Penn. Ave. one day out on pass I had my corps badge and shield on my jacket, and that was unbuttoned, when who should come along but the major, who ordered me to take off my badges and button my jacket. I did

My Own   Gov!. Cap,

I had no army cap and the one that the
Lieut. got for me was some two sizes too
large and came down over my ears

neither, only while I was in his sight. He ordered me back on one occasion, when I was going out on pass, he being at the gate, to take off my fancy cap and store boots, and put on the govt. pontoons before I could pass the guard. At the next parade I had no army cap and the one that the Lieut. got for me was some two sizes too large and came down over my ears. I made it answer by pinning it up.

On Sunday the 10th we had dress parade in the square, and it was so crowded that a detail of 25 men was made from the Regt. to keep the crowd back. As I was one of the guards I had a good view of the Regt. and a fine sight it was. Every movement in the manual of arms was executed as if by clock work and drew forth the plaudits of the spectators. On the 21st we were to have had a grand review and inspection by Col. Rush, but it began to rain and so spoilt part of the programme. Leaving our quarters in the morning, we formed platoon front on the ave. and with a band from one of the hospitals at our head, we marched to Franklin Square, keeping so good a front that we were cheered by the people congregated on the sidewalk. Upon reaching the square, we formed in column of companies and the inspection began. By the time the last company was reached, the rain came down so fast that we were ordered back to quarters. We did so in quick time. When we reached there, we had inspection of quarters and the work was over.

As there was so many new men in the ranks, who had never handled a musket (being for the most part from the cavalry and artillery branch of the service) the eve. dress parade was done away with and a half hour's drill took place instead. It was amusing to any one who knew how, to see the way in which the new men broke into fours, or made an oblique movement. Sometimes they would crush up and so break the line, or hang back and so leave a gap in the ranks. Altogether it was a nuisance for men who were up in their drill to be placed in the ranks with them.

As it was now getting warmer our men were kept bussy in fixing up our quarters to make them look as neat as possible. The barracks were scrubbed and white washed. In front of our stoop we filled in with broken stone to keep it dry and on either side along the front of the building a grass plot was laid, so that it made quite an improvement to our quarters, and more inviting to our visitors.

On Sunday Apl. 24th we had another dress parade on the square, but being overcome by the heat, I had to leave the ranks and was taken back to quarters by some of my comrades, one of whom got a glass of brandy from some of the ladies on the way that helped me along. Several of our men were lying under the trees in the park besides myself, the weather being fearfully hot. The 9th Army Corps passed through Wash. on the 25th on their way to the front. My friend A. Austin called to see me that day, being on his way home on furlough having reenlisted for 3 years more.

On the 8th of May in anticipation of a move, 20 rounds of ball cartridges were issued to the men and an extra patrol was sent out.

Another attempt was now made to get the patrol away from our company. On the 12th an order was issued that each company in the Regt. should furnish a detail for patroll and guard duty. Our company having to furnish 37 men, we had to take the men who were on guard duty the night before to fill up. When the patroll went out, the sergeant in command took them the longest way round, and as it was raining it made matters worse. When the squad finally got back, they were so tired out and wet that they gave up the idea of patroll duty. While the officers had such trouble to pick out the diferent patrolls, that they came to the conclusion that it would not pay, and so next morning, we took our place as usual.

On the 14th a part of our Regt. was detailed to guard some rebel prisoners who were expected to arrive. The detail consisted of 150 men, of which our company furnished 20. Marching to 7th St. wharf we boarded a tug and waited until after one o'clock but as there were no signs of the prisoners, we went back to quarters. The weather was wet and drizzely. The wounded were arriving in large numbers from the late battles under Grant, and long lines of ambulances could be seen almost every day, bearing them to the diferent hospitals in the city. My chum's brother was one of the unfortunate ones, and he informed me that my old division (Hooker's) was pretty well cut up.

On the 25th we were expecting to move, and requisitions were sent in for shelter tents, etc. As the boys' baggage had got pretty bulkey by laying in quarters so long, and was too heavy to carry on our backs on a march, some of the boys sent their extra clothing home by express, but I left mine at a restaurant kept by a friend of my chum's, named Mrs. Rollins, as it might come in usefull before I was ready to go home.

On June 1st A. Austin arrived from Jersey City on his way back to his regt. and calling upon me, we went over to the provost marshall's office to get a pass for the front, but none were issued, as there was no communication with the army. We then went to the office at the depot for a pass to go to the distribution camp in Va. This he got, and left the same day.

On the night of the 4th one of our squads had a little shooting scrape on 11th Street. Lieut. Tyrell of our company was on duty at the theatre, when an officer came along drunk and refused to show his pass. He was ordered by the Lieut. to report himself at the provost marshall's office in the morning, but as he became abusive, the Sergt. was ordered to take him to the guard house. When the guard had gone a short distance with him (Lieut. Tyrell being close in the rear) the officer pulled out a revolver, and turning round fired a shot a Tyrell and put a ball in his neck. The Sergt. took the revolver away from him, and fired one shot at him without effect, but the Lieut. coming up fired 5 shots, 3 of which took effect, one in the shoulder, one in the back, and another one somewhere else. Tyrell was taken to his quarters, and the other one to the hospital. The citizens turned out that night in full force, for the purpose of cleaning out the patrol, but beyond some bluster and blow, nothing came of it. The end of the matter was that Tyrell was promoted to 1st Lieut. of Co. 1st Regt. V.R.C. while his antagonist died and was buried.

The 5th our new band played for us on dress parade for the first time

One mounted cavalryman escorts each ambulance and the stars and stripes are placed over each coffin

and did very well. On Sunday the 12th the whole company had to stand at an attention in our quarters, while the Capt. read the articles of war to us, all on account [of a] fool in the company, who objected to the orders of the Capt. because he did not have his shoulder straps on when he went the inspection rounds. The man was right enough according to regulations, but as the order was proper, he should have obeyed without comment. As the boys were all down on him for it, he made no friends, but led a dog's life while he remained with us.

On the 17th a sad accident happened at the arsenal by which 17 young ladies lost their lives by being burnt to death, while many others were injured, caused by an explosion that blew up and burnt some of the buildings. The funeral of the victims took place on Sunday the 19th. The procession to the cemetry preceeded by a brass band was composed of the Sons of Temperance and the girls who worked in the arsenal. Carriages containing the President and other officials and the friends of the deceased followed, and then the hearses and ambulances containing the bodies enclosed in handsome coffins, brought up the rear.

Funerals were of daily occurance as the sick and wounded seemed to

[be] dying off very fast in the hospitals, owing I suppose to the hot weather. A new order of things took place about this time in regard to the burial of soldiers. Previous to this, the dead were coffined, put into an ambulance and carted of without any show or honor. But now, one mounted cavalryman escorts each ambulance and the stars and stripes are placed over each coffin. In this way they could be seen wending their way to the soldiers' burrial ground in strings of twelve more or less every day.

Having got acqua[i]nted with a family in the city, I could spend my time a little better than formerly by paying them a visit occasionally. On Sunday, June 8th myself and chum (Vail) paid them a visit and had a very pleasant time as well as a good dinner of roast lamb and green peas with cherry pudding for desert. Rather an improvement over the soldiers' fare, for our rations at this time were not as good as what we had while with the army at the front. We got salt pork right along for a month, then for a change we got salt horse for another month. Fresh beef we had at the most three days out of ten, rice we never saw, nor hominy, potatoes nor ham, while beef or vegatable soups were things of the past, and beans were a rare article owing I suppose to the cooks' being too lazy to make it.

Our band were getting along nicely and were handsomely uniformed in blue jackets trimmed with black facings and three rows of brass buttons, shake hat with plume, and brass eagle ornament, epaulettes, and black pants with blue, black and gilt stripe down the seam. They looked very gay, but the company funds had to sweat in rigging them out. The officers paid an assesment for that purpose and the funds did the rest. On July 4th the 1st brigade consisting of the 1st, 7th, 9th, 23rd, and 24th Regts. of V.R.C. had a review and parade in rear of our quarters and made a handsome display, having with us three bands. The officers of the 24th Regt. wore gold epauletts and showed off to advantage. The weather was very hot, so much so that it almost burnt our feet walking on the sidewalk.

In the eve. I and some others went to a picnic at 7th St. park and stopped until twelve o'clock. Notices had been given out that an inventor would walk through fire during the night. A frame of light wood had been erected, something like a house as to shape, and covered over with tar and other combustibles. When this was set on fire it made a very hot shanty. The inventor encased in clothing of his own make, walked in and out of this fire with seeming indiference, and when the fire had died out came out of it as well as ever.

In order to keep up the 4th in proper style, our company had two keggs of beer tapped, and some of the boys made good use of it by getting tight and having a free fight, which resulted in black eyes and bloody noses. As I had no relish for either, I kept out of the mus.

On the 6th we had orders to move at a moment's notice, 60 rounds of ammunition to be carried in the waggons no extra clothing to be carried by the men, and as being more servicable, for active service, each man received a blouse.

On the 7th I with some 20 men of our company under command of a lieut. were detailed to act as a military guard on an excursion boat, that was going down the Potomac to Glymont Park. Upon getting ourselves on board, we found that our excursionists were made up of the rough element of Wash. with the ladies of the town as companions. Everything went smooth until we had got some distance down the river when a fight commenced between the bruisers. The guard was ordered in line and after loading our muskets in presence of the crowd, the Lieut. told them that we had been sent by the military authorities to keep order on the boat, and that no fighting would be allowed but if they did endulge in one he would have to fire on them. He also told them that as we had nothing to do with them on land they could do as they pleased when they got off the boat. After that everything was quiet, and the gang treated the boys several times to drinks or segars. After a pleasant sail down the river, we reached our destination and the boat was tied up.

The gang plank was no sooner run out than a grand rush was made for the hotel on shore, and before the guard had fallen in previous to going on

Our band were getting along nicely and were handsomely uniformed in blue jackets trimmed with black facings

shore, a row took place in the hotel. The first thing we saw was a man flying through the window with another man's fist after him. The fist struck the window frame instead of the man, and was considerably the worse for wear on our way home, being swolen to twice its size. That ended the fight, and the parties enjoyed themselves by dancing and swinging. The women standing on the swing the same as the men, and displaying a goodly proportion of leg. Getting tired of this sport, the women proposed to have a swim, but probably on account of the soldiers looking on they did not indulge. After we had got outside of a good supper at the expense of the party, we returned to the boat, and getting under way we reached Wash. about eleven o'clock that night, the roughs having a parting slug at each other as they landed.

On the 8th we had orders to pack up and send all of our extra duds away, so getting a pass for myself and two other men I went to the express office and sent mine home. In the afternoon we had inspection with knapsacks, and received 35 rounds of ammunition which we turned in again the next day. All the members of the V.R.C. who had served in the artilery were ordered to report to brigade head-quarters at 10 p.m. Cartridges were reissued, rations cooked, and we were ordered to sleep in our uniforms and be ready to move in five minutes. On Sunday the 10th orders came to move, so

The women standing on the swing the same as the men

269

RUSH   RACKS.

Washington, D. C. *July* 1864.

Guards and Patrols:

Pass *Corpl Ballard & two men* Co. C,

1st Reg't V. R. C., through this city *to go to Express*

Office until 2 P. m. this date 1864.

M. Brohl

a er 1st Sergeant.

By order of

Hannibal D. Norton

Capt Commanding Co. C., 1st Reg't V. R. C.

Approved:

M. Brohl a er lt Serg

Commanding 1st. Reg't V. R. C.

Getting a pass for myself and two other men I went to the express office

with 35 rounds of blue pills in our cartridge boxes, and our knapsacks on our backs, we left camp at seven o'clock p.m. and forming the brigade on Pen. Ave. we marched through Georgetown and Tennallytown with bands playing and colors flying. The streets being thronged with people to see us off.

Reaching Fort Reno soon after, we halted, and the brigade was deployed out as skirmishers (about 3 feet between each man) in the rifle pits. Orders were given to keep awake and have an eye on the supposed rebels in front. We remained there all night, but as for keeping awake, I for one did not, for I had several cat naps during the night. Had the rebs made an attack on Was. that night, nothing could have saved it, as their [there] was no troops round the city but our brigade, and we were supposed to be unfit for active service.

The morning of the 11th guns were heard in our front, and long lines of dust could be seen rising above the tree tops showing that large bodies of troops were on the march. Re-enforcements now commenced to arrive, about 3,000 from camp distribution, both white and black. A squad from the hospitals and several companys of the 2nd batallion V.R.C. During the day we moved further to our right near Fort Stevens. Several large houses that stood in our front, and would have afforded protection to rebel sharp shooters, were burnt down. During the night all was quiet along the Potomac.

On the 12th the 6th Regt. V.R.C. went out on the skirmish line, as the rebels were now in our front and the artilery had got to work. By this time the 6th and 19th corps from the army had arrived and went into action at Fort Stevens. Our line was on a range of hills that surrounded the city and was well fortified with earthwork forts, armed with seige guns, the entire chain of forts being connected with rifle pits. In the afternoon our Regt. was ordered out to relieve the 6th on the skirmish line. Advancing to the edge of the hill, we were deployed out as skirmishers with our company on the extreme left. Our captain having become what he was pleased to term moon blind (whatever that is) the command devolved upon the Lieut. [Schaffel] who had left one of his arms at Fredericksburg. When we began to deploy, he asked me if I would take charge of the left. I said yes. After we had scrambled over lots of brush wood, we finally reached our position on the crest of the hill, and saw the rebel skirmishers posted on a range of hills just in front of us, but out of range so far as we were concerned, as we were armed with smooth bore muskets, while the rebels had long range rifles.

As no firing was going on in our front, I got some canteens and started down the hill to get some water, telling one of the corporals as I went, that when he heard me call, to answer, so that I could find my way back again

We were relieved by a body of dismounted cavalry who marched along the line and took our place

through the woods, that were very dense. He said he would. Finding a good spring at the bottom of the ravine, I filled the canteens and started back. Having gone as I supposed far enough, I hailed the corporal, but got no answer. Going further up the hill, I hailed again, but still no answer. Making up my mind to find the line myself, I started on and had got right over them, before I was aware of their presence. The corporal and some other non coms. with some privates had left the line to take care of itself, and taken up their position under some trees and bushes. They were out of the sun, and at the same time were out of sight of any body else.

As it seemed to me that they were afraid, I made up my mind to draw the rebel fire. So taking my gun, I stood up by the stump of a tree that stood on the brow of the hill, and taking aim at the nearest rebel that I could see, blazed away. The ball kicked up the dust about half[way] between us down in the hollow. In response to my shot, there was a puff of smoke and a rifle ball whistled over my head, passing through the clump of bushes where the corporal and his valient friends were hiding. Owing to our not having long range guns is probably the reason that we did not get into action and lose more of our men. One man of our Regt. shot through the thigh being the only victom.

A short time after my experience with the non. coms. in the bushes, we were relieved by a body of dismounted cavalry who marched along the line and took our place. The commanding officer telling us to clear out, as he could do without us. Falling back we took up our position in the rifle pits near Fort Stevens, where we lay all day with nothing to do but look on. The skirmishing was kept up by the troops from the front right along. During the day our artilery fire set fire to a mansion that was between the lines, and a company of rebels who had taken posession were dislo[d]ged. What with the burning houses, the bursting of shell and the rattle of small arms, it looked and sounded very much like old times, but with this exception, that very few men were killed or wounded.

The morning of the 13th every thing was quiet along the line, and scouting parties were sent out. They were soon marching over the ground lately held by the rebs, but not one could be seen, with the exception of two dead ones, who had been left unburried. The enemy had fled. In the afternoon the 6th corps were sent off in pursuit.

Starting about 9 o'clock that night, we took up our line of march for Wash. having halted for a rest close by a fence. I sat down by a gate, and leaning against it, was soon fast asleep, as I was pretty well tired out with marching up and down hills. When I woke up the Regt. had gone, but by following the road I soon caught up with them. About 3 o'clock in the morning we crossed the Aqueduct Bridge at Georgetown and bivouacked near the forts that commanded the bridge. A block house was also there, having been built when the war first commenced, but was of no use now. While resting here the boys took a swim in the river to wash off some of the sacred soil of Virginia. Towards night we marched along the line of breastworks for about a mile and went into camp. After pickets had been posted for the night we turned in on the ground and went to sleep.

The next morning our knapsacks were sent back to our quarters, and as we had nothing to do, we took a strol around our position. All along our front was low bushes while here and there targets had [been] placed for artilery practice from the forts, but none took place while we staid there. A short distance from our left was a large pond or mill dam that was said to be full of eels and cat fish, that is according to an old countryman's talk who was trying to catch one that had got stuck in a drain pipe. As we had no fishing tackle with us, we could not verify his statement. Small creeks abounded in the bushes, that were filled with a small and lively fish, something like a silver fish. During the day the bushes caught fire from some unknown cause and the shells that lay around loose kept exploding and sent

A block house was also there, having been built when the war first commenced

274

their fragments flying through the air, but luckily without doing any damage.

As we had been exposed to the sun for about a week without any shelter, we looked more like darkeys than white men. And when my chum came to camp on his return from New York, where he had been on furlough, we could see the diference, he looking more like a girl with his white face, than a soldier. We were melted with the sun in the day time, and nearly froze to death at night with the dew. The first night when I had got my bed made up of pine tufts and laid down, a spider or something else bit me on the lip, and it swelled up so rapidly that I could feel it puffing up, but after a little while it went down as quick, so did no harm, only feeling uncomfortable.

On the 16th a detail was sent out fully equiped for special duty. Drilling commenced without arms, and we had an order for inspection that did not come off. In the afternoon we pitched our tents in streets and made it look more like a camp than a bivouac. As it looked as if we were going to stay for some time, a guard was sent to the barracks for the prisoners. We spent our time in drilling, picketing and rambling round the country until the 20th when we struck tents, and marched back to our old quarters, passing over the Aqueduct Bridge on our rout[e]. This bridge was used before the war in passing canal boats over the river, being the connecting link for the Baltimore and Ohio Canal. The planks on the sides had been pretty well battered up by the boats chafing against them. When we got back to our quarters, the avenue patrol was sent out on duty so that we were not given much time to rest. The citizens of Wash. were glad to see the Regt. back again as they were well thought of for their efficiency and soldierly bearing.

During the raid the citizens were formed into companys and used our parade ground for drill every day. A national reserve having been formed for the protection of the city, all government clerks and employees were enrolled and formed into companys and regts. and had to drill every day. Anybody refusing to go into it was given the bounce at once.

From the time we reached our quarters until the 8th of August, we had been ordered to pack up and the knapsacks placed in the store room two or three times, it being reported that the rebels were still hanging around Penn. It seemed to me at the time as rather curious that they should be allowed to do so, knowing of the small force that was on our side of the river. Troops were passing through the city continually but no one knew where they were going. The 6th and 19th corps were still encamped near the city, besides a brigade of cavalry that had arrived too late for the raid. The government employees were also formed into a brigade, uniformed and armed the same as soldiers, and had a drill every afternoon on our parade ground. They were commanded by regular army officers and did some very good drilling, a good many of them being old soldiers. At a review held by them was a very fine display there being three regts. of whites, and one colored assisted by the band of the V.R.C. (ours). They were reviewed by Maj. Genl. Meigs (Q[uarter]. M[aster]. G[eneral].) and Brig. Genl. Rush. Wash. was now well guarded for the first time in a year, and if the Johnys had made an attack at this time, they would have met with a warm reception.

The weather was very hot, being some days over one hundred in the shade. We had two or three thunder storms that made it cooler for a time, but it was soon as hot as ever. On the 18th I had my last parade and monthly inspection. Revelie was beaton at four o'clock in the morning, [we] had our breakfast at half past four, and our inspection at half past five. This was rather early for breakfast, as our usual time was six o'clock, but as the weather was so hot, it was thought best to have the inspection in the cool of the day. I was still on patrol duty, but being on the night squad, I got clear of the heat. The day patrol had to attend dress parade at seven o'clock a.m. and guard mount at half past eight, besides making two trips on duty and answering role call morning and night. The night patrol answered no roll call, had one hour's drill every night at half past six, and had only one

Home once more

tour of patrol varying from one and a half to four hours, a slight change in the hours and squads having been made Augt. 19th, 1864.

As my three years of service had expired I reported the fact to the Capt. who after hearing what I had to say, asked me if I would not re-enlist. I told him I would not, and he made out my papers at once. Getting them into my hands I was once more a citizen, and going over to the Treasury building, I drew my bounty of one hundred dollars and seventy-three dollars monthly, clothing and transportation money. With this in my pocket I felt quite rich.

As it was reported that the 5th Regt. N.J. Volls. were expected in Wash. every day on their way home, I waited for them untill the 22nd when, as there was no signs of their comming, I bid the boys good bye and took the train for Trenton. When we arrived at the Trenton depot, I got off the train and went to the state house to get my state pay but as the Regiment had not arrived I did not get it. Taking the next train, I arrived in Jersey City that night.

The Regt. coming home on the 31st I went to Trenton with them, and received my state pay of sixty-eight dollars, but not without some questioning on the part of the Q[uarter]. M[aster]. Gen[era]l's clerk, who said that my papers were made out to private A. Bellard, while my name on the Regts'. muster roll called for corporal. I explained that I had been promoted to corporal at the Battle of Chancellorsville, Va. but being wounded and pronounced unfit for active service, had been transferred to the Veteran Reserve Corps. and of course was not with the Regiment after that. He was satisfied with my explination and handed over the spondulix.

Appendix I

Officers, Company C,
Fifth New Jersey Infantry
August 1861 – May 1863

Captains: William J. Sewell, August 1861–July 1862 (promoted to Lieut. Col.)
John Gamble, July–August 1862 (transferred to Co. H)
Henry H. Woolsey, August 1862–June 1864 (died of wounds)

1st Lieutenants: George S. Russell, August 1861–May 1862 (promoted to Capt., Co. D)
Cyrus H. Rogers, May 1862–July 1862 (promoted to Capt., Co. K)
Thomas C. Godfrey, July 1862–March 1863 (promoted to Capt., Co. F)

2nd Lieutenants: William H. Hill, August 1861–May 1862 (promoted to 1st Lieut., Co. I)
George H. Mitchell, May 1862 (promoted to 1st Lieut., Co. G)
Charles W. Arnett, May 1862–July 1862 (died of wounds)
George J. Lawyer, July 1862–March 1863 (promoted to 1st Lieut., Co. F)
Sylvester W. Nafew, March 1863–October 1864

Sergeants: Alfred H. Austin, August 1861–November 1861 (reduced to Corporal)
Edward Barrett, August 1861–February 1862 (reduced to ranks)
Edward Bessigkommer, August 1861–February 1862 (reduced to ranks)
Patrick Campbell, (November?) 1861–May 1862 (discharged)
Gustavus Goetz, August 1861–September 1864
John W. Jennings, March 1863–September 1864
George J. Lawyer, August 1861–July 1862 (promoted to 2nd Lieut.)
Edward Miller, September 1862–October 1864
Philip Russell, December 1862–May 1863 (promoted to 2nd Lieut., Co. B)
John Thomas, February 1862–December 1862 (reduced to ranks)

Corporals

.

Alfred H. Austin, November 1861–March 1863 (reduced to ranks)
James Bligh, August 1861–June 1862 (discharged for disability)
Calistro Castro, August 1861–February 1862 (reduced to ranks)
Patrick Campbell, August 1861–(November?) 1861 (promoted to Sergeant
George C. Curtis, August 1861–October 1862 (discharged to join regula
    army)
Bernard J. Deery, March 1863–September 1864
John Elberg, December 1861–December 1862 (discharged for disability)
Richard Gill, May 1862–October 1862 (discharged to join regular army)
William Heatley, August 1861–August 1862 (reduced to ranks)
John W. Jennings, August 1861–March 1863 (promoted to Sergeant)
Anthony W. Luken, August 1861–June 1862 (discharged for disability)
Edward Miller, May 1862–September 1862 (promoted to Sergeant)
Christian Rapp, November 1862–September 1864
Archibald Ritchie, November 1862–April 1863 (discharged for disability)
Philip Russell, August 1861–December 1862 (promoted to Sergeant)
Peter Wynn, August 1861–October 1862 (discharged for disability)

Appendix II

Bellard's Three Versions of the Battle of Fredericksburg

*I. From
Bellard's Pocket Diary*

[December] 13th [1862]
moved ¼ mile and rested
until about 3 o'clock
when we went across the
pontoon bridge and
marched to the front.
The first briggade took
the advance and ours the
reserve. Some smart work
going on. 14th Sunday,
fine day scirmishing go-
ing on pretty brisk. The
first briggade lost about
100 men. The firing was
stopped towards night

*II. From Bellard's Letter
to his father, Camp near
Falmouth, Va.,
December 16, 1862*

Next morning the 13th
we moved about a ½ mile
and rested until about 3
o'clock in the afternoon.
While we where [*sic*]
resting, I went over to
the batteries which where
[*sic*] hard at work, to see
how our men were making
in the direction of Fred-
ericksburg. I could see
our men charging on the
Rebel batteries, posted
on a heighth. But it was
of no use they had to fall

*III. From
Bellard's Memoir*

In the morning (13th)
we moved about a quarter
of a mile nearer the river
and halted in a wood to
draw rations and await
our turn to cross the
river.

At this time our
troops were advancing
from Fredericksburg to
storm St. Marys
[Marye's] Heights that
was in plain sight of our
position. So I went over
to one of our batteries

under a flag of truce. 15th our briggade gone to the front. The pickets posted in plain sight with the arms laying down, no firing being allowed on either side. Our Company sent out about dark. 16th a little rain. About 1 o'clock we left the line and returned across the river camping about ½ mile from it, the Rebels running over the ground we left. We marched back to our old camp that night.

back. I could see plain the Rebel infantry in a hollow and ours in another firing at each [other] as hard as they could. On the right of them I saw three lines of our men advancing on a double quick on to their infantry which was firing into them all the time. On the left of the line there was a line of battle formed by our artillery which was fired by volleys into the woods. The Rebels where [were] driven a ½ mile back at this place. We marched about three and passing over the pontoon bridge we went str[a]ight to the front. The first and second brigades were put in the advance and ours lay in a field behind them as a reserve. The Rebels commenced to shell us here so we fell back to the road and got behind the bank which formed the Rebels' first line of works in the morning but

that were hard at work to look at them. The guns of our heavy artilery were planted on the edge of the hill all along our front and were pegging away at the rebel batterys on the heights over the river, to cover our men, who were charging up the hills to drive the rebel infantry away from a stone wall that was about half way up, and used by them as a breastwork. In front of where I stood, rebel infantry occupied one hollow and our men another, and they fired away at each other as fast as they could load and fire. While another brigade was advancing to support them, one of the shells that was intended for the rebels fell short and, as I could follow it with the eye from the time it left the gun until it burst, I saw it explode right in the rear of our men but w[h]ether it killed anyone or not we could not see, but rather think it they where [were] driven back. Schirmishing went on pretty brisk all night. On Sunday the 14th the scirmishing continued until about four o'clock but brought on no engagement which pleased us very much. It was stoped about 6 o'clock by mutual consent on both sides. On the 13th [15th] our brigade was sent out to relieve the first who who [*sic*] had been in for two nights and a day. We took our position and the scirmishers [were] sent out to relieve the others. Our officers and the Rebels met togather on the lines and conversed with each other but no firing took place. About dusk our Company was sent out as pickets to relieve the others. When we got to our post, I saw the Rebels' line in front all standing up without arms about 30 yards ahead of us. We were ordered to lay down our arms and not to fire on them unless they ad-

did. On the right of these troops and directly in rear of the city, 3 lines of our troops charged up to the stone wall on the double quick, with the shot and shell flying round them like hail stones. It was of no use. They would get close to the stone wall, when they received such a volley of small arms in their faces that they had to fall back, leaving half of their number dead and wounded on the field. On the left of the line our artilery fired by battery and drove them back about half a mile into the woods.

About 3 o'clock in the afternoon we started for the front and crossing the river on a pontoon bridge we took up our possition. The river was crossed by 3 bridges. One for infantry. One for cavalry and artilery and one for waggons. When marching over these bridges we had to break step, or else break the vanced. About 11 o'clock we were ordered to put our knapsacks and everything on and to keep very still. We began to smell a rat then so we got ready for a move. About two oclock this morning we got up from our post and left for the rear in a stooping position to avoid being seen by the Rebels. When we got of[f] at a distance we straightened up and marched in time towards the river. When we got to the river we found a briggade drawn up in line of battle to cover the retreat over the bridge. We passed over the bridge and formed with the Regt. on the other side. We marched about ¼ mile and rested until late in the day when we marched to our old camp w[h]ere we are now. At the place we crossed their [there] was three bridges one for infantry and the other for artilery and waggons. While we were resting this morning I saw the

bridge. The 1st and 2nd brigades took the advance lines, while the 3rd held the reserve in the rear. We had not been there long when the rebels opened on us with artilery, and one of the shells went screaming over the Col's. head. As this was too close for him, he ordered us to fall back about 10 feet and take our position in a road that had been the rebels' first line of battle, but [they] had been driven out by our artilery. Here we were sheltered from the stray shots, as a bank had been thrown up on each side of the road forming a regular breastwork. The skirmishing was kept up pretty much all night. The 21st N.J. being on our right on the other side of the road several of us went over to see them, but as their col. had his men laying down, and ordered us to do the same or leave, we left. A few bullets were dropping amongst them but

Rebel cavalry scouting over the ground we had just left. We could hear the Rebels laughing and singing all night and some of them were cutting trees all night. They had been making rifle pitts and redoubts all the time we lay in the field and I have no doubt had we staid in that field today their [there] would [have] been a good many of us missing that is here in camp tonight. As it is I believe there is only one man shot out of our briggade. . . .

they were thrown there by some of our men for a joke.

On the morning of the 14th skirmishing commenced about 4 o'clock and continued til 4 in the afternoon, at which time it was stopped by mutual consent. Under a flag of truce the wounded were collected and the dead burried. Before the truce was ordered, one of our Jersey batterys that was planted in the open field did a little good practice. One of the officers saw a group of mounted rebel officers under some trees, and judging from the number of horses that they were of some consequence, ordered his gunners to fire into them. Taking careful aim he fired, and with such good effect that a scattering took place, leaving some of their number dead behind them. As it was afterwards learned one of their generals was killed and others

wounded. In the skir-
mishing the 1st Brigade
lost about 100 men, the
2nd a good many more,
while the 3rd had only
one man killed and none
wounded (except myself,
who had a bloody nose
while on the march.)
When the boys saw it
they sang out "There's
one man wounded, see the
blood?"

The 15th our bri-
gade was sent out to the
front line to relieve the
1st who had been there
for two nights and a day.
Taking our position, a
company was sent out as
skirmishers to relieve a
company of the 1st who
were then on duty. No
firing took place, and one
of our officers and one of
the rebs met half way
and had a friendly chat.
While we lay here, the
boys amused themselves
by playing cards, while
one of the recruits who
was a good singer gave us
some songs.

Towards dark our
company was sent out on

picket, and on arriving at
our posts witch [which]
was about 30 yards from
the rebs, I was surprised
to see them walking
about without arms in
their hands. We received
orders to lay ours down
also, and were not to fire
at them unles they ad-
vanced. So throwing my
knapsack on the ground
I placed my rifle on top
of it and had leasure to
look around. On our left
was a pile of dead men
that had been collected
previous to burrial. The
wounded were being con-
veyed to the Lacy house,
that was in our rear near
the river and was used
for a hospital (it was
afterwards burnt down).
In our front was the
rebel pickets, with our
officers and theirs talking
together, while on the hill
back of them and a little
to our right was an ugly
looking brass battery
that we had not seen be-
fore, all ready to lay us
out on the morrow. All
that night we could hear

the rebels singing and
laughing, while chopping
was going on in the
woods, showing that they
were making their de-
fences as strong as
possible.

About 11 o'clock
that night we got orders
to put on our knapsacks
and to keep very still,
which we did until about
2 o'clock in the morning
of the 16th when Major
Ramsey of our Regt.
came along and ordered
us to fall back. We did
so, marching off in a
stooping posture, getting
down as low as possible,
so as not to be seen by the
rebels. As a large black
cloud hung over us at the
time it helped us a great
deal. When we had got to
a safe distance from the
line we straightened up
and continued our march
in good order. Upon
reaching the river, we
found a brigade drawn
up in line of battle to
cover our retreat. (The
rest of the army being
already across the river.)

Forming the company, we marched over the bridge and rejoined our Regt. which then marched about a half mile from the river and halted for the night. After we had got comfortably laid down for a few hours sleep, it commenced to rain, and when I woke up in the morning I found myself laying in a puddle of water.

The morning found our entire army across the river, having been favored by black clouds that prevented the rebels from seeing what was going on. So that when they were ready to give us a dose in the morning they found nothing but open fields in front of them, with our army safe and sound on our side of the river and the bridges taken down. When I got up, the rebel cavalry were scouting over the ground we had left. After resting nearly all day we returned to camp that night.

Biographical Index

———◆———

Except where otherwise indicated, all private soldiers and noncommissioned officers in this index were members of the Fifth New Jersey Infantry Regiment. The age given for each of these soldiers is that at the time of enlistment in 1861. General officers of the Union and Confederacy have been identified only to the extent necessary to explain their relationship to Bellard's regiment. For full biographical sketches of these commanders, see two exemplary works by Ezra J. Warner: *Generals in Gray: Lives of the Confederate Commanders* (Baton Rouge: Louisiana State University Press, 1959), and *Generals in Blue: Lives of the Union Commanders* (Baton Rouge: Louisiana State University Press, 1964).

Biographical Index

Banks, General Nathaniel Prentiss (1816–1894), a former Massachusetts governor, congressman, and speaker of the House of Representatives, who commanded Union troops at Cedar Mountain. Page 159.

Beauregard, General Pierre Gustave Toutant (1818–1893), of Louisiana, who was in command at Charleston when the Confederates attacked Fort Sumter. Page 3.

Bell, John, a 36-year-old coppersmith born in Liverpool, who died of consumption on Feb. 9, 1862. Page 38.

Berdan, Colonel Hiram (c. 1823–1893), of New York, who led the 1st U.S. Sharpshooters and advocated breechloading, repeating rifles. Pages 56, 207.

Bly, Charles, a member of the Hudson Brigade, 3rd Regiment, Artillery Co. Page 22.

Boyd, Belle (1843–1900), a Confederate spy who gave information on Union troop movements to "Stonewall" Jackson during the Valley campaign. Twice arrested and imprisoned, she escaped in 1863 to England. Pages 248, 251.

Bramhall, Walter M., of Rahway, New Jersey, captain of the 6th New York Independent Artillery Battery. Page 75.

Buck, Dennis M., a 29-year-old Boonville, New York, carpenter, who transferred to the 2nd U. S. Cavalry in October 1862. Pages 21, 154–155.

Burke, Mrs. Mary A., a widow who lived in Fairfax County, Virginia, and in 1860 owned a farm valued at $6,000. Page 152.

Burnside, General Ambrose Everett (1824–1881), of Rhode Island, who headed the Union expedition against Roanoke Island, North Carolina, and led the left wing of the Union army at Antietam before succeeding McClellan, in November 1862, as commander of the Army of the Potomac. Pages 165–166, 177–178, 190, 195–196, 200.

Carr, General Joseph Bradford (1828–1895), of New York, who commanded a brigade in Hooker's division of the III Corps during the Peninsular campaign, and at Second Bull Run, Fredericksburg, and Chancellorsville. Page 226.

Casey, General Silas (1807–1882), of Rhode Island, who commanded a division of Keyes's IV Corps at Seven Pines (Fair Oaks). Pages 24–25, 72, 83, 86.

Castro, Calistro, a Mexican-born cabinetmaker, who enlisted in 1861 at the age of 33. Promoted to corporal, he was reduced to the ranks for insubordination in 1862 and was discharged for chronic rheumatism in 1863. Page 138.

Conkling, Charles, a 20-year-old wheelwright from Morristown, New Jersey, who was in Co K, 7th New Jersey Infantry. Page 22.

Couch, General Darius Nash (1822–1897), of New York, who commanded a division of Keyes's IV Corps in the Peninsular campaign. Pages 72, 83, 96.

Curtis, George C., a Monmouth, New Jersey clerk, who enlisted in 1861 at the age of 19 and became a corporal. In October 1862 he transferred to the 2nd U.S. Cavalry. Pages 24, 143.

Davis, Jefferson (1808–1889), President of the Confederate States of America. Pages 31–32, 42, 53.

Deery, Bernard, a 19-year-old papermaker, born in New York City, who became a corporal in 1863. Page 214.

Donaldson, William, a 32-year-old teamster, born in Cavan, Ireland, who died in May 1862 of wounds received at Williamsburg. Page 67.

Dugan, John, a 19-year-old Hudson City clerk, wounded at Chancellorsville, who was subsequently transferred to the Invalid Corps. Page 224.

Early, General Jubal Anderson (1816–1894), of Virginia, who served in all the engagements of the Army of Northern Virginia, 1862–1864, and led the Confederate invasion of Maryland in 1864. Page 249.

Eaton, Charles, a butcher, who served in Hexamer's Company (Battery A), New Jersey Light Artillery. Page 22.

Ellsworth, Colonel Elmer Ephraim (1837–1861), organizer of Zouave companies, who was shot while removing a Confederate flag flying over the Marshall House in Alexandria. Pages 18–20.

Fenton, Martin, a 33-year-old Washington, New York, carpenter, who was wounded and captured at Chancellorsville and paroled 11 days later. Page 224.

Flick, Joseph, a 34-year-old German-born shoemaker, who was wounded at Chancellorsville and discharged in November 1863 because of disability. Pages 214, 224.

Franklin, General William Buel (1823–1903), of Pennsylvania, who commanded the VI Corps during the Peninsular campaign and led the Left Grand Division during the battle of Fredericksburg. Pages 177–178, 181.

Frantz, Anton, a 33-year-old German-born painter, who died on May 7, 1862, from wounds received at Williamsburg. Pages 67–68.

Free, Mickey, evidently a pseudonym, since no member of the 5th N.J. Infantry bore this name. Probably Robert Harriott, aged 42, born in Monaghan, Ireland, who listed his occupation as "Pedestrian" (cf. Bellard's account of "Mickey Free" as a "walkist"). Like "Mickey Free," Harriott was wounded in the left hand at Wiliamsburg — the only Irishman in the regiment to be so wounded. Pages 17, 65.

Gamble, John, 1st Lieut. of Co. G, 5th New Jersey Infantry, who succeeded Sewell as captain of Co. C in July 1862, was transferred to Co. H in August 1862, and died on May 3, 1863, of wounds received at Chancellorsville. Page 151.

Gill, Richard, a 19-year-old "moulder" born in Galway, Ireland, who became corporal in May 1862 and was wounded at Second Bull Run. In October 1862 he transferred to the 2nd U.S. Cavalry. Page 27.

Goetz, Gustavus, a 41-year-old jeweler, born in Germany, who as sergeant of Co. C attempted to discipline Bellard. Page 112.

Gould, Robert, Captain of Co. E, 5th New Jersey Infantry, whose record of sickness, absence without leave, and arrests led to his discharge in April 1863. Pages 187–188.

Grant, General Ulysses Simpson (1822–1885), who, after victories in the West, became lieutenant general in command of all the Union armies in March 1864 and made his headquarters with the Army of the Potomac, commanded by Meade. Pages 236, 242, 249, 263.

Grover, General Cuvier (1828–1885), of Maine, who led the 1st Brigade of Hooker's 2nd Division, Heintzelman's III Corps, in the Peninsular campaign. Pages 87, 94.

Hancock, General Winfield Scott (1824–1886), of Pennsylvania, who led brigades in the IV and VI Corps in the Peninsular campaign. Page 70.

Healy, Virgil, who rose from 2nd lieut. to captain of Co. B, 5th New Jersey Infantry, was wounded at Williamsburg, Chancellorsville, and Gettysburg, and in November 1863 became major in the 8th New Jersey Infantry. Page 138.

Heatley, William, a 24-year-old New York City bricklayer, who became corporal and was then demoted for conduct prejudicial to good order and military discipline. He was wounded at Second Bull Run and died of further wounds received at Chancellorsville. Pages 189, 224.

Heintzelman, Samuel Peter (1805–1880), of Pennsylvania, who commanded the III Corps during the Peninsular campaign and at Second Bull Run. Pages 71–72, 87, 100, 125, 128, 134, 159.

Heslen, Peter, a 30-year-old laborer, born in West Meath, Ireland, who was seriously wounded at Chancellorsville and discharged because of disability in May 1864. Page 224.

Hexamer, William, captain of Battery A, New Jersey Light Artillery Regiment. Pages 176, 195, 203.

Hill, William H., a Paterson, New Jersey, laborer, who served as 2nd lieut., Co. C, and captain, Co. I. Wounded at Williamsburg, he was absent on sick leave for most of the next five months. Pages 4, 68, 74, 158, 171.

Hooker, General Joseph (1814–1879), of Massachusetts, to whose division of Heint-zelman's III Corps Bellard's regiment belonged during the Peninsular campaign and Second Bull Run. The 5th New Jersey Infantry was also part of Hooker's Grand Central Division at Fredericksburg. Named commander of the Army of the Potomac on Jan. 26, 1863, he led the army in the disastrous battle of Chancellors-ville. Pages 43, 62, 67, 70, 72, 78, 81, 87, 131, 165, 170, 176, 177, 179, 200–201, 207, 209–211, 218, 223, 226, 264.

Howard, General Oliver Otis (1830–1909), of Maine, who succeeded Sigel as com-mander of the XI Corps and was routed by "Stonewall" Jackson at Chancellors-ville. Page 201.

Jackson, General Thomas Jonathan ("Stonewall") (1824–1863), Lee's daring lieu-tenant, who led the Confederate campaign in the Shenandoah Valley, helped drive McClellan back to Harrison's Landing, was instrumental in defeating Pope at Second Bull Run and Burnside at Fredericksburg, and was largely responsible for the Confederate victory at the battle of Chancellorsville, during which he lost his life. Pages 87, 124–125, 128–129, 132, 133, 201.

Johnston, General Joseph Eggleston (1807–1891), of Virginia, commander of the Army of Northern Virginia until wounded at Seven Pines, May 1862. Pages 50, 71–72.

Kearny, General Philip (1815–1862), of New York, who commanded a division of Heintzelman's III Corps during the Peninsular campaign and at Second Bull Run and was killed at Chantilly. Pages 67, 71, 88, 95, 134, 135, 145, 210.

Keyes, General Erasmus Darwin (1810–1895), of Maine, who commanded the IV Corps during the Peninsular campaign. Pages 71–72.

Larkins, Patrick, an 18-year-old rope-maker, born in Limerick, Ireland, who was promoted to corporal in July 1863 and in November 1863 went on detached service to recruit in New Jersey. Pages 189, 246.

Lawyer, George J., a 23-year-old New York City clerk, who served as 1st sergeant (or "sergeant dresser," as Bellard called him) and 2nd lieut. of Co. C, and as 1st lieut. of Co. F. He was wounded at Chancellorsville, and discharged on Nov. 6 1863, because of disability. Pages 215, 225.

Lee, General Robert Edward (1807–1870), who became commander of the Army of Northern Virginia after Joseph E. Johnston was wounded at Seven Pines. Pages 87–88, 99, 124, 134, 149, 177, 190, 201, 236, 249.

Lincoln, Abraham (1809–1865), 16th President of the United States. Pages 11, 18, 24, 31–32, 71, 124, 149, 159, 165, 200, 207–209, 247, 249, 265.

Longstreet, General James (1821–1904), of South Carolina, one of Lee's major lieutenants in the Peninsular campaign, at Second Bull Run, and at Fredericksburg. Page 134.

McClellan, General George Brinton (1826–1885), who became commander of the Army of the Potomac after the disaster at First Bull Run, led it during the Peninsular and Antietam campaigns, and was replaced by Burnside in November 1862. Pages 11, 18, 25–26, 31–32, 49–50, 62–63, 70, 83, 87–89, 99, 115, 124–125, 149, 165, 169–170.

Magruder, General John Bankhead (1807–1871), of Virginia, who commanded the Confederate forces during the early stages of the Peninsular campaign. Pages 50, 74.

Meade, General George Gordon (1815–1872), who commanded a division of Franklin's Left Grand Division at Fredericksburg and led the V Corps at Chancellorsville. On June 28, 1863, he succeeded Hooker as commander of the Army of the Potomac and continued in that position until the end of the war, though overshadowed by Lt.-Gen. Grant, who made his headquarters with that army. Pages 236, 243–244.

Meigs, General Montgomery Cunningham (1816–1892), of Pennsylvania, the highly efficient Union quartermaster general. Page 276.

Mitchell, George H., a 22-year-old carriage maker, from Charleston, South Carolina, who served as sergeant of Co. K until May 1862, when he was promoted to 2nd lieut. He was subsequently promoted to 1st lieut. and assigned to Co. G. Page 113.

Mott, General Gershom (1822–1884), of New Jersey, who commanded the 6th N.J. Infantry during the Peninsular campaign and led a brigade of Hiram G. Berry's division of Sickles's III Corps at Chancellorsville. Pages 37, 190–191, 195.

Newell, William J., a 30-year-old clerk, born in London, who died Dec. 24, 1862, of consumption. Page 189.

Patrick, General Marsena Rudolph (1811–1888), of New York, provost marshal general of the Army of the Potomac under McClellan, Burnside, Hooker, and Meade. Page 244.

Parker, Joel (1816–1888), who was elected, as a Democrat, governor of New Jersey in 1862 and served until 1866. Page 210.

Patterson, General Francis Engle (1821–1862), of Pennsylvania, who commanded the 3rd Brigade (to which Bellard's regiment belonged) of Hooker's division of